Design Methods in Engineering and Product Design

DESIGN METHODS IN ENGINEERING AND PRODUCT DESIGN

Dr. I.C. Wright

Engineering Design Institute
Department of Mechanical Engineering
Loughborough University

The McGraw-Hill Companies

London • New York • St Louis • San Francisco • Auckland
Bogatá • Caracas • Lisbon • Madrid • Mexico • Milan
Montreal • New Delhi • Panama • Paris • San Juan • São Paulo
Singapore • Sydney • Tokyo • Toronto

Published by
McGRAW-HILL Publishing Company
Shoppenhangers Road, Maidenhead, Berkshire, S16 2Q1, England
Telephone 01628 502500
Fax: 01628 770224

The LOC data for this book has been applied for and may be obtained from the
Library of Congress, Washington, D.C.

A catalogue record for this book is available from the British Library

1990813

**Further information on this and other McGraw-Hill titles is to be found at
http://www.mcgraw-hill.co.uk**

ISBN 0 07 709376 3

McGraw-Hill

A Division of The McGraw-Hill Companies

1 2 3 4 5 CUP 2 1 0 9 8

Typeset by WestKey Limited, Falmouth, Cornwall
Printed and bound in Great Britain at the University Press, Cambridge

To Irena my wife, and Nicola my daughter for endless support
and patience while I was writing this book.
Also, to all of my students who have helped me
to develop many of the examples and assignments
over years of teaching 'methods'.

CONTENTS

PREFACE

This book is primarily intended for undergraduate students who are studying design as a part of their course. Although many of the methods that are described are considered to be of principal use to engineers, this is an ill-informed view. One of the greatest benefits to be gained from using the methods is to encourage interaction between disparate groups within a company, and thereby encourage effective communication between everyone involved in the design of products. The methods provide a 'common forum' for the interchange of ideas and information between the marketing, industrial design, and commercial and financial functions, as well as between engineers of all disciplines. For this reason, the book should be useful for all students who will be involved with the specification and development of products, and the management of product innovation. The book also provides an introduction to product design methods for practising engineers and designers.

The methods described in the book are:

- Product feature charts
- Customer perception charts
- Market information gathering
- Requirement trees
- Requirement weighting
- Product design specifications
- Brainstorming
- Problem diagrams
- Morphology charts
- Concept evaluation matrices
- Market and technology risk analysis
- Fault trees
- Failure mode analysis
- Value engineering and analysis
- Quality function deployment

To illustrate the diversity of situations in which the methods can be applied, I have provided case studies from a variety of backgrounds. While some of these are concerned with products that can be classified as consumer durables, e.g. audio equipment, kitchen appliances and DIY tools, others use examples from industry such as aeroengines, packaging machinery, and process control systems. Despite this broad spread of application, students in the second or subsequent years of any industrial design or engineering undergraduate level course should have the background to cope with the case studies and assignments. Only a short section in Chapter 10 dealing with the application of Boolean algebra to fault trees is likely to test non-engineers, although the reader is taken through the analysis on a step-by-step basis. Leaving this section out entirely has no detrimental effect on anything that follows.

To understand fully the strengths and limitations of the methods described, the student must undertake the assignments provided, for only by solving problems will the difficulties and benefits become clear. Because the methods encourage interaction between members of the 'design team', the greatest understanding of the benefits is gained by working on the assignments in groups of between three and six people. Although most of the methods described are widely used in industry, this does not mean that effective application of them is easy to achieve. It needs to be remembered that working together as a team is something that has to be learned. This is true for the individual, and for the team as a whole. When inexperience in team working is combined with an imposed methodology, it is understandable that problems will arise. However, conscientious effort in working on the assignments should prepare the reader to apply the methods in project work.

Because the outcome from applying the methods depend on the background and experiences of the user, each person's solution to an assignment will be different to anyone else's. This recognition that no two solutions will be the same is, at the same time, comforting and worrying to the learner. Because of this, I have provided a set of model answers in Appendix 2. Although your answers will be different for the reasons just given, the model solution will enable you to check the structure and completeness of your work. Do not be tempted to look at a solution before attempting an assignment. The principal benefits and the major problems associated with the application of methods are to be found in the process of application. In most cases, the solution in the form of a chart, table, or matrix looks deceptively obvious. Hence, it is easy to fool yourself into thinking that you can apply a method just because you agree with and understand the end result. Nothing could be further from the truth.

Some of the charts and matrices used for the entry of data are quite complicated in form. Appendix 1, contains masters of some of the more complicated charts so that they can be photocopied for use in answering assignments. Some charts, like the one used for QFD, will benefit by increasing them to A3 size, although this does tend to make the lines rather heavy.

The methods are concerned with ensuring that information about customer requirements are built into the products that are designed and manufactured for them. This information and the frequently conflicting commercial constraints under which a company operates are substantial and complex, as is the design process itself. Chapters 1 and 2 provide a foundation of understanding about the product design process and its information requirements, and Chapter 3 explains the nature of teamwork in a modern company environment.

THE PRODUCT DESIGN PROCESS

OVERVIEW

Although many authors have produced models of the **product design process** (PDP), diagrammatic representations of these models all fail to reflect fully the complexity of the process as it exists in a commercial setting. Simple diagrams, that represent the process as a series of linked stages, are a useful starting point in understanding the various activities that are involved. When other aspects of the process such as iteration and information handling are included, the models become so involved and case dependent that they cease to be useful other than as a means of illustrating the degree of complexity that is frequently present. Chapter 1 sets out to provide an insight into the form and complexity of the product design process, particularly from the points of view of iteration and information. In so doing, it forms a basis for Chapter 2, which looks in detail at the process's information requirements.

OBJECTIVES

When you have finished studying this chapter, you will be able to:

- understand the essence of the design process;
- understand the limitations of design process models;
- appreciate the importance of iteration during design;
- recognise the need for information during the process of designing a product.

STAGES OF THE PRODUCT DESIGN PROCESS

Product design is concerned with the definition of products that will be commercially successful. Products are any combination of components that together provide the functionality required by the customer. Products might be domestic items such as hi-fi or washing machines, automobiles and their constituent systems, civil or military aircraft, chemical process plant, manufacturing machinery and processes plant, industrial products such as gearboxes and turbines, medical instrumentation etc.

A commercially successful product can simply be defined as one that makes an acceptable level of profit for the company. What is acceptable depends upon many factors including the uniqueness of the product, the investment provided by the company, and the total size of the markets into which it is being sold. However, profitability is the key, and the contribution that product-generated income makes to this will be seen as the most important factor in assessing the worth of the product to the company.

The various stages that a product goes through during its design is frequently depicted as a linear sequence of events. The simple diagrammatic model of the various stages represented in Figure 1.1 (broadly attributed to French, 1971) indicates that the first part of the process is the determination of customer requirements. This is entirely reasonable, since a necessary prerequisite for profitability is that a sufficient number of customers will actually hand over money in return for ownership of the product. Obviously this will not be the case if the product does not provide the required functionality at the right price. Because it can only be the customer who decides what is required, and what is an acceptable price, it is vitally important for the company to discover what these factors are before making decisions that will influence them.

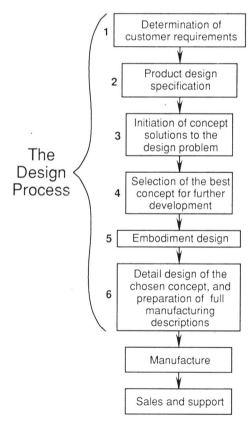

Figure 1.1 The design process as a linear activity

Although a company must know what the customer requires and the price that is acceptable, this knowledge is rarely sufficient to allow solutions to be developed immediately. There are a number of reasons for this. First, engineers frequently need customer preferences to be expressed in very explicit ways. For example, a company might know that there is a demand for a new hair-dryer that will dry hair more quickly than others that are already available. However, engineers will have to interpret this primitive need in a way that enables them to propose and evaluate a number of alternative ways of satisfying it. In this case, they will need to ask 'what does "more quickly" mean', and whether this can be converted into engineering characteristics like air velocity and temperature?

The business of converting the frequently non-technical, non-quantified customer requirements into a set of product characteristics expressed in engineering terms leads to the product design specification (PDS), which is identified as stage 2 in Figure 1.1.

The PDS lays out the customer requirements in as a complete manner as possible. When this has been completed, the design team can commence the innovative activity of proposing product configurations to satisfy customer needs. Almost inevitably, a number of alternative product configurations will be proposed. Indeed, the greater the number of alternatives, the more likely it is that one of them will offer acceptable or even outstanding attributes when assessed against the requirements stated in the PDS. This is the concept initiation phase identified at stage 3 in Figure 1.1.

The output from the concept initiation stage should comprise a number of alternative product configurations. Those configurations that do not meet the product design specification will be rejected, or modified until they do. In the case of the hair-dryer problem, we might end up with two possible designs, both of which satisfy the known customer preferences. However, the first may have better reliability than the second but at a higher cost. Which one should be chosen to manufacture and sell? It all depends on which one would provide the company with better profits, and there are many factors that would combine to determine this final choice. The business of evaluating concepts and selecting the best is represented at stage 4 in Figure 1.1. Making the correct decision at this stage is vitally important, and we will be looking at ways of evaluating and choosing concepts later in the book.

When the decision has been made to adopt a particular concept for development, the next stage in the design process is embodiment.

Definition

embody **1.** give a concrete or discernible form to (an idea, concept etc.).

Although it will have been necessary for designers to think in detail about many aspects of the design concepts to enable a full evaluation to be made, many of the final decisions will only be made during embodiment. The product design team will apply a wide range of skills, knowledge and methods during this stage. Just as in stage 3, the team will be called upon to contribute creative thinking to solve the problems, and engineers will use mathematical methods to analyse the performance of the various options. If appropriate, computer-based techniques will be used to synthesise solutions and simulate the performance of various systems within the product. The effect of manufacturing and material options will be considered, in addition to the cost implications. At all times, the team must be acutely aware of the needs of the product's potential customers, and the implications of all of their decisions on product sales and profits. The purpose of these activities is to enable the company to arrive at a description of the product that can be detailed for production. Figure 1.1 identifies this final stage of the product design process as detail design. Detail design is concerned with providing a description of each component and sub-assembly, all of the materials and tolerances, and the positioning and means of fixing of all elements of the product. All of this information must be given in sufficient detail and in such a way that the product can be produced without ambiguity. The outcome from this final stage will be a complete set of instructions for the manufacture of components and assemblies, and the purchase of items that are 'bought-out' by the company.

Although Figure 1.1 provides a reasonable description of the major stages of the product design process, it is a simplification of what actually happens. In reality, the linear progression of the stages is complicated by a large degree of overlap between them. In addition to it frequently being difficult to identify which stage has been reached, the design team will probably work simultaneously on several stages. This is because although the design process is progressive, it is also iterative in nature, as shown in Figure 1.2.

Although the stages shown in Figure 1.2 are identical to those in Figure 1.1, it represents a more realistic representation of the product design process because it identifies both feedback and feed-forward elements. These connections indicate an almost infinite

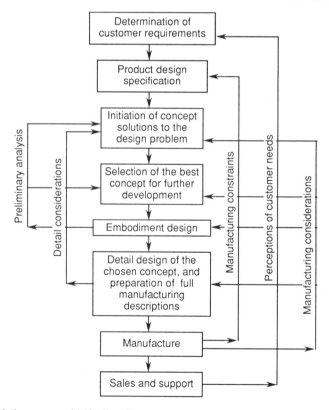

Figure 1.2 The design process with 'feedback' loops

number of possibilities in the way that the stages can be combined. The following case study will give an insight into the complexity of the process.

CASE STUDY 1.1

A manufacturer of aids for the elderly and disabled decided to produce a new product to make it easier for infirm people to take a shower. Its marketing department discovered that there was a need to use a standard bath with wall mounted shower attachments. They provided the engineering project team with a list of features that the customer would value, and the preferred selling price. They also obtained information on products produced by other companies against which they would have to compete. The most successful product already on the market was a simple seat that was positioned over the bath and rested on hooks located over the sides.

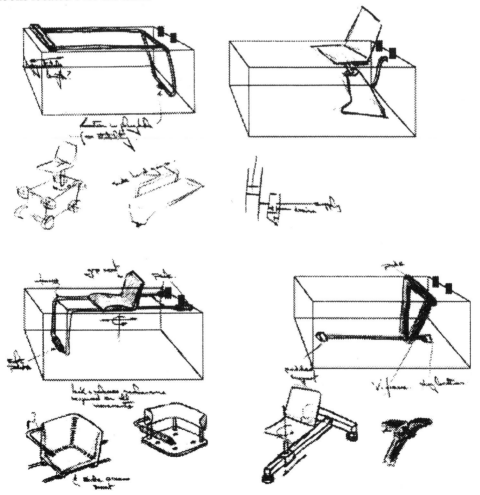

Figure 1.3 Concept sketches for the shower aid

When presented with this information, the company's design team produced 14 concept ideas. Some of the original concept sketches are shown in Figure 1.3 The concepts included:

1. A seat which fitted inside the bath and which could be raised level with the top edge of the bath to facilitate access, and lowered for showering. The seat was powered by water pressure via a connection to the tap.
2. A seat mounted on a light-weight frame that rested on the top edge of the bath. The seat rotated to facilitate access, and could slide along the frame to enable the user to move under and away from the shower zone.
3. A frame mounted on the floor by the side of the bath, to carry a seat that could be positioned over the floor or over the bath by moving it on a slideway.

Following discussions between the marketing department and design engineers, concept 3 was eliminated. There were several reasons for this. First, it was thought that the floor-mounted frame would get in the way of a carer who, in certain circumstances might have to be present to help the user. Second, after preliminary calculations of moments, the engineers had concerns about the stability of the device. Either the frame would need bolting to the floor, and this could create an obstacle for other users; or the device would need to be stabilised by locating it on the far edge of the bath. After examining various suggestions on how this might be done, the basic concept was rejected on the grounds of safety.

Although it was estimated that concept 1 would cost 50% more than the main competitor, it was decided to investigate it further because of the additional benefits that it provided. Calculations were undertaken to establish what sizes of piston could be used in the hydraulic cylinder. Basically, a small diameter cylinder would provide a greater maximum velocity to the chair than a large diameter cylinder, but a higher water pressure would be required to lift the mass of the person. The larger the diameter of the cylinder, and the greater the weight and cost of the device.

Because many baths have a 'vanity bar' running along one side to hold toiletries, it was decided that the concept 2 frame would have to rest on the ends of the bath. This meant that there would be a long span, with the mass of the person being supported on a seat near the middle. The question of whether adequate strength and rigidity could be provided whilst keeping the weight within acceptable limits needed investigating. Again, engineers undertook calculations to get a feel for the effect of changing the values of the variables.

In addition to the strength and performance calculations carried out for concepts 1 and 2, the design engineers worked with industrial designers, and manufacturing engineers, as well as with marketing department staff during the process of identifying the most promising concept. This process took several weeks, but when it was complete company staff were agreed that concept 2 offered them the most promising way forward in terms of meeting customer needs and company profitability.

At the embodiment stage, 'scheme' (or 'layout') drawings were produced for several different versions of concept 2. These schemes showed all of the component parts with sufficient detail to ensure that they would fit together correctly and function in the way envisaged. Company staff from marketing, sales, design, manufacturing, purchasing, and

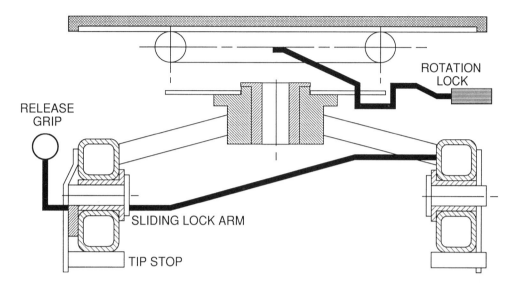

ROTATION
LOCK

RELEASE
GRIP

SLIDING LOCK ARM

TIP STOP

Figure 1.4 Prototype seat locking mechanism

customer support functions were involved in the assessment of the various options that arose during the development of the schemes.

It had been decided that the frame would be supported on the ends of the bath, and that the seat would slide along the frame as well as rotate to facilitate access. An important problem that required solving was the design of a mechanism by which the user could control the sliding and rotating motion. Several alternatives were proposed, some relying on positive mechanical locking, whilst others relied on friction. There were considerable doubts about the reliability of the friction-based devices, particularly since slideways might become coated with water and soap. To investigate this, prototype devices were built and tested. The result of this was the selection of a positive locking and release system which the designers considered to be fail safe. Figure 1.4 shows details from one of the drawings specifying a prototype seat locking and release mechanism.

The process of developing several solutions to the scheme stage, and the parallel activities of prototype building, testing and evaluation, enabled the design team to make decisions about the final form of the product in an informed and confident manner. Hence, most of the information required to select appropriate materials and finishes, manufacturing processes, bought out items, and limits and fits was available by the time that work was commenced on the preparation of detailed manufacturing drawings.

The product was offered to customers approximately 18 months after the marketing function first identified the opportunity for the company.

COMPLEX DESIGN PROCESS MODELS

The shower seat case study indicates some of the complexities of the design process. In particular it shows that design is not a neat linear activity with one well defined task following another in predictable order. The activities and their order of application depend

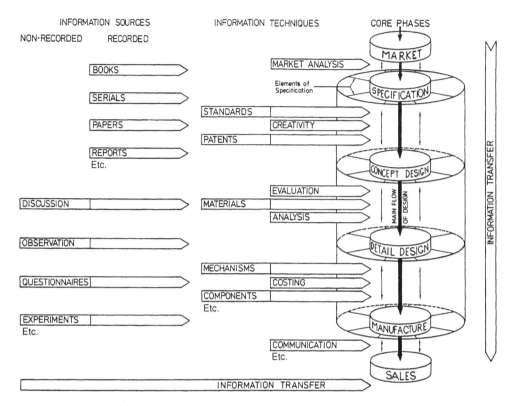

Figure 1.5 Pugh's model of the design process with information requirements

upon the nature of the design task, the objectives and constraints, and the preferences of the people involved. With all of these elements interacting in a complex and unpredictable way, it is not surprising that all models of the design process have their limitations.

One of the best known and most extensive models of the process is that proposed by Pugh (1991). Figure 1.5 shows a variant of the basic model that Pugh produced to indicate the information requirements of the PDP.

The acquisition and manipulation of information is a key activity within the product design process. One of the central roles of the designer is to pull together all the information required to enable the process to proceed. Information will be required from many sources including the customer via marketing and other company functions, technical experts such as mechanical and electronics engineers, ergonomists, industrial designers, manufacturing engineers, and research staff. Figure 1.5 indicates that although some information will be available from recorded sources, there will probably be a need to obtain additional information by means of various techniques including experiments, questionnaires, and observation. Discussion is also necessary to evaluate information, and produce the synergy that is so valuable when creative progress is required. The figure also shows that in addition to a flow of information **into** the PDP, the information flows **along** the process as the product develops. Pugh's background as an engineer comes across in his choice of terminology. Other than for that, the model shown in Figure 1.5 might be used to explain elements in the process of design for any type of product.

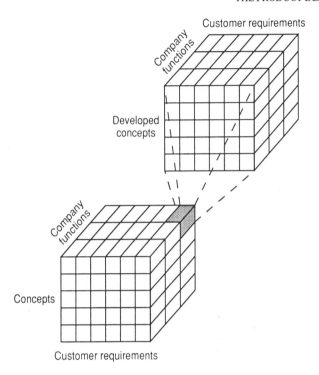

Figure 1.6 Growth of information with time

Being aware of the need for all this information is one thing, obtaining it and making the correct decisions as a result of it is another. For the process to work effectively, the providers of information need to be involved in the decision-making process, and the discussions that precede it. Wright & Swain (1995) examined the way that information flowing along the PDP grows in volume and complexity. Figure 1.6 shows one way that this growth can be visualised. The four dimensions of this information model are customer requirements, concepts, company functions, and time. The lower part of Figure 1.6 represents the information matrix at an early stage of concept generation, with each cell representing the perception of a person or company-function of the extent to which a concept meets particular customer requirements. To be able to compare concepts, it is necessary to include information from all the functions within the organisation, such as purchasing and manufacturing, as well as the technical design disciplines. As the evaluation – selection – modification cycle proceeds, the information matrix grows and changes in content. The upper part of Figure 1.6 shows how a small part of the 'early concept' matrix has grown due to the additional information that has been generated over time. In general, the nature of the information changes from informal and opinionated to formal and factual as the embryonic product moves closer to full definition.

None of the design process models shown so far indicate the effect of project complexity or size. Perhaps the best attempt to illustrate this is the 'VDI 2221' model. The Verein Deutscher Ingenieure (VDI) is the professional body for German engineers, and VDI 2221 is their guideline for *Systematic Approach to the Design of Technical Systems and Products*. This guideline recognises that complex problems are not solved as a whole, but are broken

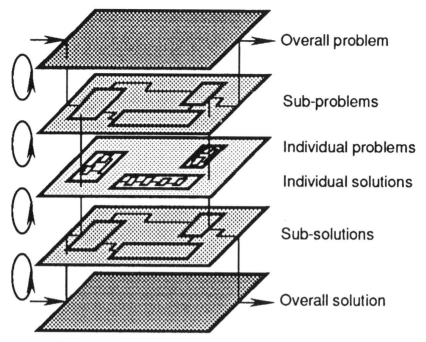

Figure 1.7 The VDI model with iteration loops

down into a number of sub-problems that are solved individually. Nevertheless, because the solutions to the sub-problems must be compatible with each other when combined into an overall solution, the needs of the sub-problem interfaces and their effect on overall system performance must be considered throughout the process. Figure 1.7 shows the VDI 2221 design process model with the addition of feedback loops.

The general progression of the design process is downwards through the five planes shown in Figure 1.7. The overall design problem is broken down into interconnected sub-problems represented on level 2. Next, these sub-problems are broken down further into individual problems for which solutions are found. The individual solutions are then combined into sub-solutions which, in turn, combine to form an overall solution to the problem. The addition of circular arrows between the stages merely indicates that an iteration is always required to some extent between the phases. For example, the overall problem for the previous case study was the provision of a shower aid. However, a single set of sub-problems could not be identified immediately until it became clear which concepts were to be developed. The circular arrow between the 'overall problem' and 'sub-problem' stages illustrates this circular process of problem definition, concept generation, and concept evaluation. Only when this process is at least partly complete can the sub-problems be sufficiently defined for work to begin on them. This backward and forward interaction takes place not only between adjacent stages of the VDI model, but in some cases between non-adjacent stages. For example, if viable solutions to some individual problems cannot be found, it may be necessary to go right back to overall problem definition to examine if all of the objectives and constraints are valid. Similarly, when sub-solutions are combined into the overall solution, it may be found that overall system performance is not satisfactory, despite the care that was taken in evaluating sub-solution performance. This may necessitate reworking several previous stages of the design process.

The difficulty involved with ensuring that several sub-systems combine to give a satisfactory overall product performance can be substantial where complex system inter-actions are concerned. Automobiles and aircraft provide good examples of this type of product. In the case of a motor car, the overall problem is to provide a vehicle that will meet the requirements of a defined segment of the market. At sub-problem level will be the long list of attributes desired by the purchasers in respect of ergonomics, aesthetics, performance, and cost. Many of these sub-problems and their eventual sub-solutions interact strongly. The decisions made by an ergonomist working on interior design will be influenced by the decisions of engineers working on the car's suspension system. In turn, the suspension system design will be influenced by the characteristics of the engine, gearbox, and brakes. For a designer to work alone on his or her particular problem would result in a totally unsatisfactory product because of the inevitable mismatch between sub-systems.

Many undergraduate engineers are given experience of solving these type of problems as a part of their course. A popular study is based upon some kind of transmission unit such as a speed reduction gearbox. Here, the overall problem might be to design a unit that will provide a reduction in rotational speed from R_1 revolutions per minute to R_2, and transmit a power of W watts with certain fixed configurations of the input and output shafts.

Even if the problem is constrained to the utilisation of gears rather than being left open to include consideration of belt and chain drives, the possibilities are almost endless. The solution to the problem will incorporate gears, shafts, bearings, seals, a housing, and fasteners, all of which can be individually and jointly configured in a myriad of ways. Many of these elements or sub-problems interact. Although the equations that describe the behaviour of gears, shafts and bearings are well known, it is not always obvious where to start the process of calculating appropriate parameter values. The size of shafts cannot be calculated until the gear design has been progressed to a stage where the separation and axial forces are known. Gear calculations cannot be finalised until the limits on the distance

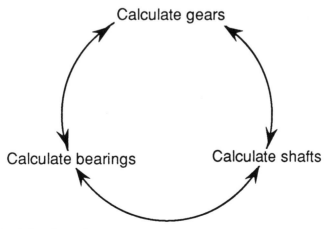

Figure 1.8 Iterative design of a gearbox

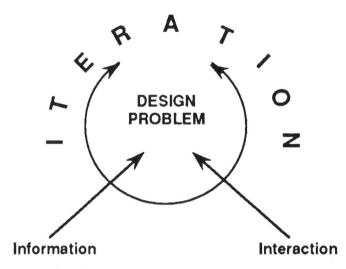

Figure 1.9 The nature of the design activity

between shaft centres are calculated. Shaft centres may depend upon the size of bearings that are required, and this cannot be fixed until the shaft forces have been calculated. The engineer seems to be trapped in a circular problem, with insufficient knowledge to start at any point in the process.

The way forward is to 'cut-and-try'. This rather appropriate Americanism accurately describes the process of taking one's best shot at assigning starting values at some point in the process. For example, by making an initial estimate of gear type and sizes, the designer can proceed to the calculation of forces, shaft sizes and bearings. In all probability, the initial choice of gear parameters will subsequently be found to be not ideal or even downright impossible. Several iterations around the loop (Figure 1.8) will be necessary to see if a solution is possible, and what the best solution is. However, each iteration will provide the designer with a better understanding of the problem and its possible solutions. Experience with similar problems is obviously a considerable advantage because it improves the chances of the first 'guess' being close to the final solution.

The important conclusion is that design is an iterative process at all levels (Figure 1.9). Iteration is present at the problem definition, concept generation and evaluation, embodiment, and detail definition stages. In general, the larger and more complex the product, the greater will be the number of iterations required. In the vast majority of cases, each of these iterations will require information from multiple sources and the involvement of many people to innovate, evaluate, analyse, and make decisions. Case studies of product design reveal that the details of the iterative process are never the same from product to product, or company to company. For this reason, all of the design process models that we have examined merely show a highly simplified description of the linkage between the basic elements of the process.

Whilst accepting that the design process models that we have examined illustrate the general progression of development of the product over a period of time, Figure 1.10 more accurately shows the nature of the activity viewed through the eyes of those involved. This model by Acar (1996), attempts to show the ongoing interaction between specification,

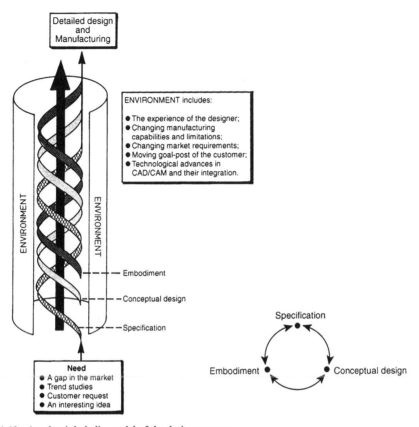

Figure 1.10   Acar's triple-helix model of the design process

conceptual design, and embodiment throughout the PDP by means of a triple helix existing within the product development environment. As time passes, the product development passes along the helix, but at any given moment a slice through the helix shows that there is always interaction between the three aspects of the process.

THE PRODUCT LIFE-CYCLE

Having completed the introduction to the PDP and its information requirements, we will now consider the relationship between the PDP and the product life-cycle. This is necessary to enable you to grasp why companies need to employ the PDP to remain in a competitive market position.

All products have a life-cycle, which is the period of time between their initial launch onto the market and their final withdrawal. The length of the **product life-cycle** (PLC) depends upon the nature of the product and the market into which it is sold. In the case of some products, the life-cycle may be only a year or a few months. This is particularly likely in the case of products like computers where the technology is developing so quickly that it leads to rapid obsolescence. Other products such as civil aircraft may be sold in virtually the same form for a decade or more.

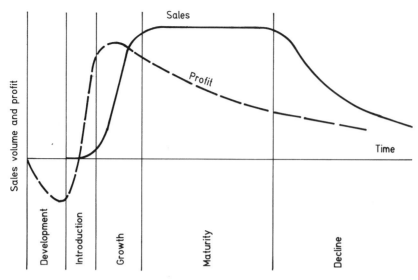

Figure 1.11 A life-cycle curve for sales volume and profit

A valuable insight into the way that a product is selling at a particular point in its life-cycle can be obtained by plotting its life-cycle curve. The usual way of presenting this is by plotting sales volume and profit against time. Figure 1.11 shows what is generally considered to be the basic form or typical life-cycle curve.

A typical curve has five phases: Product development, product introduction, product growth, product maturity, and product decline.

Product Development

Product development is the period between commencing investigation into a new product and launching that product onto the market. It includes the costly activities of market research, technological research, design, prototype testing, and preparation for manufacture. Because the product is not generating income from sales during this phase, the company needs to redirect assets and/or secure loans to finance the development stage.

The principal role of marketing during product development is to ensure: (1) that the company understands the needs of the future customers, (2) that the market for the product and the potential to make profits are large enough to warrant the investment that the company is making, and (3) that the company has developed advertising strategies that will support the product in the market, and has used appropriate advertising to prepare the market ahead of product launch.

Product Introduction

The product introduction phase starts with the first sale and covers the subsequent period of time during which the product is becoming established. Unlike the product development phase, it is impossible to produce a unique description of the product introduction and subsequent phases that identifies precisely where they begin and end.

The product introduction phase can be long or short, both in absolute terms and in comparison to the overall life of the product. Revolutionary products can take a long time to become accepted, and need time before a sufficient number of customers are persuaded to buy. Advertising is frequently very important in getting sales volumes to pick up quickly.

In addition to customer resistance, the product introduction phase sometimes suffers from other problems including the use of untested distribution channels, early product failures due to unforeseen modes of product usage, and manufacturing reliability and quality control difficulties. All of these problems cost the company money at a time when sales volumes are low. Inevitably, there will be a period at the start of product introduction where costs exceed income and the company will continue to accumulate losses.

There are many good examples of well known products that went through a difficult introduction phase. Powdered coffee creamers, frozen orange juice, and even instant coffee all needed long and expensive campaigns before they managed to overcome consumer reticence.

Some products fail during the introduction phase, and are withdrawn from the market to be redesigned, repackaged, or dropped altogether. If the product is to succeed, the company will want to pass through this high-cost – low-volume phase as quickly as possible so that they can enter the promised land of the growth phase.

Product Growth

If the new product satisfies the market and it is well backed by the company, it will enter the growth phase during which sales accelerate. During this phase of the product's life the increase in sales volume will mean that the cost of supporting it is shared between an ever increasing number of units. Cost per unit decreases and profits can increase dramatically.

In response to seeing the company having success with its new product, competitors will try to enter the market with their version of the product. The company will need to switch some of its advertising to encourage existing customers to stay loyal in addition to continuing to attract new buyers. The company will also need to consider adding improvements to the product so it remains attractive against the offerings of the competition. With a new product, the appearance of competition need not be a bad thing. The extra advertising provided by the competitors will widen the market, and all the companies involved in selling similar products may benefit. Reticent customers who resisted the advertising campaign of a sole supplier may be persuaded to experiment when other companies enter the arena.

The main problem that companies frequently face during the product growth phase is making the three-way decision between maximising profits, adding product features, or reducing prices. Competitors will invariably enter the market with improved product features and/or lower prices than the innovating company. If the company decides that the best strategy is to establish itself as a long-term player in the market it will need to ensure that its product remains competitive, and to do this it must respond with stronger advertising, improved product features, competitive pricing, or a combination of these. All these options will cost money and will reduce the short-term profitability of the company in the hope of improving profit in the next phase. As Figure 1.11 shows, the profit curve may peak and start to decline during the growth phase of the life-cycle because of the extra costs that the company is starting to incur.

Product Maturity

During the maturity phase of the product's life, sales volume is level relative to the rapid rise during the growth phase. If the company decided to go for the long-term view during the growth phase, it may now have a healthy market share because of its earlier decisions relating to price and product features. Sales are level because the company and its competitors are, between them, satisfying the needs of a fully developed market. Although it will be difficult for new competitors to break into this market, the company will need to be careful to protect its share of the market by advertising, and well thought out pricing and product feature strategies. Chapter 4 looks at these strategies in more detail.

The length of the maturity phase depends largely on the nature of the product. The first hand-held calculators with graph plotting capabilities were available for a little over six months before they were replaced by better products with improved features at a lower price. The life-cycle curve of these innovative products was almost straight up and down with no identifiable maturity phase. The maturity phase for many household white goods (fridges, washing machines etc.) is from one to three years, whilst that of some industrial products like transmission elements is over 10 years.

Product Decline

Although recognition that the eventual decline and demise of a product is an integral part of planning strategy for most companies making consumer products, it is often overlooked by companies selling industrial products. To a large extent, this is because the maturity phase of industrial products tends to be very long, and the future seems to be distant and hence unimportant prospect. Nevertheless, the time **will** come when the product can no longer be made available on the market.

In some cases, sales may rapidly drop to zero because of the unforeseen introduction of a much improved product by a competitor. More frequently, the decline will be a gradual decrease to a level at which it might remain for many years. In this situation, the company may attempt to hang on to the vestiges of its market by reducing prices even further, but this can drastically erode profits. Inevitably, the end result is one where no longer continuing to make the product makes economic sense, and withdrawal from the market is the only option.

Although there are options that may be taken in the early or middle decline phase, carrying a weak product can be very costly to the company. This cost is not only in terms of profit from the product, but also in respect to the demand that it places on company managers, the marketing function, inventory, and manufacturing. The time spent by these staff may be better applied to the development of new products that will generate a much higher level of profit. Keeping a weak product delays the search for replacement products, reduces profitability, and loosens the company's grip on the future.

The PDP and the PLC Curve

It is interesting to look at the relationship between the design of products and the PLC curve. The curve illustrates the problem faced by a single-product company. If such a company were to wait until its current product was in the decline phase before looking for a replacement it would be likely to meet very serious difficulties. As we have already seen, the product development phase can be very costly from both financial and staff time points of view. If the company delays the new product development phase until the old product is in terminal decline, the company may be so weakened financially that it is doomed to failure. Indeed, strong arguments can be made that the best time to develop a new product is during the growth or early maturity phases of a current product when the company is strong, resources are available, and the profit curve is reaching its peak. The problem with this strategy is that the company is usually under enormous pressure in the growth phase simply to tune its manufacturing capabilities to meet the continuously increasing sales demand. This, combined with an uncertainty about the exact shape that the PLC will take for a product persuades some companies to make hay whilst the sun shines and postpone difficult and expensive decisions until things become clearer in the future. Of course, things have a terrible way of not becoming clearer, and the main chance may be lost for good.

In addition to having influence on the timing of new product development, the PLC curve also illustrates the need for continuous design improvements to existing products. Improved features (some of which might lead to lower costs) are one of the ways that a company can respond to the inevitable competition. Incremental design improvement is therefore a necessity and not an option, with the initiative for the improvements being found in market function analysis of competitors and market trends, faults identified in use, warranty claims, manufacturing problems, etc.

RECAP

The PDP is a progression of activities complicated by the presence of repeated iterations in the search for the best solution to a series of design problems. The need to consider the influence of factors like manufacturing and overall system performance, even during the earliest stages of the process, makes a holistic approach necessary. To facilitate this approach, the designer needs continuous access to information and the knowledge, skills, and opinions of many people.

Recognising the need for information, being able to identify the sources from which it is available, and ensuring that it is taken into account during the PDP is essential for good design. For this reason, information management is one of the most important activities of an accomplished product designer.

The combination of market knowledge and good design is the foundation of long-term success in a company, and an important aspect of this is to recognise the need to develop new products as a strategy and not as a tactical response to growing failure in the market.

INTERFACES WITH DESIGN

OVERVIEW

Chapter 1 showed that the PDP is extremely complex, and involves the flow of information between many functions within the company, and across the company boundaries. This chapter looks in more detail at the information that crosses the design function interface.

Many of the methods that are described in later chapters provide structured ways of improving the effectiveness with which information is passed to the design function, and for processing and recording the information within the design function itself. Therefore, it is important to understand the nature of the information used by designers and what needs to be done with the information when it reaches its destination. Making this information passing activity effective and efficient is a vitally important aspect of design management, although in many companies the implications are not well understood.

OBJECTIVES

When you have finished studying this chapter, you will be able to:

- understand the nature of the information that crosses the design process boundaries;
- understand the need to manage the information flow;
- understand the complexity of the information and staff management implications;
- appreciate the consequences of inadequate interface management.

MARKETING AND DESIGN

Put simply, it is the responsibility of the marketing function to inform the company about the needs of the customer and the competitive products that are on offer. Without this information, it is impossible for engineers to define and produce products that will be commercially successful. The role of marketing and its relationship to design is so important that Chapter 4 deals solely with some of the techniques that marketing personnel use.

The extent to which an identifiable marketing function exists within a company varies widely. In some companies, the marketing function is represented at board level by a marketing director, who is responsible for one or more marketing managers (e.g. European marketing manager, American marketing manager, and Far East marketing manager). Each of these managers might be responsible for 5, 10, 20 or more staff who are concerned with collecting and analysing information, and compiling the results into a form that is useful to other functions within the organisation. Marketing is an expensive activity, and the type of marketing function outlined could only be supported in a large company. Typically, such a company would be selling to the domestic consumer market in products like motor cars, audio systems, and white goods such as washing machines and refrigerators.

At the other end of the scale, many small companies have no identifiable marketing function whatsoever. This does not necessarily mean that such a company is unaware of the need for market information. Frequently, a sales manager is made the *de facto* marketing expert, and sales staff are given the task of feeding back customer-generated information on product preferences, usage problems, suggestions for improvement etc. Companies with this type of marketing activity tend to be small and involved with the selling of specialised industrial products into niche markets where competition is negligible and/or the technology incorporated into the product is at a low level.

Of course, the marketing function is not the only path by which market-related information enters the company. The service department, which is concerned with the provision of spare parts and the processing of repairs, can contribute much useful information on product reliability, areas of superiority and inferiority in comparison to competitors, and the cost to the company of product faults. Sales, if it exists as a separate function, can provide information on why potential customers choose particular products, and developing trends in the market place. The breadth of market-related information, and the various company activities that can be used to provide it, identify the principal advantage gained from a well organised marketing department, i.e. coordination and the provision of a single point of contact between the design function and the market information that it needs.

What then is the nature of the information that crosses the marketing/design interface? Figure 2.1 shows some of the most obvious elements in this flow.

The first thing to notice is that there is flow in both directions. Although, in this case, it seems obvious that it is the responsibility of the marketing function to provide design with vital information about the needs of the market, the task of the marketing function can be made much easier if it has information about the constraints under which the design function is operating. For example, under the heading of 'market potential', the marketing function might attempt to establish what types of product variants will be in demand several years in the future. Whilst the company will want to keep its options open, and consider all possibilities, it might be useful for marketing to be aware of the current manufacturing and technological limitations of the company so that it can pay particular attention to products that fall within these limitations. This two-way flow of information and constraints is always present across functional interfaces. Figure 2.1 sets out some of the information that marketing can supply to the design function.

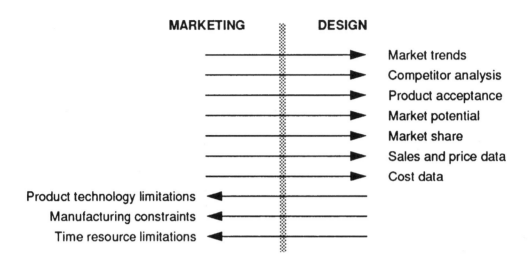

Figure 2.1 Information crossing the marketing/design interface

Market Trends

With the best will in the world, the smartest designer cannot define a commercially successful product unless the requirements of the customer have previously been established. One of the core activities of the marketing function is to provide designers with information about these customer requirements through market trend information. This covers a very wide range of knowledge about customer behaviour but can be categorised as follows: What the customers want now; how these requirements are likely to change in the future; and what can be done to influence current and future customer perceptions.

A team that is working on the design of a computer system needs to know about the applications that the final product is likely to be used for. How many purchasers would want to use graphics packages or word processors? How many would want to write their own software and in which programming languages? What type of output devices do they prefer, and how do prices influence these preferences? Information like this, on what the customer wants now is essential, but equally important is what will be required in the future. Will developments in Internet capability mean that other features will have to be incorporated? Should possible future changes in leisure activities or business systems influence the design? The probability of such information having an important influence on design decisions is even more likely to be the case when the product in question has a long lead time like an aircraft, or motor vehicle.

The requirements of customers are influenced by the environment and culture in which they live and work. Knowledge about the influence of these factors on buyer behaviour are essential so that appropriate features can be built into the product. Indeed, it may be necessary for designers to provide several variants of a product to meet the needs of different groups of customer, not only on the basis of environmental and cultural differences, but also in regard to other groupings such as age, sex, geographical location etc. The division of the market into groupings which exhibit different buyer behaviour is called 'market segmentation', and it is important that designers are provided with relevant information about the differing needs of each segment.

Competitor Analysis

Although company sales staff, service function staff, and other customer-orientated personnel can easily provide information relating to the performance and 'saleability' of their company's products in service, the ability of a company to secure an acceptable share of the market also depends on the attributes of competitor products.

There are instances where the objective of the design function is to improve some aspect of the company's product simply because it has failed to come up to expectations in service. If the reason for this is a basic design fault (e.g. the service department identify that an unacceptably high number of products returned for repair under warranty are due to the failure of a particular component or sub-assembly), the design function will attempt to rectify this problem by changing the geometry or material of the relevant parts. This type of design change is frequently carried out without any need to evaluate the performance of competitor products available to customers. However, when the aim is to introduce a design that is new to the company, or alter an existing design in such a way that it changes the performance, appearance, or purchase price of the product, it is important that decisions are not made without analysing what the competitors have to offer. Indeed, a constantly updated knowledge of competitor products should be one of the major driving forces for continuous design improvement.

From a designer's point of view, the most important competitor product information relates to functional attributes and cost, and the value that customers place on these. For example, designers who were involved with the design of a new or improved washing machine would certainly need to know about the capacities, available programmes, control options and panel layouts, safety systems, power and water consumption, and styling strategies of other manufacturers. They should also be aware of the methods by which competitors provide these features, and the implications for product cost. This information, plus an understanding of the importance placed by customers on each of these features provides an essential element of design knowledge.

Market Characteristics (Acceptance, Potential, and Share)

At the most basic level, the degree to which a company's product has been accepted by the market at which it was aimed, can be assessed passively by collecting data from personnel who interact with the customer. In particular, sales staff will be able to relate the responses that they get from potential customers, and this information can be used by the design team to ensure that any design failings are rectified. However, this type of information only provides a part of the picture.

Assuming that the new or modified product is being sold in competition with similar products from other manufacturers, a good measure of success is the share of the total market that is secured. If there are 20 different mid-range dishwashers being sold in the United Kingdom, each might be expected to secure in the region of 5% of the total sales for this type of product. In all probability, this equal share will not be the case because some products will offer better attributes and/or a more competitive price than others. Information about the total size of the market, the share of that market held by a particular product, the reasons for the variations in market share, and strategies for improving and fulfilling a product's full potential is the stuff of which business survival is made. Without it, the design function is working with its hands tied behind its back, in a sealed room, with the lights off.

To expect sales staff to collect data relating to their own company's products is one thing, but the collection of data that can be used to estimate market size and the share claimed by the various participants is another. The collection of information of this type usually requires active market function involvement via surveys of the customers, retailers, and distributors.

Cost Data

One of the most difficult problems that designers have to overcome is the balancing of 'trade-offs'. In the case of a structural component in an aircraft there might be a trade-off between weight and strength. To maximise load carrying capacity, the unladen weight of the aircraft must be as small as possible, and one way of achieving this is to minimise the amount of material in each component. However, there comes a point where a particular component cannot be made any lighter without reducing its load carrying capacity to a point where structural failure is an unacceptable risk. Unless there is a very precise definition of 'unacceptable', there will be a grey area where the best combination of weight and strength is a matter for discussion and possible disagreement. In such cases, engineers will attempt to arrive at a well considered decision by careful analysis of all of the factors involved. Regardless of this, the final decision may still turn out to rest upon art as much as science.

In the case of the aircraft component problem, it is probable that a third factor would complicate the decision-making process even more. By choosing stronger, lighter material, the engineers may be able to reduce weight and increase strength at the same time. The problem would be that such a material choice would invariably be more expensive than the heavier and weaker material. The decision then rests upon a judgement of whether the customers would prefer a low-cost aircraft with low load carrying capacity, or a more expensive aircraft with a higher payload capacity.

Frequently, cost is the most demanding and complicated constraint that the designer has to face. From a product sales point of view, the important issue is the price that the customer has to pay for the desirable attributes that the product provides. Although there is a connection between the cost of providing the product and the selling price, the rules governing this connection are complex and by no means obvious. One of the roles of marketing is to help determine the selling price that will maximise profits for the company, or to provide the company with a strategic market advantage. For example, in a situation where a particular product has no strong competition, it may be possible to pitch the selling price much higher than when competition is strong. Such decisions are usually beyond the sphere of influence of engineers. However, although it is frequently difficult to estimate the cost to the company of providing a product from knowledge of its selling price, there is no doubt that costs built into the product by design decisions will ultimately affect the price at which it is sold. Therefore, it is essential that designers have the information that they need to make decisions that influence product cost.

Ideally, this information will include not only the total cost that competitors are building into their products, but also the cost that they are building into each of the functions that customers see as being desirable. Designers can then set about the task of seeking design alternatives, not only with an ability to make functional evaluations and comparisons, but also with the possibility of assessing the implications for competitive costing.

Earlier in this chapter, I drew your attention to the two way nature of information flows across the marketing/design interface in both directions. To illustrate this Figure 2.1 shows three different types of information flowing from design to marketing. Each of these is provided to help the marketing function undertake its information gathering and analysis role efficiently. Briefly, the nature and purpose of this information is as follows:

Product Technology Limitations

The marketing function needs to know the strengths and limitations of the technology base within the company. The technology base is characterised by the experience and skills of the company's staff and, to a lesser extent by its technological product development facilities such as computer-aided design systems, research laboratories, and test equipment. Although the technology based attributes of the company can be improved and added to, the fact remains that this will cost money and take time, and either or both of these may be in short supply.

Manufacturing Constraints

The manufacturing facilities that a company uses to produce its products might be owned by the company itself or it may use the facilities provided by another company. If the company has invested heavily in purchasing general purpose or specialised manufacturing facilities, it needs to use them effectively. Therefore there is a pressure to make sure that expensive machine tools are heavily loaded, and not standing idle for a large proportion of their working lives. This pressure means that companies have to balance the benefits that may be gained from designing a product that utilises existing manufacturing facilities, against a design that would need new facilities or work being placed elsewhere. The choice will be made on the basis of company economics, and it is quite possible that large investment in new plant can easily be justified.

Time Resource Limitations

Although functional attributes and cost are vital elements in a commercially successful product, an equally important factor is the time taken to get the product to market. The marketing function will help the company to identify market opportunities, but these opportunities will only remain available over a limited time period. Delay in taking the opportunity can result in competitors entering the market first, or the market situation changing so that the identified needs no longer hold true. In this respect, time is a company resource. The length of time that will be taken from market definition or product concept to product launch will depend upon the ability of the design and other functions to respond. In addition to the technology limitations already described, there is the number of staff hours available to complete the project. Armed with this sort of information, the marketing function can help the company to identify windows of opportunity for product development.

The sources and destinations of the information that I have shown crossing the marketing/design interface may, in reality, be different. In some organisations it is the design function itself that is responsible for collecting competitor-related information. Companies frequently obtain examples of competitor products and place them in their development or research department for disassembly and assessment. Information regarding product acceptance may go to design directly from the sales or service functions, and external marketing consultants might be used to provide information on market characteristics. The important thing is that appropriate information enters the product design function to enable it to make informed decisions about current and future products upon which the economic health of the company will rely.

MANUFACTURING AND DESIGN

Manufacturing means those company functions that are concerned with the processing of materials as a means to producing the product. This broad definition includes:

- **Process planning** which has the responsibility for deciding the most appropriate methods for manufacture and assembly.
- **Production control** which is concerned with ensuring that production targets can be achieved by judicious loading of work onto the various elements of the manufacturing facilities.
- **Manufacturing systems** which is concerned with the specification and design of manufacturing facilities to meet the needs of the company.

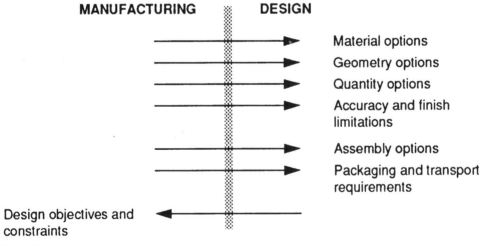

Figure 2.2 Information crossing the manufacturing/design interface

In some companies these three manufacturing functions will exist (possibly with different names) as separate entities, whilst in others the boundaries between them will be blurred or non-existent. Regardless of this they are the source of essential information for the product design process. Indeed, in many modern organisations, their role is seen as being so central to the PDP that their role is fully integrated at all stages. We will look at the implications for these types of structures in Chapter 3.

Figure 2.2 shows some of the most important information that crosses the manufacturing/design interface. Many of the elements identified in the figure are interdependent. For example, it is impossible to consider material options without giving regard to quantity. Hence, a component that was required in very large quantities might be restricted to manufacture by a choice of two or three alternative processes, and these processes might limit the designer to choose from a limited range of materials (e.g. injection moulding would limit the choice to thermoplastics).

Material Options

Design staff will want to choose the best combination of materials and manufacturing processes for the product under development. However, there could be several reasons why the list from which they make their choices might be restricted or at least biased. The company's in-house manufacturing processes will be suitable for some materials but not others. Foundry facilities may be geared up to handle ferrous rather than non-ferrous metals, the investment made in plastic processing might have been directed at thermosets rather than thermoplastics, or the company might have made a significant investment in processes to handle ceramics or sintered metal components. Whilst no one would propose that the company should limit its material choices to those that it could handle without new investment, an awareness of current manufacturing capabilities is important if alternative options are to be thought through properly.

Geometry Options

Certain manufacturing processes are limited to the production of particular shapes. For example, lathes produce cylindrical forms, whilst shaping machines and many milling machines are limited to the production of flat surfaces. It may be that a company's stock manufacturing processes restrict the design function to combinations of certain geometrical forms. If this is the case, the company will have to decide whether to restrict the design options to what it has available, purchase additional manufacturing facilities, or arranging for all or part of the manufacturing to be contracted out to other companies.

Regardless of where the manufacturing is to be done, design staff will need information that will allow them to decide the best geometries for the processes that are going to be used. If a decision has been made to make a component out of zinc alloy on a high pressure die-casting machine, the designer needs advice on the geometrical limitations of the process. If this information is not available at an early stage of the PDP, the resulting component may be impossible or at least costly to make by that process. The aim is to ensure that 'design for manufacture' considerations are incorporated from the start of the PDP, and never as a corrective measure at a later date.

Figure 2.3 Two designs of date stamp

Quantity Options

For almost all manufacturing processes, a range of component throughput can be identified over which the processes provides the most economic conditions. There are many reasons why this is the case, but the most significant are maximum production rates, set up costs, and labour costs.

As an example, consider the two items shown in Figure 2.3. Each is a version of a date stamp, used in offices to record the date of arrival of incoming mail. Despite minor design differences, each provides essentially the same function as the other, and yet, the two manufacturers have chosen different manufacturing methods. The stamp on the left is manufactured principally from steel, whilst that on the right is mainly injection moulded plastic. Frequently, the decision that leads to such differences rests upon the number of components that will be made per year. Figure 2.4 helps to explain the basis for the decision.

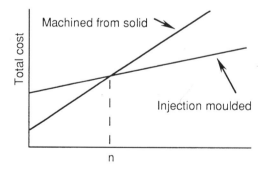

Figure 2.4 The relationship between total cost and quantity for two different processes

Manufacturing the mould into which the plastic is injected can be very expensive. This means that the company has to invest a large amount of money before the first component can be made. However, once in production, this process is highly automated, and the labour and factory overhead costs associated with each individual component is low. On the other hand the cost of making jigs and fixtures for machined component will be relatively low, but the process is likely to carry a higher labour cost.

In Figure 2.4, the relatively high point at which the 'injection moulded' line crosses the cost axis shows the implication of expensive tooling. The 'machined from solid' line starts lower, but rises more steeply because the labour cost per component is higher. In this illustration, the two lines cross, which suggests that if the total number of components to be produced are less than n, the machining from solid option will yield the lower unit cost. If the total number of components to be produced is greater than n, the injection moulded option would be the most economical. The number of components at which the two lines cross is called the 'break even point'.

The information that the designer needs to enable full account to be given to these factors is complicated by the presence of other factors including the availability of machines, and the frequency with which new tooling will be required. The availability of this information is essential if the correct product design decisions are to be made.

Accuracy and Finish Limitations

Broadly speaking, each manufacturing process has a range of accuracy and surface finish over which it can be used most economically. If a component has a requirement for size tolerances that are smaller, or surface finishes that are smoother than the inherent capabilities of a particular process, it is usually best to consider an alternative process with suitable capabilities. Attempts to make a process produce tighter tolerances or smoother surfaces than standard usually result in significant added cost. Conversely, choosing a process that offers better capabilities than those required, is usually an incorrect decision from a cost point of view. In many cases, the only way to overcome this type of problem is to use several different processes to manufacture a single component. Again, the availability of this information at the very earliest stages of the PDP is essential for good design.

Assembly Options

Potentially, component assembly decisions can have a significant effect upon overall product cost. The decision that needs to be made is similar to that of choosing between alternative manufacturing processes. In this case the choice is frequently between various degrees of automatic and manual assembly. The difference in setup costs between these two options is usually considerable. Automatic assembly can require very large investments in automated equipment, but manual assembly can involve high labour costs. Once again, the key is quantity; but whatever the decision, the designer has a vital role in minimising assembly costs by the application of appropriate product geometries and handling features.

'ackaging and Transport Requirements

For many products, adequate consideration of the need for appropriate packaging and transportation plays an important role in defining a commercially successful product. In instances where these factors are considered as an afterthought, the results can be far from satisfactory.

From a transportation point of view, the designer needs to ask if:

(a) the product is sufficiently robust to be transported by the preferred method, and if not can this be rectified by judicious design of the product or its packaging;

(b) the product needs special protective packaging;

(c) special lifting provisions need to be built in.

The interaction between manufacturing and design is two-way. The form of the information from manufacturing to design will be modified by the objectives, constraints, and options available to the design function. Therefore, the interface is essentially concerned with determining the optimum balance between the demands of the market place, the design options on offer, and the manufacturing options available to the company.

PURCHASING AND DESIGN

The role of the purchasing or buying function is to act as the interface between the company and the suppliers of bought-out components and materials. In addition to the placing of orders, it is likely to be concerned with determining the best sources of supplies from the company's point of view. In this case, determination of 'best' is likely to be influenced by a potential supplier's capacity to provide the required goods at the right quality and at the right price. However, other issues may be important such as the ability of the supplier to provide the goods at the right time and in the right quantity for the buyer. This is particularly important when a company is attempting to keep its stock of parts down to a minimum, and only wishes to purchase goods that will suffice for a month or week of production. Purchasing departments will also be concerned with determining the reliability and commercial integrity of suppliers, and establishing alternative sources of key components and materials in case usual suppliers fail to meet the company's needs.

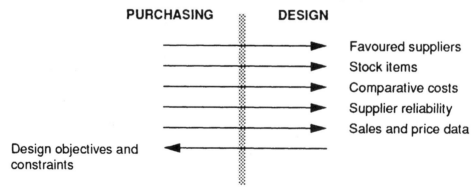

Figure 2.5 Information crossing the purchasing/design interface

Figure 2.5 shows the flow of information from the purchasing to the design function. The information from purchasing need not present restrictions to the design activity, but awareness of existing chains of supply, favoured suppliers, and components in stock might lead to design decisions that will have beneficial downstream consequences for product cost and quality.

OTHER SOURCES OF DESIGN INFORMATION

Some of the ways that marketing, manufacturing, and purchasing will be involved with the PDP have already been described. However, developing a product that will make a profit for the company is such a basic requirement for survival that every function in the company will be involved in some way.

Although, in a company with a well constituted marketing function, most of the customer-orientated information will enter the PDP via that function, other routes will also be utilised. Direct contact between design staff and personnel from sales, service, spares, and technical support functions will provide information on customer perceptions about product strengths and weaknesses. The commercial or finance functions within the company will play the key role in assessing the implications of design options on cash flow, borrowing requirements and profitability, and continuous sharing of information will be necessary throughout the PDP.

In some companies, the roles of the design and product development functions are classified as united from an organisational point of view. Many companies emphasise this link by establishing a 'design and development department' with the prime responsibility of putting new or improved products into the market. In this context, design is concerned with defining the nature of a new or modified product, whilst development is concerned with taking production or prototype versions and improving them by a testing and modification. Although the objectives of the design and development functions may be considered the same, the activities are quite different and usually take place in different locations. Even when the two functions are controlled by a single manager, the regular interchange of information is required to facilitate effective progress. Figure 2.6 shows the nature of a large proportion of this information.

In addition to the testing of the company's own products, the development function is frequently concerned with testing competitor products to provide a 'benchmark' against

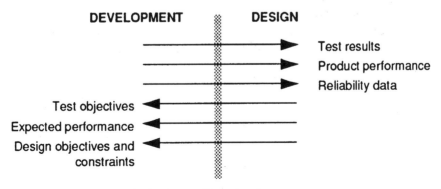

Figure 2.6 Information crossing the development/design interface

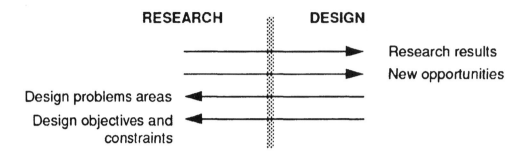

Figure 2.7 Information crossing the research/design interface

which the company's product can be evaluated. This information is valuable to the design and marketing functions.

Companies with their own research capabilities generate information that they hope will provide them with a competitive edge over their competitors. However, this information will not benefit the company unless it is disseminated effectively to other functions. Equally, the activities of the research function need to be based upon the requirements of other company functions, and design plays a key role in determining the research activity. Figure 2.7 indicates the nature of some of the information flowing between the research and design functions.

INFORMATION PROCESSING METHODS

Because conflict resolution is a primary activity of the PDP, the information that flows into the process from elsewhere needs to be processed, analysed, and negotiated before being accepted for incorporation into a list of product requirements. As an example, the design function in a company that produces telephone handsets may be instructed by the marketing function to develop a new product with a 'warm feel' to it. From a design point of view, the easiest way of achieving this might be to use a different type of plastic to that used previously. However, such a decision may be resisted by manufacturing because of the absence of suitable production machines, and by finance because of the need for additional investment. This conflict can only be resolved effectively by first ensuring that all relevant information is available, and then by taking a decision that considers the best interests of the company. This information processing activity can be represented as shown in Figure 2.8.

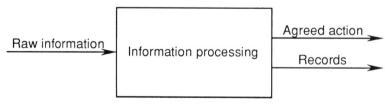

Figure 2.8 Design involves information transfer and processing

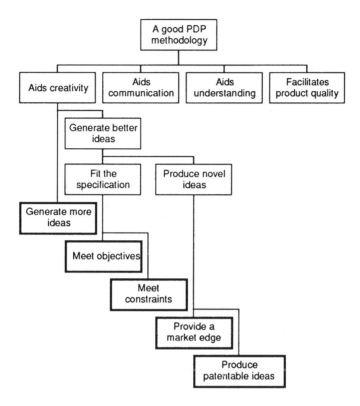

Figure 2.9   Creativity benefits from design methods

The raw information being provided for the PDP by one or more company functions must lead to a set of agreed product design actions. It is these actions that will lead to the development of the new or improved product that meets all of the company's objectives and constraints in the best possible way. At the same time, the processing of the information should lead to the generation of suitable records, so that the rationale for arriving at the decisions, and the identification of the person(s) responsible can be retrieved at a later date.

The methods that are used for the processing of the information are varied. However, because conflict resolution is a key requirement, the process will almost certainly involve negotiation between the interested parties. This recognition of the central role played by direct communication between the interested parties provides a basis for determining the attributes that a good method should exhibit. Figures 2.9 to 2.11 show a logical mapping of these attributes.

There are four key benefits that can be gained by the application of appropriate design methodologies during the PDP. The benefits will comprise one or more of the following:

- an improved environment for the generation of creative ideas which may be used for the solution of problems associated with product design;
- improved means by which staff involved in the PDP can communicate their ideas and views to others;

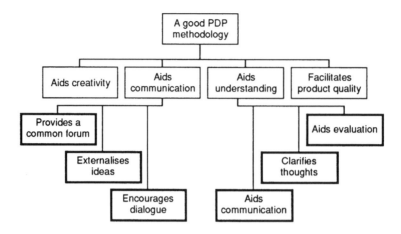

Figure 2.10 Communication and understanding benefits from design methods

- improved conditions in which staff can understand problems, evaluate solutions to problems and agree courses of action with colleagues;
- the provision of agreed formats that can be used for recording the objectives, activities, and outcomes of the PDP.

Figure 2.9 shows these four principal areas of benefit emanating from the application of a good PDP methodology. The figure also contains an expansion of the 'aids creativity' branch to show what the result of this benefit is likely to be. Thus, aiding creativity leads to the generation of more and better ideas; with some of the ideas being novel, and an overall

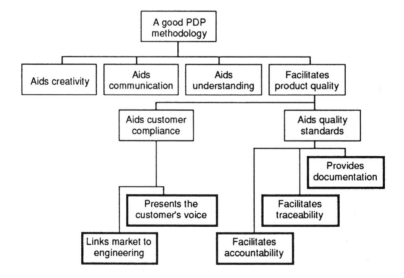

Figure 2.11 Quality benefits from design methods

improvement in the probability that ideas will fit the product specification. These ideas (we would hope) would meet the objectives and constraints, and might provide the company with a commercial market edge against its competitors, and ideas that could be patented. The figure shows the final benefits that might accrue from using a method for creativity enhancement in boxes with bold outlines. Figure 2.10 expands the 'aids communication' and 'aids understanding' benefits to show what the outcomes of these are likely to be.

The three benefits under the 'aids communication' heading are clearly important in any attempt to improve the flow and processing of information. To enable communication to take place effectively, people need a set of rules, whether this be related to verbal, paper or electronic interactions. Communication rules might involve things like the way that product specifications are formatted, or the way in which market needs are defined. If you don't have any rules, or you don't apply the rules consistently, the result is a bit like playing a football match without a game plan. The match will proceed after a fashion, and individual performances may be excellent, but there will be many misunderstandings, mistakes, and lost opportunities. The methods described later in this book provide a game plan for the transfer and processing of product information in a design environment by establishing a common forum for these activities.

In the football match analogy, the introduction of a game plan would help the players to cooperate with each other, and lead to a better understanding of what everyone was trying to do. In the company, the introduction of methods actually encourages dialogue. In this sort of environment, staff tend to be more confident in putting their views forward, and this externalisation of ideas can contribute enormously to making the PDP more effective and efficient.

To a certain extent, the 'aids understanding' benefit springs out of the communication benefits. After all, one of the main stumbling blocks to lack of understanding is inadequate communication. However, the increased understanding that can result from using methods is so important that it is worth identifying separately at the second level in the benefit map. Obvious sub-benefits from an increase in understanding are that it helps staff to evaluate options, and enables them to think more clearly about problems and their solutions. Interestingly, people who are well informed and understand the issues are also likely to communicate the issues more effectively than less well informed colleagues. Therefore the map arrives at the communication benefit at two levels, suggesting that it is of special importance. The logical mapping of ideas in the way presented in Figures 2.9 to 2.11 is one of the methods described later, and detailed analysis is given in Chapter 5.

The remaining principal benefit from method utilisation is that it facilitates consideration of product quality. Figure 2.11 expands this particular branch.

The common definition of the word 'quality' implies that it is concerned with some inherent characteristic present in all products.

Definition

quality **1.** degree of excellence . . .

However, this is not the definition of quality that industry uses when referring to its products or systems. For us, the appropriate definition is provided by the International Quality

Assurance Management System Standard as contained in International Standard ISO 9000 and European Standard EN 29000. Quite simply, their definition of quality is 'fitness for purpose'. In other words a quality product is fit for the purpose for which it was designed and produced. And 'purpose' is the use to which the product may be put as described by the company and expected by the customer. Hence, by this definition, a Lada may be determined to be a better quality product than a Rolls Royce if it meets the needs of **its** customers more closely than the Rolls Royce meets the needs of **its** customers. The achievement of this match between customer needs and product attributes requires two principal actions by the company. First, the company has to establish what the customer really wants. And second, appropriate procedures must be established within the company to ensure that actions are taken to incorporate the customer needs into the product. The first of these actions is concerned with customer compliance, and the second with quality standards.

The keys to achieving customer compliance are to determine what the needs are, then to make sure that all decisions that influence the attributes of the product are assessed in the light of these needs. Most of the methods that we will consider address both of these issues by linking engineering to the market and constantly placing the needs in front of the design team. The Japanese coined the phrase the 'voice of the customer' for the sum total of the attributes that the customer values. Spreading the voice of the customer is a key objective of most design methods.

The introduction of appropriate procedures for ensuring that product quality is fully considered at all stages of the design process is essential. An important aspect of these procedures is to ensure that decision makers take every reasonable precaution to ensure that product quality is upheld. An ability to determine who made decisions, and why a decision was made is essential if adequate control of the PDP is to be maintained. Hence, the provision of appropriate documentation and the facilitation of traceability and accountability are important benefits from methods utilisation. The bottom level of Figure 2.11 identifies these features.

RECAP

For the PDP to work effectively, a large amount of information must be passed between members of the design team, and between the team and other company functions. The communication of this information, and the dialogue that needs to take place to reach understanding and agreement is a vitally important aspect in the production of a quality product. The use of PDP methods provide a means of making this information handling more effective than would be the case if they were not utilised.

The methods bring many benefits to product development, but the following list summarises the principal ones:

- generation of more creative ideas;
- increased opportunities of meeting project objectives and constraints;
- can give the company a market edge over competitors;
- increased potential to produce novel patentable ideas;
- provides a common forum for dialogue;
- helps staff to externalise ideas;

- encourages dialogue;
- aids evaluation of options;
- clarifies thoughts;
- aids communication;
- provides a link between marketing and engineering;
- spreads the voice of the customer throughout the company;
- provides documentation for quality procedures;
- assists traceability and accountability.

THREE

ORGANISATION AND TEAMWORK

OVERVIEW

Chapter 2 identified some of the information that the design function requires, and possible sources for this information from within and outside the company. In doing this, the impression might have been given that each of these functions exists as a totally separate entity, perhaps located in different office space, and relying on the communication of information across departmental boundaries. Although this type of organisational structure exists in many companies, there are alternative strategies that can be adopted. This chapter looks at different approaches to organising the way that people work with each other, and considers the advantages and problems associated with each from the point of view of team interactions.

Despite the advances that have been made in electronic communications and computer-based information systems, team working is still the most essential element in the processing of information during the PDP. This chapter examines the role of teams in providing cross functional communication, and the requirements for the effective team work necessary to achieve maximum benefits from the use of methods described in subsequent chapters.

OBJECTIVES

When you have finished studying this chapter, you will be able to:

- understand the difference between functional and matrix organisational structures;
- understand the concepts of total quality management;
- understand the purpose and requirements of the simultaneous engineering approach;
- understand the role of teams in the PDP;
- understand how methods might assist team operation.

ORGANISATIONAL STRUCTURES

When Thomas Boulton and James Watt set up their factory to make stationary steam engines in the latter part of the 18th century, the issues involved in ensuring that the venture was successful were much the same as is the case in industry today (Baynes & Pugh), 1981. Materials and parts had to be purchased, and a product made with the attributes and price required by a customer. Watt employed only a few people at his Birmingham works, and kept tight control over all aspects of the venture from design, to manufacture and installation. His background as an engineering craft apprentice ensured that he was a practical engineer with a thorough understanding of the capabilities and limitations of manufacturing processes. Prior to 1781, he did all of the design work himself, including the preparation of the working drawings. Even after that date, when a small drawing office was added to the works, he worked with only one assistant in his own home, and kept personal control over all aspects of his company's operations. At the time, Watt's work on steam engines was at the cutting edge of technological achievement, in a similar way to the position occupied by certain aspects of space flight and automobiles at the start of the 21st century. Yet, it would be almost inconceivable to envisage a high-tech company today where all of the company's functions were under the direct control of a single person. Why is this, and what has changed?

There is no single reason why the organisational structures of modern companies are so different from those previously found to be acceptable. Many factors have contributed to the need for change, and the process of change itself has been gradual. The key to understanding the change is the way that information is held and communicated. In Watt's day, and through until the early 20th century, companies tended to be much smaller than they are today, and this lower employee count in itself meant that communication was easier. Secondly, the technological basis of products was less diverse. Although Watt's engines were incredible works of innovative engineering, they did not demand the breadth of technological expertise demanded in (say) a modern motor car. This growth in technological content has meant that it is difficult, and in many cases impossible to avoid employing large numbers of people each with specialised technical skills.

An additional factor that has brought about the change is the high production volumes required for some products. This demand, together with new manufacturing methods has meant that specialists are required to optimise the manufacturing routes that will provide the required quantities at a competitive price. Finally, the increase in wealth in the industrially developed countries has brought about a large increase in choice, not only for the consumer, but also for the companies that are a part of the manufacturing chain. A company that purchases components to incorporate in its products has many other companies competing for its business. This makes careful decision making essential if expensive mistakes are not to be made.

COMPANY ORGANISATION

A Functional Structure

Even today, small concerns often have a structure that Watt would be familiar with, that is a single person controlling the smallest detail of company operations as in Figure 3.1.

Figure 3.1 One man and a dog

For a small business this type of organisation can be the most effective because coordination between all of the different activities is ensured. However, if the business grows beyond a certain size, it is impossible for a single person to manage all of the concern's affairs without making mistakes. At this point, the owner is likely to employ some staff in a managerial role to take care of functions under his or her direction (Figure 3.2). This relinquishing of control to others is sometimes difficult, but is necessary if the various activities are to be managed properly.

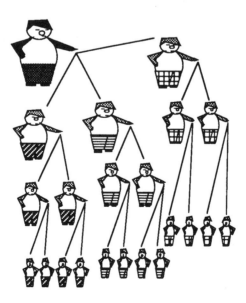

Figure 3.2 A functional organisation

The delegation of responsibilities to managers brings the benefits of specialisation, e.g. the person put in charge of sales is likely to be an experienced sales manager, and will give 100% of their working life to ensuring that the sales function operates effectively. The down-side of this distribution of management responsibility is that it introduces the risk of misunderstandings between different managers, and between individual managers and the owners of the company, i.e., both across and up and down the organisation. When these misunderstandings are of a serious nature, the consequences can be expensive or even disastrous for the company.

Eventually, the company might grow to a point where the executive control is vested not in a single person, but in a group of directors. At that point, there are likely to be many managers, some at senior level who will be responsible for several junior managers each of whom in turn will be responsible for several members of staff. The type of company growth and evolution just described gives rise to a functional departmental structure. The staff and junior managers who are under the control of the senior sales manager will form the 'sales department', where all the sales expertise of the company resides. Even if the sales activity is divided into two sub-departments, one for European sales and the other for North American sales, the expertise available in the department will be principally sales oriented. To a very large extent, this functional organisation of the company owes nothing to the type of product that the company is manufacturing, and two companies with totally different products might have almost identical functional structures.

A visitor, taking a walk around many companies will quickly see evidence of the functional basis of its organisation. There will be doors with legends such as 'sales manager', whilst next door will be an office space with workers busily progressing the work of the sales function. Further along the corridor, a design manager might have control of an office of engineers, clerks and secretaries. As we have seen in Chapter 2, all of these functions have access to information which must be shared with others for the PDP to proceed effectively.

One of the fundamental problems with functionally based organisations is that of communication between the separate departments (Figure 3.3). In badly managed companies, communication is inadequate, and staff adopt an 'over-the-wall' attitude to staff in functions other than their own.

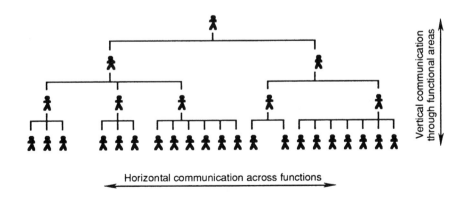

Figure 3.3 Communication needs to flow horizontally as well as vertically

This tends to manifest itself in an excess of paper communication at the expense of discussion, negotiation, and group decision making. The result is that each function tends to work as a separate entity that does not take account of what other functions need. This is analogous to the single owner of the company that has grown too big to be kept under effective control. In this type of situation, a marketing function might not provide the information that design require; not because the marketing function is ineffective, but simply because of a lack of good communication in both directions. Similarly, engineers might design and produce drawings for components that are expensive or even impossible to manufacture because the communication links between the design and manufacturing functions are inadequate. When a company operates in this way, its achievements will be way below what could be attained even though each individual function might be working hard and effectively. From the point of view of product design, a badly managed functional organisation is a disaster. The vital information exchanges identified in Chapter 2 will be very difficult to achieve, with the result that the PDP will take longer than it should, and the end result will be of lower quality than might have been the case.

Over recent years, many companies have had to slim down their organisations to remain competitive. A common strategy in this slimming down process has been the removal of one or more middle management layers within the functional structure as shown in Figure 3.4. Theoretically, in addition to reducing staff costs, this 'delayering' procedure makes vertical communication between senior managers and junior staff quicker and less prone to transmission errors. Whatever the broad effect of these 'flat' organisations, they have interesting implications for the use of teams.

The reduction in middle management layers should mean that companies move towards Total Quality Management (TQM) philosophies by involving and empowering junior staff (see the next section in this chapter). After all, if this is not the case, the effect of delayering may be to place an unmanageable burden on senior staff. On the other hand, if staff empowerment **is** a consequence of delayering, there are positive implications for effective teamwork because of increased motivation to solve product-oriented problems.

Even after delayering, strategies are still required to ensure that functional barriers do not present impenetrable barriers to horizontal communication. Many companies now use an alternative organisational approach to the functional one previously described. This alternative is called a matrix organisation, and it can provide the mechanism to break down functional barriers.

A Matrix Structure

The objective of a matrix structure is to take account of the communication needs of individual projects. The central theme is the formation of teams which set out to meet

Figure 3.4 Delayered companies are slimmed down by the selective removal of middle management

	Product team 1	Product team 2	Product team 3
Sales	1	-	-
Design	3	1	1
Manufacturing	2	1	1
Marketing	2	-	1
Purchasing	1	-	1

Figure 3.5   Teams based on a matrix structure

pre-defined objectives. These teams have members drawn from any of the functional groups that are necessary for the effective operation of the project. In Figure 3.5, product team 1 might have the task of undertaking all of the work for a new product, and have been constituted from one member of staff from sales, three design engineers, two manufacturing engineers, two marketing personnel, and someone from purchasing. Product team 2, consisting of one design engineer and one manufacturing engineer might be seeking a solution to a difficult design for manufacture problem, and product team 3 might have been formed to formulate broad policy for product improvement in response to a new improved design from a competitor. The way that cross-functional teams operate in industry varies between companies. In some instances, if the project is of a suitably long duration, members of the team are placed in the same geographical area. In an open-plan office layout, this can lead to particularly effective communication. In other cases, team members will be more remote from each other, and will need more careful managing to ensure that effective communications are maintained.

Cross-functional teams tend to form and reform as required by the workload. Some teams may work together for months or years on the design, development, and support of a particular product. Others come together to solve relatively short duration problems, and are then reassigned to other tasks. Frequently, an engineer will be a member of several teams between which his or her total effort will be shared. Hence, in Figure 3.5, an individual engineer may be a member of all 3 of the product teams identified.

A matrix system requires management along project lines as shown in Figure 3.6. Project managers might not be a part of the normal hierarchical functional structure, and if this is the case they will not owe allegiance to functional managers. Alternatively, they may be drawn from within the functional structure, usually from a department that has a key role to play in the project. Frequently, project managers are called 'product managers' and are identified as being the product 'champions' whose role it is to bring the product successfully to market.

Although cross-functional teams frequently provide effective means of breaking down the communication barriers, the matrix organisation has some peculiar management problems. One of these problems stems from the potential for conflict between project managers for the services of team members. In a matrix organisation, the functional design

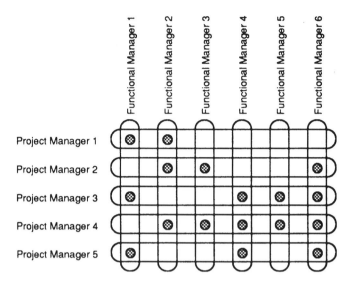

Figure 3.6   A matrix organisation has functional and project managers

manager will be responsible for all of the staff resources in the design area. However, the managers of project or product teams are principally concerned with the rapid resolution of tasks, and will want sufficient staff resources to complete them in the allotted time. Inevitably, it happens that team managers are sometimes in competition with each other for limited staff resources, whilst functional managers have the task of finding a solution to the limited resource problem.

TOTAL QUALITY MANAGEMENT

Chapter 1 introduced the concept of product quality being the attainment of the product attributes required by the customer at an acceptable price. Meeting this goal is the objective of the PDP, and **all** of the people who are concerned with it. The key word in the preceding sentence is 'all' because, as we now understand, design is a team effort.

The use of TQM to bring about the fulfilment of the quality objective goes back to just before the second world war. In the 1920s, the term 'quality' was restricted to manufacturing quality control. At that time, quality was concerned with reducing the number of defective components produced by a manufacturing system. This business of measuring and controlling defective components by the application of statistical techniques still plays a vital role in companies today. In the 1940s pioneering work by Deming and others indicated that a more holistic view of quality was required, i.e. prevention where possible was cheaper and more effective than cure. Strangely, although Deming was an American management consultant, it was the Japanese who adopted his ideas with the most enthusiasm. The destruction of the Japanese industrial base in 1945, and the decision by the Americans to rebuild it, took Deming to Japan in the 1950s where his ideas were readily adopted (Deming, 1986). From the 1960s onwards, TQM was 're-discovered' in the United States, and has since been adopted by many companies worldwide. Deming's

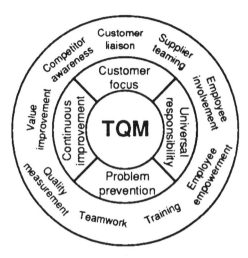

Figure 3.7 Important features of Total Quality Management

vision of quality was concerned with improving the fit between the attributes that a product has, and the attributes that the customer wants. This is much more than the narrower definition that is concerned with ensuring that the output from the manufacturing process is within the limits laid down in detail design documentation. Because of the obvious risk of confusion over which of these definitions are being applied, a broadly adopted convention is to use the upper case convention 'Quality' to mean customer needs compliance, and the lower case convention 'quality' to mean process output control. These conventions are used throughout this book.

As shown in Figure 3.7, TQM adopts the objectives of customer focus, continuous improvement, problem prevention, and universal responsibility (Oakland (1997) and Berk (1993)). The attainment of these objectives requires the company to adopt the actions in the outer ring of Figure 3.7, but above all the successful implementation of TQM requires sustained management commitment.

Each of the actions in the outer circle merits a brief examination.

Customer Liaison

Knowledge of what the customer really wants is a basic precept to the establishment of the TQM strategy. This knowledge may be through direct contact with customers or via broad based market evaluations carried out by the marketing function or other customer-related functions. Chapters 4 and 5 examine some of the methods that are used.

Competitor Awareness

The other half of market awareness is knowledge about competitors. If another company is already selling a good product then extra care must be taken in providing the additional features that will persuade the customer to buy your product. Again, this information is frequently acquired by the marketing function, and appropriate methods are dealt with in Chapter 4.

Value Improvement

In the end, customers will decide which product to buy on the basis of their value to them as individuals and/or their company. Information on the way that customers assess the value of your product and competitors' products is an essential pre-requisite to product design. Chapter 10 deals with the analysis of product value.

Quality Measurement

If you can't measure Quality you don't know when you have enough of it. Because product design is a team effort, everyone involved needs to know where they are and where they are going in terms that are sufficiently measurable to allow them all to have the same perception of achievements and targets. Chapters 8, 9, 11 and 12 introduce some commonly used methods.

Teamwork

Teamwork is central to product design and TQM systems. All of the methods dealt with in this book from Chapter 4 onwards involve the use of teams.

Training

TQM is about people working effectively. It is not, essentially, about paperwork or computer systems, or management directives issued from upon high. Companies that successfully employ TQM strategies report that staff training is probably the single most important factor in their success. People need to know what the company objectives are and how their role in the company helps to meet these objectives. An important aspect of TQM is that staff must realise that they **all** have a customer or even several customers. In many cases, these customers will be other staff working in the same company. Nevertheless, it is vital that the needs of these internal customers are satisfied if the external product buying customer is to be given full satisfaction.

Employee Involvement and Empowerment

To some managers, employee involvement and empowerment seems to be a frightening encroachment on their responsibility as a manager. In practice, if carried out properly, involvement and empowerment **does** lead to a partial delegation of a traditional manager's responsibility, but requires additional skills and techniques to be adopted in their place (Weaver, 1995).

The person who holds the most knowledge about a particular task is invariably the person who carries it out on a day-to-day basis. It is this person, not their manager, who knows what aspects of the task are working well or badly. To ignore this knowledge is to impoverish the company, but many managers fail to utilise this valuable source of information in their decision-making activities. The first stage of rectifying the problem is to involve the employee in the decision-making process by at least making sure that their knowledge is taken into account. This not only benefits the company but also motivates the employee to think about their task.

The stage after involvement is empowerment, which means giving staff the responsibility to fix problems. To a certain extent, empowerment is even more frightening but eventually more beneficial than involvement. Together with empowerment comes the increased sense of worth and the recognition of joint objectives that is the ultimate objective of TQM.

Supplier Teaming

An objective of companies with more advanced TQM strategies is to form strong relationships with good suppliers. Evidence suggests that, in the long run, a company will do better by working closely with a small number of suppliers than by changing suppliers every time one comes along with a better price. The reason for this is that a familiar relationship with a trusted supplier makes it easier to involve them from an early phase of the product design process. In turn, this makes it more likely that the supplier will be able to provide the right product at the right price.

SIMULTANEOUS ENGINEERING

The concept of simultaneous or concurrent engineering is that the design of a product and the systems by which it is to be manufactured should be developed in parallel. Many studies have been carried out that show the economic benefits that can be gained by following such a practice. Hauser & Clausing (1988) stated that costs incurred in getting manufacturing and Quality issues right prior to product launch were subsequently paid back many times over via reduced lead times and downstream problems.

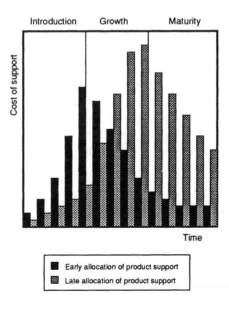

Figure 3.8 The early allocation of money to overcome product design problems reduces cost downstream

From Hauser & Clausing (1988)

Figure 3.8 suggests that the area under the cost curve is reduced if early expenditure is increased to 'design-out' problems that might otherwise have been ignored or overlooked until later. In addition to avoiding expensive redesign and the possible recall of products in service, this approach avoids the associated problem of redesigning the manufacturing system with costly implications for modified jigs, fixtures, and tools. Getting it right before product launch also tends to reduce the lead time between the decision to go ahead with a product development and launching that product onto the market. Arguably the most important benefit of all is that the problems are solved 'in-house' without the customer being involved in or aware of a series of potentially embarrassing incidents.

Improving the linkage between design and manufacturing at the early stage of the PDP has been the subject of a great deal of research over recent years. Much of this work has been based upon an analysis of information requirements and the development of computer-based systems to facilitate information storage and exchange. The developments have several objectives, four of which will be mentioned here in the way of examples.

Group Technology

The purpose of group technology is to identify individual components as being members of one or more groups of similar components on the basis of either their geometry, material, or process route. The descriptions of these groups and the individuals from which they are formed are recorded on data bases that are made available to designers. During the PDP, designers are encouraged to access the data base to establish whether similar components are already being manufactured for another purpose. If similar components can be utilised instead of manufacturing a completely new component, cost savings can accrue from reduced manufacturing effort and decreased inventories.

Automated Process Planning

Several software systems developed over recent years provide the designer with information on possible routes by which a proposed component may be manufactured. The data base behind the software contains information on the manufacturing processes available within the company and, if appropriate in sub-contracting companies. Some of these software packages provide knowledge-based systems that propose alternative manufacturing routes, give estimates of production costs, and allow designers to play 'what if' analyses by altering component geometry, tolerances, and surface finish.

Information Viewpoints

One of the problems associated with information requirements at the early design stage is the rapidity with which the information changes and grows (Wright & Swain, 1995). Each person involved in the process needs access to only a part of this dynamic set of information, but also needs the ability to add, modify, or erase information in keeping with their role and rights in the process. The subset of information used by a particular person or group is called a 'viewpoint' (Kotonya & Sommerville, 1996). There are many problems in attempting to computerise this dynamic information data base including the provision of mechanisms to ensure that users are kept aware of the most up-to-date state of the data that affects them, and that all the people who have a stake in certain viewpoints are consulted before changes are made. Most of the work on viewpoint systems has been carried out by information technologists and software engineers, although some preliminary evaluations have been carried out on engineering design problems.

Design for Assembly

There are now many Design for X (DFX) systems available, where X can be any objective that is deemed to be desirable. Hence, you can purchase paper- or computer-based systems where X is assembly, disassembly, strength, reliability, etc. Like many other DFX systems, Design for Assembly (DFA) attempts to provide the product designer with specialised knowledge so that best practice can be achieved. In general, DFA systems work by eliciting information on the number of components, their size, symmetry, and handleability, and then provide the designer with a measure (usually based upon a numerical assessment) of the assemblability of the constituent parts. Designers can play 'what if' analyses by trying alternative configurations and, in so doing, arrive at an improved understanding of the options available.

DFA and other DFX systems can be invaluable during the design of some products, but care is needed to ensure that all of the associated factors not included in the system are taken into account. For example, whilst current DFA systems deal effectively with the assembly costs of a design, many give scant regard to the implications of their recommendations for individual component cost.

The above examples show that software systems are being developed to assist the simultaneous engineering (SE) activity work by improving access to information and/or providing the opportunity to use information to evaluate design options. This focus addresses not just the requirements of SE, but one of the central problems of the PDP.

Whilst computer-based systems offer much promise for the future, the role of human interaction in the passing, transformation, evaluation, and recording of information is likely to remain predominant in the foreseeable future. The next section examines the role of teams in this interaction process.

TEAMS

There is a saying which goes 'a trouble shared is a trouble halved'. Most people would agree that there is an underlying truth in the saying, and would be able to recall an experience where a psychological load was lightened simply by sharing or discussing it with someone else. Such a benefit can be felt even when the problem is intractable, and no solution can be found, but in many cases discussion of a problem with a colleague leads to the generation of a solution. Sometimes, this will simply be due to the colleague knowing the answer, but in other cases it will be due to the combination of effort and experience that both parties bring to the discussion. This type of serendipity, where the outcome is greater than the capability of each individual alone is due to the synergistic effect of working together.

Definitions

serendipity, *n.*   the faculty of making happy and unexpected discoveries by accident.
synergy, *n.*   combined or co-ordinated action.

The formation of teams of employees to identify and solve problems is a vital issue for companies. Much has been written on the subject of choosing the right team members and enabling them to get on with their task (Eales-White, 1995), but it is not the purpose of this book to deal in depth with the issue of group dynamics. What we are going to do is examine the role that groups play in the passing of information between company functions, and in the processing of this information as a part of the PDP.

With the need to provide a Quality product, reduce lead times, and maintain profit margins at an acceptable level, staff involved in the PDP need to address the following issues:

- What are the PDP objectives?
- What constraints need to be applied (e.g., technological, resources)?
- What information is required and where can it be found?
- What problems need to be solved?
- What are the best solutions to the problems bearing in mind the constraints?
- How can information and decisions be best communicated?
- How can decisions be recorded and made available for future reference?
- How can the actions mandated by the decisions best be implemented?

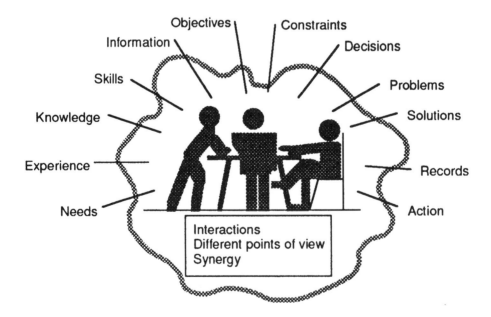

Figure 3.9   The benefits and functions of teams

Figure 3.9 shows a generalised representation of the role that teams play in a company's organisation.

The role of teams in combining knowledge and skills, reaching understanding, generating solutions, and communicating information is not limited to 'in-company' activity. Teams can also involve representatives from outside the company in the form of suppliers, sub-contractors, and customers. We even have the concept of 'virtual teams' where some members who cannot attend in person have their views represented by means of appropriate communication techniques. This may be achieved by ensuring that the views of absent team members are represented by a third party (in the way that the marketing function represents the customer), or by written, telephone, or e-mail contact. Perhaps the most up-to-date technology for supporting virtual teams is video conferencing, where participants from around the world can take part via a system which transmits audio and visual images of team members to everyone involved.

FOCUS TEAMS

Focus teams are formed to deal with specific well defined problems that a company needs to solve. They are made up from members who have the knowledge necessary to address all aspects of the problem, and are hence likely to contain members from several functional departments. To ensure that the objectives of the team are focused on well defined problems, company management at an appropriate level is frequently represented. Because the involvement of senior management can force the team into accepting the pre-conceived ideas of the manager, it is often advantageous to select a team leader who is lower down the hierarchy but closer to the problem. Hence, focus team leaders might be designers, machine operators, or development engineers.

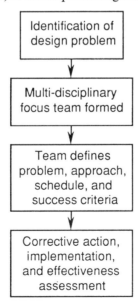

Figure 3.10 Focus teams

One of the major contribution of focus teams to product design is in the solution of problems associated with continual improvement. Such problems might be concerned with changing certain aspects of a product's design to avoid a problem reported by the sales or support functions, or in response to concerns about a new superior product introduced by a competitor. Figure 3.10, which is adapted from Joseph and Berk (1955), illustrates the focus team approach to the solution of design-related problems. Joseph and Berk also propose a methodology by which focus teams can report their progress and problems to senior company management. This methodology involves four different types of report:

1. **The problem statement.** Time and hence money will be wasted if the team does not focus on a precise problem for which a solution is sought. The problem statement report should define exactly what the problem is, and what criteria will be used to assess whether the outcome is successful. Figure 3.11 shows the problem statement for a team that was given the task of solving a stability problem on a fork-lift truck.

PROBLEM STATEMENT

The prototype RXT24 fork-lift truck fails to meet European legislation regarding dynamic stability when cornering. The company requires a solution to this problem which will not reduce load or reach capacity in time for incorporation in the second prototype by 1 May. A solution needs to be found within current cost limits due to the competitive nature of the market.

SUCCESS CRITERIA

1. Satisfy current European stability legislation.
2. No increase in manufacturing cost.
3. Detail design complete by 1 May.

TEAM MEMBERS

H. Pugh - Marketing
B. McGrew - Engineering
A. Cuthburt - Development
C. Dibble - Manufacturing
B. Grubb - Research

Figure 3.11 Focus team problem statement

2. **The approach.** All members of the team need to understand the approach that they are adopting in their attempt to solve the problem. This is essential if all members of the team are to pull together in the same direction. Senior company managers, who may or may not be members of the team will also need to be assured that the team has a well defined plan to help it meet its objectives. The approach can be presented as a list or in the form of a map as shown in Figure 3.12.

3. **The schedule.** In addition to having a clear understanding of what is required and how the requirements are to be attained, the team will need to determine how long each stage of the problem-solving process will take. In turn, these individual times will allow the team to estimate the overall completion time for their project. Figure 3.13 shows the schedule for the solution of the fork-lift truck problem.

APPROACH

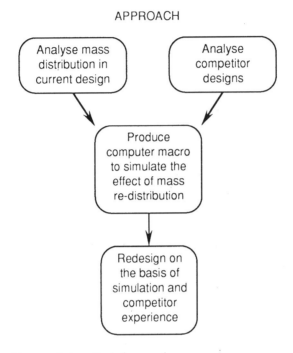

Figure 3.12   Teams need to agree their method of approach

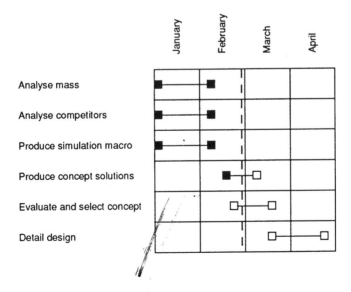

Figure 3.13   The schedule for the truck problem

4. **Obstacle identification statement.** Although the team will produce its first schedule on the basis of what needs to be achieved and the resources available, unforeseen obstacles will almost certainly occur that will push the process off course. These obstacles will cause earlier attempts at scheduling the work to be disrupted, and the team will have to decide whether to accept the delays, seek additional resources to enable earlier time estimates to be met, or work around the problems in other ways. Whatever the decisions, it is important that the team recognises the obstacles so that they can take appropriate action and keep senior managers informed. Figure 3.14 shows a typical obstacle identification statement.

RECAP

The availability, flow and processing of information is the life blood of the PDP. Information must be able to pass easily across the functional boundaries that exist in all companies to some extent. Companies can adopt one or more strategies to facilitate this horizontal flow, and this chapter has briefly examined the principles, strengths and problems associated with TQM and simultaneous engineering. Both of these address the problem, TQM from a broad company 'culture' point of view, and simultaneous engineering from a more narrow frequently computer system direction.

Whatever strategies may be adopted, getting people to work together in teams is the key element. However, simply telling employees to work together, or even sitting them down around a table will not work unless objectives, method of approach, and scheduling of work are managed correctly. The formation of focus teams is one way of dealing with the setting up of effective team working provided that a methodological approach is adopted.

OBSTACLE STATEMENT - 26 February
The 2-week delay in completing the simulation macro resulted in the start of the "produce concept solutions" phase being delayed until19 February. Although this stage is now proceeding well, it appears that the evaluation of concepts will not be able to commence until the end of the first week in March. This may result in the time initially allocated to detail design being squeezed.

PROPOSED ACTION
The team believe that providing additional design staff to either the concept initiation or concept evaluation phases would do little to reduce the scheduled time. The best solution is to make an extra member of staff available for the detail design phase. This team member would need to be available from the l
week in M_____h until th__

Figure 3.14 Teams need to identify obstacles for themselves and senior management

FOUR

MARKET RESEARCH METHODS

OVERVIEW

This chapter introduces some of the fundamentals of marketing that are of particular importance to the PDP. These are the concepts of **segmentation, targeting**, and **positioning**, knowledge of which can enable the designer to understand the impact of product attributes on sales.

Methods of collecting and presenting information on customer needs and competitors are illustrated in a case study which provides an integrating thread through the chapter. The purpose here is not to turn designers into marketing specialists but to provide an understanding of the role and importance of market research in relation to the PDP. The references provide routes into specialised marketing literature for readers who need to seek in-depth information.

OBJECTIVES

When you have finished studying this chapter, you will be able to:

- understand the marketing concepts of segmentation, targeting, and positioning.
- understand the need to analyse competitor products.
- present the competitor information in a manner helpful to designers.
- understand the use of questionnaires, interviews, and focus group meetings to elicit customer requirements.
- Present customer requirement information in a clear manner.

THE MARKETING FUNCTION

Philip Kotler in his book *Principles of Marketing* (1996) defines marketing as:

> A social and managerial process by which individuals and groups obtain what they need and want through creating and exchanging products and value with others.

Kotler goes on to explain his definition by saying that marketing requires an understanding of human needs, human wants, human demands, product definition and provision, exchange on the basis of perceived value, and the individuals or groups who are actual or potential buyers of the product. This definition indicates something of the breadth of involvement of a marketing department in the activities of a company. Particularly in the case of a company selling consumer goods, this involvement would include:

- **Analysing market opportunities**. Using market research to identify new markets for existing products, and opportunities for new products. Considering the impact of competitor products.
- **Selecting target markets**. Measuring and forecasting market demand for existing and future products. Identifying groups of purchasers and potential purchasers in a way that helps the company to meet their requirements.
- **Developing the marketing mix**. Identifying the best strategy for increasing demand for a product. This might include making decisions about product attributes, channels of distribution, and advertising.

From the point of view of the design function, the principal interaction with marketing is through the information provided by marketing, which influences the attributes of the product. This information about the needs of the buyer in terms of product attributes, together with the influence of competitor products on the buyers is the stimulus for the development of good products for the future.

For the design function to respond effectively to this information, it must be presented in a way that enables the designer to interpret it in an appropriate way. In many cases, the marketing information needs to be analysed and re-formatted by the designer. In the case of an engineering designer, unquantified customer perceptions of requirement may have to be interpreted to give quantified performance descriptions. Such re-formatting carries the potential danger of misinterpretation, leading to a final product that does not meet market requirements.

MARKET SEGMENTATION

Markets are made up of people who buy products, which may be artifacts or services. For various reasons, some people will be more likely to buy certain products than others and it is in the interests of the seller to be knowledgeable about the buyers and potential buyers of their product. To help this understanding, one of the aims of market research is to identify groups of buyers and see what makes them behave in the way that they do in relation to the product. The purpose of this is to ascertain if sales of the product can be increased by modifying its attributes, or by changing the advertising or distribution strategies that are used or envisaged. This splitting of the total market into identifiable groups that behave differently in regard to the product is called 'segmentation'.

A market can be segmented on the basis of any variable or group of variables that proves to be useful in identifying market opportunities. Hence, it may be beneficial to look at how the buying behaviour of men differs from that of women in respect to a particular product. Alternatively, it might be found that young adults between the ages of 18 and 25 years have different preferences in regard to a product that people in other age ranges.

Knowledge of this type can be invaluable in enabling companies to identify ways of improving sales of an existing product, or in enabling them to design a completely new or modified product. In many cases, a useful segmentation of the market will be made using several variables. For example, it may be found that there is a distinct difference in buyer preferences within a four-segment market identified on the basis of gender **and** age; e.g. 18 to 25 year-old males, 18 to 25 year-old females, 26 to 35 year-old males, and 26 to 35 year-old females might all look for different attributes in a particular type of product or be influenced by different advertising strategies. Of course, not everyone in each segment will have the same preferences, but market segmentation aims to identify tendencies which can influence strategy.

VARIABLE	**EXAMPLE DEFINITION**
Geographic	
Region	North America, Europe, South East Asia, South America
Country	United States of America, United Kingdom, Singapore, Brazil
Population density	Either quantified densities or general categories like urban, suburban, and rural
Demographic	
Age	Under 12, 12–15, 15–17, 18–25, 26–35, 36–45, 46–55, 56–65, 66–75, Over 75.
Sex	Male, female.
Stage of family life-cycle	Single; married, no children, married with youngest child under 10; married with youngest child between 10 and 18; married with youngest child over 18; widowed.
Income (individual or family)	Under £7000, £7000–£10000, £10000–£15000, £15000–£25000, £25000–£35000, £35000–£45000, £45000–65000 etc.
Occupation	Professional and technical; managers and supervisors; clerical; craftsmen; operatives; farmers; retired; students; homemakers; unemployed.
Race	Hispanic, Black, White, Asian.
Nationality	American, British, Chinese, German, Japanese, Mexican.
Psychographic	
Personality	Compulsive, gregarious, authoritarian, ambitious.
Social class	Higher, upper, middle, lower.
Life style	Integrated, belonger, achiever.
Behaviouristic	
Purchase occasion	Regular, special.
Benefits sought	Quality, service, economy.
User status	Non-user, ex-user, potential user, first-time user, regular user.
Usage rate	Quantified, or light, medium, heavy.
Loyalty to product	None, medium, strong, absolute.
Awareness	Unaware, aware, informed, interested, desirous, intending to buy.
Attitude to product	Enthusiastic, positive, indifferent, negative, hostile.

Figure 4.1 Some segmentation variables for consumer products

We are all familiar with being stopped in the street and asked questions about our preferences for certain types of product, where and when we shop, and our lifestyle. Many of these surveys are carried out by market research organisations that are seeking segmentation information. These studies can be undertaken in an investigative mode where there is minimal perception of what the study might reveal. Alternatively, the study may seek to prove or disprove previously held but unverified perceptions of buyer behaviour.

Figure 4.1 lists some segmentation variables frequently used for consumer products. For certain types of product, the difference in needs between segments will be obvious. If a company selling bungee jumping as a service decided to carry out a segmentation study

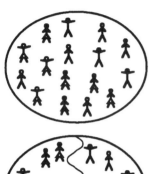 The market is made up from all of the people who purchase or might purchase a particular product. Unless a segmentation study has been carried out, there is no basis on which to assess if different groups of people behave differently with respect to the product. In other words 'everyone looks the same'.

 Following a segmentation study, it may be found that males and females behave differently with respect to the product. This may help the company to develop an appropriate strategy for increasing sales to the segment which is already the principal market, or to investigate another segment that is currently not purchasing the product.

 Of course, the study might reveal that gender has no influence on the buyer behaviour for the product. Perhaps age, marital status, income, or racial background are more important.

 Frequently, segmentation of the market will be based upon more than one variable. Perhaps Afro-Caribbean females turn out to be a distinct group, with quite different buyer behaviour than Caucasian males.

Figure 4.2 A market can be segmented in various ways depending upon the nature of the product being considered

using age as a variable, it would probably find that a 18 to 23 segment had a considerably different view of their product than the over 65 segment. The company might ask if this apparent lack of interest by the over 65s was due to the absence of some desirable feature in their product, whether they were falling down on their advertising, or whether there was a more fundamental reason why it did not catch the imagination of this large and sometimes affluent group.

Particularly with consumer products, the identification of segments with differing needs sometimes leads to companies selling identical products to them purely on the basis of a different advertising approach. A company marketing shampoo can place one series of advertisements aimed at selling the product to parents with young children, and a second series aimed at the teenage market. The first series might concentrate on gentle care whilst the second may stress that using the product will lead to an improved appearance and a better social life. The product sold into to each of these segments may be the same, although it **may** be packaged differently. Alternative strategies would be to produce two totally different products, or to ignore one of the segments completely.

The way that a company perceives market segmentation in regard to its product will do much to determine its strategy for the provision of product attributes, quality, service and support. Two competitive companies that are trying to sell products that are essentially the same might each see the same segments, but may decide to adopt very different strategies for their products. Company A might decide to tailor their product to a very large segment with the potential for high volume sales with a small profit margin, whilst company B may decide to attack a smaller segment that demands high quality but is prepared to pay a higher price. In both cases, the aim is to maximise profits for the company, bearing in mind the market opportunities and the constraints under which they are operating. Figure 4.2 indicates how a market may show different segmentation characteristics, depending upon the viewpoint of the company and the product that it is capable of supplying.

After a segmentation study has been completed, four conditions have to be met before the study can be deemed to have been successful:

1. Customers within each segment should be as alike as possible in regard to product purchasing behaviour.

2. Customers within a segment should behave differently to those outside it.

3. It must be possible to reach the group effectively by tailoring the product or advertising strategy.

4. The number of customers in the segment must be large enough for it to be of commercial importance.

It is important to remember that the end user of a consumer product is not the only person who makes the decision to buy. Between the manufacturer and the user, there is likely to be a chain of organisations made up of wholesalers and retailers. Any one of these that decides not to buy will break a link between manufacturer and the end user and potentially damage overall sales performance. These intermediate customers will also have requirements that must be considered by the company, and a study of their differing needs is also necessary to maximise the probability of success. In the case of industrial products, the 'user' is rarely the buyer, and because of this segmentation can be more difficult.

VARIABLE	EXAMPLE DEFINITION
Geographic	
Region:	North America, Europe, South East Asia, South America.
Demographic	
Industry type:	Automobile, aerospace, computers.
Company size:	Large, medium, small.
Operating variables	
Technology:	Nano-technology, electronics, optical sensors.
User status:	Non-user, ex-user, potential user, first-time user, regular user.
Purchasing approach	
Purchasing function organisation:	Centralised, decentralised.
Power structure:	Marketing dominated, technology dominated, manufacturing dominated.
Purchasing policy:	Prefer leasing, prefer purchase.
Purchasing criteria:	Quality, service, price.
Situational factors	
Urgency:	Quick service, long lead time.
Product application:	Some or many applications of our product?
Size of order:	Large, small.
Personal characteristics	
Attitudes to risk:	Should we concentrate on risk-taking or risk-avoiding customers?
Loyalty:	Should we concentrate on customers who show loyalty to their customers?

Figure 4.3 Some segmentation variables for industrial products

Although some of the variables listed in Figure 4.1 can be used for both consumer and industrial products (e.g., the geographic variables), there are some segmentation variables that are particularly relevant for industrial products. Figure 4.3 indicates some of these.

COLLECTING SEGMENTATION INFORMATION

Focus Group Meetings

In focus group meetings, a team of between 6 and 12 people are brought together to discuss various aspects of a product. The work of the group is overseen by a trained interviewer who allows free discussion but makes sure that it is focused upon a particular topic or range of topics. Meetings are held in pleasant surroundings, refreshments are made available, and the participants are usually paid for their time and any costs that they incur.

The purpose of the meeting is to elicit information on the participants' perceptions about an existing product and/or a proposed product. Because of the large amount of unstructured information that is generated by focus group meetings, they are frequently recorded on audio or video tape. Subsequently, the recorded information is analysed to identify important issues on which the participants expressed views.

Problems with focus group meetings are that they are expensive to run, and the sample is rather small. As a result, the information extracted from the technique is often tested for validity on a larger sample by the use of mail questionnaires or telephone interviews.

Mail Questionnaires

Mail questionnaires are used to seek the opinions of large numbers of people at minimum cost. However, great care needs to be taken with their design if the information that they generate is to be useful. Because the respondent will be answering the questions without the opportunity of seeking clarification, all of the questions must be unambiguous. If this is not the case, it will be impossible to know what meaning the respondent read into the question.

Mail questionnaires must be concise. There is usually no reward to the respondent for providing answers to the questions. Even when companies do provide incentives, a long and tedious questionnaire will be placed with the trash, or skipped through to the detriment of accurate answers. It is a good maxim to assume that no one will spend more than a total of 5 minutes with the questionnaire, including the reading of introductory material and placing it into the reply envelope.

Advantages of mail questionnaires are that they avoid the variations in interviewer bias that can occur in direct contact, and that some people are more willing to provide personal information on an anonymous form than they are to an unknown person at interview or over the phone.

Because of the importance of good questionnaire design, it is essential that questionnaires are piloted before being distributed to the full sample. The pilot version should be identical to the final version in every detail. The people in the pilot sample should be representative of the full sample, and the method of distribution and collection should be the same. The size of the pilot sample is not critical, but should be large enough to give the researchers confidence that problems will be identified. A pilot sample that is between 2% and 10% of the size of the full sample is common. Researchers will usually try to interview some or all of the people responding to the pilot survey to ensure that the questions were easy to understand, that they all interpreted the questions in the same way, and that the length of time taken to complete the questionnaire was acceptable. If required, the lessons learned from the pilot can be incorporated into a modified questionnaire for further piloting or release, depending upon the seriousness of the problems identified.

Telephone Interviews

Telephone interviewing overcomes some of the disadvantages of mail questionnaires. Uncertainties about the meaning of questions can be avoided if the interviewer is prepared to offer an explanation. The method has an in-built flexibility that is absent from the mail questionnaire. If the respondent has something of value to say about a particular line of questioning, the interviewer can explore that avenue in more depth. It is also possible to control the sample more accurately. One of the problems with mail questionnaires is that you can never be sure who filled them in, even when they are addressed to the respondent by name. Telephone interviewing overcomes this problem.

There are three principal problems with telephone interviewing. Firstly, there is a possibility of interviewer bias caused by the way that questions are asked particularly if this is in response to the attitude of the respondent. Secondly, many people do not welcome being contacted by telephone for the purpose of a survey because they see it as an attempt to 'pin them down' at a time when they may be preoccupied by other things. This may influence the reliability of their answers. Finally, cost per respondent is from 2 to 12 times higher than with mail questionnaires.

CASE STUDY 4.1

A study of retailers in 1995 showed that over 90% of hairdryers were purchased by women (Wright, 1995). This is reflected in the packaging and advertising of hairdryers which tend to show pictures of women using the product. In addition, many of the product features including attachments to wave and volumise hair are provided with women in mind.

It was decided to undertake a study of the market to find out if there were opportunities to sell a hairdryer into a male-dominated segment of the market. The study commenced with a series of 'focus group' meetings. These meetings identified issues that seemed to be important to the participants when buying and using hairdryers. Focus groups were representative of: both sexes; age groups from young teenagers to senior citizens; and white Caucasian, Asian, and Afro-Caribbean. The findings from the study that were identified as important for more detailed investigation were that:

1. There was an identifiable group of 18 to 25 year old males who were impressed by implied quality which, by their interpretation was evidenced by heavier weight and 'precise' switch positions.

2. This group had little interest in attachments, but were concerned about being able to dry their hair quickly. They preferred the chrome look, and seemed to associate this with being 'solid' and 'reliable'.

3. The group perceived an advantage in being able to use a hairdryer some distance away from a plug.

4. Males and females in the 18 to 25 year group were less influenced by cost in their choice of hair dryer than people in older age groups.

On the basis of the focus group findings, it was decided to plan a postal survey to establish buyer behaviour in a sample of 5000 individuals. In addition to identifying behaviouristic factors, the questionnaire was designed to establish links with demographic and psychographic variables. The questionnaire was piloted with a sample of 150 people to ensure that it was as concise and unambiguous as possible. Figure 4.4 shows that part of the two page questionnaire that dealt with customer preferences.

The survey enabled researchers to identify a potential need for a different product by males in the 18 to 25 year age segment. Of the members of this segment who took part in the survey, 63% said that they did not use a hairdryer at all. Even allowing for the possibility that some respondents denied using a 'non-macho' product when they actually did, the survey had revealed a marketing possibility if an appropriate product could be formulated. The researchers called the 18 to 25 male group 'segment M', and identified some of its characteristics in the product field as follows:

Hairdryer features	No importance	Little importance	Quite important	Very important
Easy to control Choice of air temperature settings	☐	☐	☐	☐
Choice of air speed settings	☐	☐	☐	☐
Cold air for style setting	☐	☐	☐	☐
Easy one handed use	☐	☐	☐	☐
Cannot accidentally burn the hair	☐	☐	☐	☐
Hair styling Accessories enable you to set lots of different styles	☐	☐	☐	☐
Can be used for long and short hair styles	☐	☐	☐	☐
Ergonomics Can be used for long periods without getting tired	☐	☐	☐	☐
Comfortable to hold	☐	☐	☐	☐
Controls are easy to use	☐	☐	☐	☐
Accessories are easy to fit and remove	☐	☐	☐	☐
Can be used at some distance from electrical socket	☐	☐	☐	☐
Does not scratch furniture	☐	☐	☐	☐
Aesthetics Pleasing colour	☐	☐	☐	☐
Pleasing shape	☐	☐	☐	☐
Hygiene Easy to keep clean	☐	☐	☐	☐
Air is filtered to remove dust and fluff	☐	☐	☐	☐
Packaging Detailed written description on the box	☐	☐	☐	☐
Pictures of various ways of using the hairdryer	☐	☐	☐	☐
Implied quality Reliable manufacturer	☐	☐	☐	☐
Strong	☐	☐	☐	☐
Will not break down	☐	☐	☐	☐
A guarantee of more than one year at purchase	☐	☐	☐	☐
Feels solid	☐	☐	☐	☐

Figure 4.4 Establishing user preferences in hairdryer attributes

1. Impressed by implied quality (this confirmed the focus group study).
2. Tended not to use the attachments provided.
3. Would like to use the product 'some distance' from a power point. To some extent this was seen to support a proposition that men did not sit down at a mirror to dry their hair. Rather, it is a secondary activity, carried out rapidly, and possibly whilst doing something else at the same time.

4. Cost was not identified as being as important a purchase factor for segment M as for non-segment M people.

5. Segment M preferred a small and portable hairdryer, which might suggest that they saw a need for mobility.

We will return to the hairdryer case study later in this chapter. In the meantime, it has served to illustrate how a study of customers and potential customers can identify market opportunities. Whether it is feasible to take up the opportunities depend upon many factors, one of which is competitor activity.

ASSESSING COMPETITOR PRODUCTS

No company which is serious about making profit from its product can afford to be anything other than well informed about the offerings of its competitors. This knowledge falls into two main categories: product attributes, and buyer perceptions.

Products sell on the basis of the attributes that they offer, and the perceptions that potential customers hold. In most cases, a purchaser of a product will have options. In other words there will be choices between competing products from alternative manufacturers. The product chosen will be the one that, in the eyes of the purchaser, offers the best combination of attributes for him or her, or the organisation that they represent. Hence, products are assessed by a prospective buyer on a comparative and not an absolute basis. Clearly, when a company is in the process of developing a new product, or modifying an existing one, it needs access to all of the information available to the purchaser in terms of competitive choices. Information on competitor products are available from several sources. In the case of consumer products, current competition can be seen in the shops and other distribution outlets. For industrial products, company sales staff will usually have opportunities to see competitor products in operation when they are attempting to sell their own company's wares. Catalogues, brochures, and price lists are as available to competitors as they are to buyers. Sometimes, these sources are sufficient to enable companies to build a profile of the competition, and Case Study 4.2 examines how this was done in the case of the hairdryer.

In the case of complex competitor products and those involving advanced technology, a company may feel that it needs a 'hands-on' study to assess its attributes more closely. An example of this approach is when Quality and reliability are purchasing issues. Attributes like these are difficult to assess visually, and the company may feel that the only option is to purchase competitor products and subject them to a detailed analysis including prolonged testing and strip-down. This 'benchmarking' of competitor products can also reveal vital information on the cost incurred by competitors in building their product, and the profit margins under which they are operating. Competitor benchmarking strategies are widely adopted by the majority of companies working in the consumer product market. Companies like Ford, General Motors, and Toyota are invariably the first 'owners' of new models produced by other car companies.

Companies also obtain examples of competitor products to enable them to assess customer perceptions of these and their own products. Assessing and comparing products can be carried out in focus group meetings, or by allowing selected users to assess the products over an extended period of time. Our hair-dryer case study provides an example of the use of focus groups to provide customer evaluations of competitor products.

CASE STUDY 4.2

PRODUCT (Underlined product features are advertised on the outside of the packaging.)	Power rating (Watts)	Number of heat settings	Number of airflow settings	Hanging-up loop	Anti-scratch pads	Removable filter	Washable filter	Fitted plug	Automatic overheat cutout	Automatic overheat reset	Cool button	Automatic air temperature control	Cost (£)	Cord length (m)	Weight (grams)	Guarantee (years)	Separate on/off switch	Attachments	Comments (Comments in normal text are obtained from the product packaging. Comments in italics are observations resulting from inspection of the product.)
Braun 1600 Electronic. Soft Diffuser Plus	1600	∞	3	✓	✓	✓	✓	✓	✓	✓	✗	✓	23.50	1.7	600	1	✗	Nozzle Volumiser	Warm air flows from the tips of the diffuser fingers which reach down into the hair giving more body for beautiful hair. The extra long fingers of the new diffuser can handle the thickest hair, and root dry full styles without crushing them. Quiet but powerful. Electronics provide constant temperature
BaByliss Chrome Salon Professional	1100	3	2	✓	✗	✓	✓	✓	✓	✓	✓	✗	34.95	2.9	650	2	✓	Nozzle Diffusor	*The package says 6 heat/speed settings, the instructions say 4. Uses A.C. motor which they claim has longer life and is more powerful. The implication is that high air flow rate gives fast drying without high temperature. Packaging shows the device but not the user*
Philips Salon Classic	1600	3	2	✓	✓	✓	✓	✓	✓	✓	✓	✗	29.50	2.3	575	1	✗	Nozzle Volumiser	*Very little wordage on the package. The cool button allows the user to override the heat setting when it is depressed. The package claims by icon that the device is quiet. Major graphics are of the hairdryer itself. Little human interest.*
Braun Supervolume Twist	1600	3	2	✓	✓	✓	✓	✓	✓	✓	✗	✗	29.99	1.7	500	?	✗	Nozzle Volumiser/ waver	Especially for short to medium hair. Easily creates different exciting styles by adding movement and waves. The unique Supervolume Twist attachment for straight hair is designed to give the hairstyle you want while drying. *Package shows a woman with medium length hair.*
Remington Volumiser Plus	1650	3	2	✓	✓	✗	✓	✓	✓	✗	✗	26.25	1.7	530	2	✗	Nozzle Volumiser Pulsator	Unique 3-stage drying system adds maximum volume and lift to straight hair. Pulsator builds body and removes excess moisture fast. Volumiser directs air to the roots for maximum root lift and volume. *Complies with 89/336 EEC radio interference. Low voltage reg's 1996*

Figure 4.5 A product feature chart for four hairdryers

In addition to undertaking the postal survey of a sample of the potential buyers, the market research investigation for the hair dryer set out to establish competitor product attributes and customer perceptions of these products. Figure 4.5 shows a product feature chart that identifies the attributes of five products from four major competitive players in hairdryer marketing. Figure 4.6 shows these products and their packaging. The product feature chart provides factual information in the sense that it is not subjective. For each hairdryer, the chart states:

1. The power rating.
2. Number of heat settings.
3. Number of airflow settings.
4. Purchase price (cost).
5. Mains cable length.
6. Weight.

7. The length of guarantee.
8. The type of attachments provided.
9. The presence or absence of:
   - a 'hanging up' loop;
   - anti-scratch pads;
   - a renewable air filter;
   - a washable filter;
   - a fitted plug;
   - an automatic over-heat cut-out;
   - a 'cool button';
   - automatic air temperature control;
   - a separate on/off switch.

The chart also records a small number of comments about more subjective issues like the segmentation strategy implied by images and text on the packaging. The chart provides a

Braun 1600 Electronic   **BaByliss Chrome Salon Professional**   **Philips Salon Classic**

Braun Supervolume Twist   **Remington Volumiser Plus**

Figure 4.6   The five products included in the product attribute study

Segment M ▬▬▬
Non segment M ▬▬▬
HAIRDRYER FEATURES

		Braun 1600				Babyliss			
		Poor	Good	Very poor	Excellent	Poor	Good	Very poor	Excellent
Easy to control	Air temperature control								
	Air speed control								
	Cold air for style setting								
	Easy one-handed use								
	Cannot accidentally burn the hair								
Hair styling	Accessories enable you to set lots of different styles								
	Suitable for long and short hair styles								
Ergonomics	Can use for long periods without getting tired								
	Comfortable to hold								
	Controls are easy to use								
	Accessories easy to fit and remove								
	Used remote from electrical socket								
	Does not scratch furniture								
Aesthetics	Pleasing colour								
	Pleasing shape								
Hygiene	Easy to keep clean								
	Air is filtered to remove dust and fluff								
Packaging	Written description on the box								
	Useful pictures on outside of box								
	Quality of packing								
Implied quality	Reliable manufacturer								
	Strong								
	Will not break down								
	A guarantee of 1 year or more								
	Feels solid								

Figure 4.7   A customer perception chart for two hairdryers

concise statement of what the competition are providing, and this can make it a valuable reference for designers. However, what are really important are the views held by customers about the attributes, and customer perception charts constructed as a result of focus group meetings are one way of collecting and presenting this information.

Figure 4.7 shows a customer perception chart for two of the products identified in Figure 4.5. In this case five focus group meetings were arranged, each involving ten people in addition to the interviewer. Group members were asked to handle the products and provide evaluations of the listed attributes. Obviously this assessment is subjective, and although there was an attempt to reach consensus, the rating eventually arrived at for each product attribute is an averaged figure. In this case, the chart has been constructed to show the difference in ratings awarded by members of the segment M and non-segment M members.

In general the segment M members awarded an overall lower average rating than the others. This might be expected because of the lower percentage of segment M members who profess interest in this type of product. Segment M members were largely unimpressed by accessories and the fact that they were constrained to use the device within a short distance from a power point. The chart confirms the earlier perceptions that a 'solid' look is important for segment M. They were also unconcerned that this attribute went hand-in-hand with increased weight. Indeed, the relatively high weight of the BaByliss Chrome Salon Professional may have influenced their perception that this product was the strongest and most reliable.

TARGETING THE MARKET

Having identified the segmentation of the market in regard to their product, companies have to make strategic decisions about targeting. These decisions will determine whether the company directs their product to a single segment, several segments, or to the entire market. These alternative strategies are called concentrated, differentiated, and undifferentiated marketing respectively. Figure 4.8 shows the difference between these three strategic options.

Each targeting strategy has its advantages and disadvantages. A decision to adopt a concentrated marketing approach can lead to the company establishing a very strong position in the segment that it concentrates on. In turn this strong position can result in good profit margins if the competition find it difficult to challenge the company's supremacy. A good example of the concentrated marketing approach is the strategy adopted by Ferrari which sells to a small but very lucrative clientèle. The main risk for the concentrated marketing strategy is that there will be a fundamental shift in the market segmentation that will leave the product high and dry. It is rather difficult to imagine something that might affect Ferrari's market in this way; perhaps public pressure on politicians may, some time in the future, result in a ban on vehicles with engines over a certain size. The point is that these sort of fundamental changes are usually difficult to foresee, and therein lies the problem.

The majority of large automobile companies adopt a differentiated marketing strategy for their products. Their segmentation studies help them to identify a range of products, each of which is designed to meet the needs of a particular segment. Each product is then advertised separately with the characteristics of the segment in mind. Looking at the offerings of the major car companies, it is clear that they all perceive the market segments in much the same way. With few exceptions a model from one manufacturer is closely matched in attributes by models from the other manufacturers. Expensive models, at or near the 'top of the range' are advertised on the basis of their comfort, status, and exclusivity, while cheaper models are advertised on the basis of fun and economy. There are several consequences of taking the differentiated marketing strategy. Overall sales are likely to be high because of the company's presence in several segments, and a strong position might be obtained in several of these segments. On the down-side, it is possible that the company might try to develop many products to suit the needs of a large number of segments. If this is taken too far, the sales of each product will reduce to a point where unit costs rise and profit margins decrease. This is called 'over segmentation'.

Usually, an undifferentiated marketing strategy is adopted when the product has universal market appeal. Within the consumer market, oranges and pears are good examples of products that are sold using an undifferentiated marketing approach, whilst mechanical fasteners are about as near as it is possible to get for an industrial product. Inevitably, this type of product will be sold to a mass market with the benefit of large production numbers and economies of scale. Unit distribution costs are also likely to be low because of the large quantities being moved. The main disadvantage is that competition is likely to be tough, with many competitors operating at small profit margins.

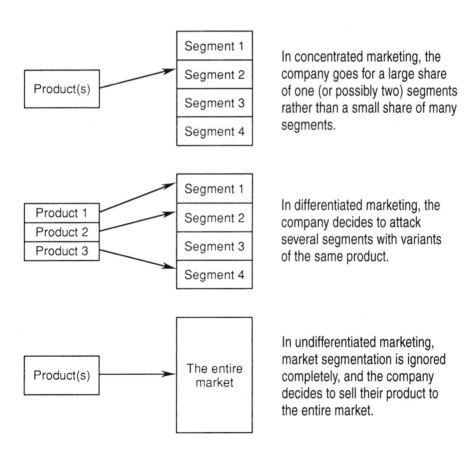

Figure 4.8 Concentrated, differentiated, and undifferentiated marketing

MARKET POSITIONING

A product's position in the market is the place occupied by that product in relation to other products in the mind of the customers. Consumers organise products into categories as an aid to making a decision to purchase, and companies use positioning to establish a strong identity in the segments that they are selling to. Categorisation takes place on the basis of product attributes and perceptions brought about by advertising strategies. Advertising strategies can help the customer to define market position by providing information on:

- Product attributes.
- Usage occasions.
- Competitor comparisons.
- Competitor remoteness.
- Product classes.

Product Attributes

By telling prospective customers about the features and cost of a product, the advertiser is helping them to place or position the product against competitors. The advertisement will be structured to position the product favourably in the segment that the company has decided to attack. Hence, BMW which sells its cars to a generally affluent market, stresses those attributes associated with luxury and quality, and even makes advantage from telling customers about the relatively high price of the product. Ford also makes as much advantage as possible from the luxury issue, but pays more attention than BMW to value for money. Perhaps there **are** quality differences between BMW and Ford, and the advertising strategies are merely drawing the customers' attention to real differences. Nevertheless, it is important for the companies to continually reinforce these different positions in the minds of their customers to be sure of remaining strong in their respective market segments.

Usage Occasions

When there are few real differences between two competing products, marketing will frequently attempt to persuade customers to the contrary. One way of doing this is to tell the customer that a particular product is specially made for a particular use.

Confectionery bars of chocolate-covered mint have long been available in the shops. These bars were originally sold to a broad public for consumption in the same way as other chocolate products. The decision by Terry's to market After Eight as a luxury product to be eaten after dinner was a highly successful positioning strategy that captured the company a large new market with a product that was essentially the same as generations of similar products that had gone before. Although Terry's now has competition, it still remains strong in its segment because of its positioning strategy.

Competitor Comparisons

Telling customers about the attributes of a product and the occasions on which it can be used may be achieved without any reference to competitors. However, in some cases companies feel that they can position their product more strongly by making a direct comparison with the competition. This policy can be dangerous because it invites a 'tit-for-tat' response from competitor companies. Untrue comparisons may even attract legal redress from aggrieved manufacturers. Direct comparisons can also draw customers' attention to the existence of competitors about which they were previously unaware, not always with the desired results.

For these reasons, companies very rarely name their competitors in their advertisements unless they are very confident that they can benefit from the heat that will be generated. In 1985, Coca-Cola changed the taste of their product in an attempt to win back the market share that they had lost to Pepsi. Pepsi gambled that a significant number of people would not like the new flavoured Coke, and put out a series of advertisement purporting to show unhappy Coca-Cola customers registering disapproval with the new product.

More frequently, customer comparisons are made discreetly. For example, in 1996 when building societies were competing for the shrinking mortgage market, the Cheltenham and Gloucester launched a television advertisement which listed the 'gimmicks' offered by other societies without saying which society offered which gimmick. The objective was to position the Cheltenham and Gloucester as a 'gimmick free' Society that looked after its customers with long-term value for money.

Competitor Remoteness

Frequently, a product will have few or no competitors during the introduction and growth stages of its life-cycle. Whilst competitors are non-existent or few and far between, a company will usually want to advertise the product on the basis of its uniqueness. Of course, the purpose of adopting this strategy is to position the product as far as possible from anything else on the market, and so avoid confusion in the minds of customers. Competitor remoteness is often linked to product attributes when attempting to establish product position. This approach was adopted by Motorola when introducing the Pentium processor for personal computers in 1995 and 1996.

Product Classes

One of the ways that customers categorise products is on the basis of class. A familiar example of the use of classes to distinguish between products is automobiles. Manufacturers provide classes with different attributes, and then help customers to position them by means of advertising. The advertisements will stress the difference in attributes between the models and use images to suggest different usage occasions.

CASE STUDY 4.3

Having considered segmentation, targeting, and positioning, we will now examine how one company responded to the segment M opportunity introduced in Case Study 4.1. In 1994, following their own market survey, Braun introduced the 'Control Shaper' for this male-dominated segment. The Control Shaper, which is shown in Figure 4.9 has no

Figure 4.9   The Braun Control Shaper for segment M

attachments other than a comb mounted on a tilting head. This gives a similar type of adjustment to that already familiar with swivel head electric shavers. The device does not provide the wide range of control functions common on other hair dryer products and is available in black, the preferred colour for the majority of men. The Control Shaper has been a considerable success for Braun, and clearly illustrates the importance of under-standing the market place in which you are operating so that opportunities can be identified and products and marketing strategies developed to take advantage of them.

MARKETING INFORMATION

One of the principal activities of the marketing function is to provide the information that the company needs to develop and sell its products. This activity demands that information about the market is identified, selected, obtained and analysed, prior to being disseminated in a form suitable for other functions. Later in this chapter we will look at the systems that are required to deal with this information, but first we need to consider what these requirements are and where the information can be found.

Information Needs

Company managers have little opportunity to read and assess information that they need to carry out their tasks, and simply cannot afford the time to sift through information that is unnecessary or verbose. This, and the fact that information gathering is expensive, makes it essential that the information needs of PDP staff are assessed carefully. The first stage of assessment is to determine what information the managers need to do their jobs effectively. This might be done by seeking answers to the following questions:

1.   What market-related decisions do PDP managers have to make?
2.   What are the information requirements of these decisions?

Some types of information are readily available whilst others are difficult to obtain. Surveys of the market can be undertaken by company staff or commissioned from external consultants. In certain circumstances, it may also be purchased directly from market research companies who continually collect information and sell it to anyone who is prepared to buy it. Similarly, information can be compiled or bought that relates to market views of competitors' customers, existing competitor products, and advertising methods. Much more difficult to obtain is information about the future activities of competitors because this will be considered confidential due to its commercial significance. The usual trade off between need and cost applies, and a company will have to decide upon the overall commercial benefits that can be achieved.

Information Sources

Sources and the means of collection of market information fall into one of the following three categories:

- Internal company records.
- Market intelligence.
- Market research.

Internal Company Records

Many companies neglect the large amounts of market-related information that is contained in their own records. This is a mistake of almost tragic proportions since little overhead is involved in its collection. Extracting and analysing the information is not always easy, and requires a well thought out set of procedures to ensure that it is put in front of managers in an acceptable format. In a company with low market awareness, it is probable that much valuable information will not be recorded at all, or internal records will be incomplete and in a form that makes analysis difficult.

Examples of records that should be available for analysis are:

- All written and telephone sales enquiries by potential customers.
- Successful and unsuccessful customer contacts by sales staff in the field. It is just as important to know why the company failed to clinch a sale as it is to have information about successful deals.
- Sales data broken down on the basis of product, product variations, and whatever segmentation variables have been determined as being significant.
- Service information relating to the cause and effect of malfunctions. This information is essential for design improvement regardless of whether the malfunction was caused by a design fault, misuse, or wear and tear. Repairs under warranty are particularly costly for a supplier and need careful analysis to establish if design changes are necessary.
- Field engineer reports. In cases where the product requires a field engineer to install equipment, records can help identify problems associated with poor design that is costing the company money or damaging customer relationships.

All of this information must be extracted, collated, and presented in an easily assimilated format using tables or graphs whenever possible. In this form, the information can be presented in a report for evaluation by managers and/or at monthly product review meetings.

Market Intelligence

Market intelligence involves looking beyond the boundary of the company to collect information about the environment into which the company sells its products. Whilst market research sets out to acquire information by experimentation and survey, market intelligence is passive in the sense that it seeks information that is readily available. Using market intelligence will ensure that the company has possession of the following:

- Competitor reports, advertisements and brochures.
- Publications targeted by competitors for advertising and editorial.
- Competitor profiles at exhibitions and conferences.
- Financial information from published company accounts.
- Chief executives' reports.
- Information on competitor products.

Again, the information needs to be collated and presented in a digestible form for consumption by appropriate company staff.

Market Research

In many cases, a company will need specific information to enable it to make informed decisions about its product development strategy. In these circumstances, market intelligence may not be sufficient, and a conscious effort is required to:

- Specify the information required.
- Establish the best methods of collecting the information.
- Manage and implement the collection.
- Analyse the results.
- Communicate the findings in a satisfactory way.

This process is called 'market research'.

Figure 4.10 shows a table that identifies some of the information sought by market research investigations.

Broad area	Typical information sought
Advertising	What motivates customers? Which media are effective? Strategies adopted by competitors
Business economics	Short/long range advertising Pricing studies
Product research	New product acceptance and potential Competitor products Packaging
Market factors	Market potential Market share Market segmentation characteristics Distribution studies Promotional studies

Figure 4.10 Types of information sought by market research

Basically, there are three types of market research investigation. Exploratory research sets out to collect preliminary information that will help to define what the problem is, and suggest an appropriate course of action. Descriptive research is used to help describe things like customer reaction and market potential. Causal research tests cause and effect, such as the relationships between price, sales volume, and profit. Depending upon the desired outcome, different approaches to market research may be adopted.

Observational research is concerned with gathering information by observing relevant people, their actions, and the situation. The people may be aware or unaware that they are being observed, depending upon the requirements of the researcher. Observational research can be useful in obtaining information that would be difficult to obtain by other means due to either a reluctance on the part of the person to give the information, or because the person does not know the reason for his/her behaviour.

Survey research is best used for gathering descriptive information. Various contact methods can be used, and these may be either direct (interview) or indirect (postal questionnaire). Survey research can provide information more quickly and at a lower cost than by other approaches, but people are frequently unwilling to take part or deliberately give misleading information.

Experimental research is best suited to gathering causal information. The techniques include selecting matched groups of subjects, giving them different treatments, controlling unrelated factors, and checking for differences in response. For example, Tandy might want to test the price sensitivity of one of their CD players. To do this, it might fix the price differently at a number of outlets and see how sales volumes varied. The company would need to take care that other influencing variables such as the proximity to competitor outlets and the affluence of the different areas were controlled or at least known.

MARKETING INFORMATION SYSTEMS

The marketing information system (MIS) is concerned with determining information needs, and the collection, analysis, and distribution of that information in an accurate, appropriate, and timely manner to those who need it. Figure 4.11 shows the essential elements of a MIS and its relationship with the market environment.

Paradoxically, it is the distribution of information from the MIS to PDP managers that often falls short of the ideal. Sometimes, this is due to marketing managers being unaware of the needs of managers in other functions. This may be due to inadequate research by the marketing function or, equally likely because managers have not told marketing what they need. One of the problems, particularly for the product design functions is that needs change frequently, and then require rapid servicing so that problems can be overcome and the PDP moved forward. This is often the case during the early stages of the PDP when the objectives and constraints are being modified in response to the evaluation of concept ideas. At this stage, the initial design objectives frequently prove to be unrealistic because they are either too demanding or can be surpassed. Product design managers need to know what the market implications will be of meeting revised objectives, and the provision of this information is clearly a responsibility of the MIS. Therefore, the provision of information involves a two-way process between the MIS and product design managers.

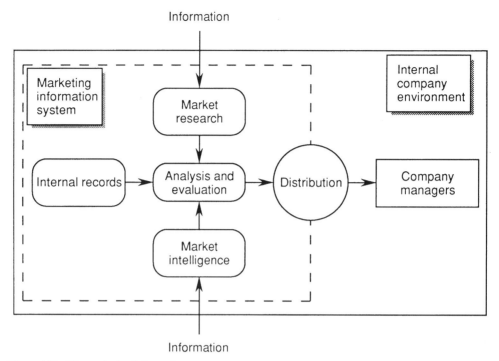

Figure 4.11   The marketing information system

Available information needs to be made available on-call, and although personal contact is still the most effective way of resolving conflicts between information needs and the resources available for its collection, computer-based data bases are now used extensively to put managers in contact with marketing information. This electronic availability of information requires the company to decide which information should be made available as raw data, and which should only be put out in the form of evaluations, conclusions, and directives by the MIS. The key to this is whether the information defines strategic policy in which case it cannot be made available for interpretation by product managers, or as background information.

RECAP

It is the role of the marketing function to provide the company with the information that it needs to maximise the sales of its products. The information is used to guide product development and the advertising that is required to secure and maintain a strong position in the market. An important aspect of the information relates to market segmentation in the product area, and the best ways of targeting the segments and positioning the product against the competition.

The MIS, which has the responsibility of collecting, analysing, and distributing the information within the company, uses internal company records, market intelligence, and market research to assemble the data required. Collection methods might involve the use of focus group meetings, interviews, telephone surveys, and mailed questionnaires.

Information will be distributed to managers in the form of reports or marketing briefs that make good use of tables and graphs to put forward the information in a palatable way. Presentation methods like user preference, product feature, and customer perception charts are particularly useful for product managers when combined with evaluations from the marketing function.

ASSIGNMENTS

These assignments are to help you think about markets in the same way that a marketing manager might when considering the needs of a company product. Because most people have easy access to television or magazines the questions are structured so that they relate particularly to consumer products. The best way to look for answers to the assignments is to read a pile of magazines or watch television for a few hours. Remember that you are looking at the advertisements, so you can get up and do something else useful when the programmes come on.

Assignment 4.1

Automobile manufacturers identify many segments for their products. Three segments that are often identifiable in their advertisements are the following:

1. Young, single, first time buyers of new vehicles. These customers are often identified as adventurous, open-minded, and risk-taking, with a considerable amount of disposable income.
2. Married with a young family. This segment demonstrates interest in safety, economy, and space for the accoutrements of family travel.
3. Middle or late middle-aged. This segment can be seen to include people at the peak of their earning power, and with diminishing demands imposed by their children. Disposable income tends to be higher in this segment than in segment 2.

Which publications might an automobile manufacturer use to reach each of the above segments? Although some publications will overlap two or all three of the segments most will only be suitable for reaching one. Obtain one or more issues of different publications that are targeted at the segments and look at the automobile advertisements. In most cases, the company will use a form of words and images that will attempt to make the product attractive to the relevant segment. In each case, make a list of the attributes and usage occasions that are introduced in the advertisement that address the needs of the segment.

Can you find examples of the same model being sold on the basis of different attributes and usage occasions to two segments? Even companies that sell pain-killers do this when selling their product to young or old, and men or women.

Assignment 4.2

Read some computer magazines and look through any popular computer retailer's window in the high street. On the basis of the products that are available, what can you say about market segmentation for PCs? Make a list of these segments, identifying some of the characteristics of the people that make them up. Complete the study by identifying one or more computers that seem to be targeting each segment. You will almost certainly find that each manufacturer attempts to broaden the appeal of its product by providing attributes that are attractive to more than one segment. Include at least one industrial segment in your study.

Assignment 4.3

From your experience, and based upon the examples given earlier, identify three consumer products that are targeted using each of the following strategies:

1. Undifferentiated marketing.
2. Differentiated marketing.
3. Concentrated marketing.

In each case, explain why that targeting strategy had been chosen. Repeat this exercise for industrial products.

Assignment 4.4

Using the product feature chart in Figure 4.5 as a guide, produce a similar chart for one of the product classes in the following list. Limit your chart to eight brands.

1. Domestic food-mixers.
2. Electric shavers for men and women (four of each).
3. Compact disc players.
4. Electric kettles.
5. Electric drills.

Remember to include price as an attribute, and identify those attributes that are mentioned on the packaging.

Assignment 4.5

Make a list of the attributes identified in your study from Assignment 4.4 and present it in a similar way to that shown in Figure 4.4. Provide a copy of the form to a small sample of 20 people or more (the more the better) and collate the results into a single sheet summary. It will help in getting some consistency in your results if the members of your sample are of a similar age or background, i.e. all students, parents, male, female etc. In other words, try to identify a segment on which to carry out your customer preference survey.

Rank the preferences in descending order, i.e., the most highly valued attribute at the top. Is it likely that a study of a different segment would show a different ranking? Is this reflected in the product range or advertising? If not, why is there a range of product brands for this class?

FIVE

REQUIREMENT TREES

OVERVIEW

In Chapter 4, we looked at some of the methods that the marketing function uses to analyse customer needs and competitor products. Ideally, the marketing function should provide designers with a concise description of their findings in the form of a brief. However, the market requirements as described in the brief are frequently expressed in a way that need some modification before being useful. The formal document that designers use to describe the required attributes of a product is called the **product design specification** (PDS), and Chapter 6 deals with the preparation of this document. Because of the difference in style and content of a marketing brief and a PDS, great care must be taken in the conversion process. This chapter examines the use of **requirement trees** to bridge the gap between market brief and PDS.

OBJECTIVES

When you have finished studying this chapter, you will be able to:

- use requirement trees to determine the objectives and constraints for the design of a product.
- use the method to establish and/or improve communication between marketing and design when determining objectives and constraints.
- apply the principles and techniques to any market requirement in any engineering discipline.
- assign weightings to objectives to signify their relative importance.

SETTING REQUIREMENTS

The needs of the customer can be defined in terms of objectives and constraints, and we will consider the difference between these more fully later. For the time being, an objective can be considered to be a requirement written in unquantified terms, while a constraint is a requirement written in quantified terms.

Definition

objectives *adj* **1.** existing independently of perception; being a material object as opposed to a concept, idea, etc. **2.** undistorted by emotion or personal bias **3.** of or relating to actual and external phenomena as opposed to thoughts, feelings, etc. **4.** . . . **6.** of or relating to a goal or aim −*n* **7.** the object of one's endeavours; goal; aim. **8.** . . .
constraint *n.* Compulsion; confinement . . .

The definition of 'objective' makes it clear that a design objective should be stated in terms that are independent of the perceptions of the designer. This is a good axiom, because it reduces the risk of ruling out possible design solutions before all of the requirements are established. Of course, in reality such a viewpoint is impossible because we are all limited and influenced by our experiences. Nevertheless, it is important during the early stages of the PDP to keep an open mind. For this reason, the purpose of a requirement tree is to explore the problem rather than look for solutions.

Someone who was setting out to design a domestic food-mixer might start with the list of requirements in Figure 5.1.

You can see that the requirement types listed in the right hand column conform to our definition. Requirements 1 and 2 are stated in a non-quantified manner, and meet the definition of objectives, whilst requirements 3, 4 and 5 are quantified, and therefore qualify as constraints. On more careful consideration, you might feel uneasy about one or both of the objective type requirements. For example, 'ergonomic design' might be partially defined in terms of knob and handle dimensions, torques, forces etc., and these would be constraints. This process of looking for opportunities of quantifying requirements (i.e. converting objective requirements to constraint requirements) is an important aspect of coming to terms with customer needs. It is sufficient to say that 'at the moment' the requirement for an ergonomic design is stated in objective terms.

A requirement tree can provide a means of 'thought ordering' for an individual designer working alone. It also provides a means of communicating thoughts on objectives and constraints to other designers, marketing personnel, and sometimes the customer. In most cases, a team of people working together jointly produce requirement trees to communicate and record their developing views on the product's requirements. In each of these cases, it is important that designers are fully conversant with the needs of the customer.

Requirement	Type
1. Aesthetically pleasing	objective
2. Ergonomic design	objective
3. Bowl to contain at least 1 litre	constraint
4. Three speed-settings	constraint
5. Built-in storage cable	constraint

Figure 5.1 An initial requirement list for a food-mixer

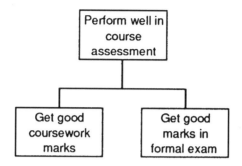

Figure 5.2 A Requirement Tree based on the need to do well in course assessment

Figure 5.2 illustrates the use of a requirement tree to examine a problem that we have all had to overcome.

The starting point for the construction of a requirement tree is to define the **top-level requirement** (TLR). In the case of Figure 5.2, the TLR is to 'Perform well in course assessment'. The next stage of tree development is to expand the TLR by asking the question 'what do we mean by this?'. In the example, the question is answered by expanding the tree into two branches which identify additional sub-requirements. In other words, the tree suggests that getting good coursework marks and good formal examination marks are requirements that must be achieved if the TLR is to be attained. The logic of the tree can be checked by asking the question 'why do we need to do that?' when moving from a lower level requirement to one at the next level up. For example, asking the question 'why do we need to get good coursework marks?' should be answerable by 'so that we can perform well in course assessment'.

This example is so simple that it is difficult to extend it much further, so a case study of a slightly more extensive problem follows. This study is an example on which you are bound to be able to volunteer your own views. These views are almost certain to be different to anyone else's. You should remember that investigating disagreement is something that requirement trees are particularly good for, so the fact that your tree would be different to someone else's is a good thing, not an indication that they are ineffective!

CASE STUDY 5.1

I don't know about you, but I hate cleaning shoes. I come home from work and go into the garden to pull some weeds up. I know that I should change my shoes before I get the spade but sometimes it seems too much trouble. The result is that I end up with dirty shoes that I need for work the following day. Now, what I really need is some sort of automatic 'machine' that will make my shoes look good. The market for such a machine at the right price must be huge. We might be able to make millions, and retire, and, and . . . anyway, perhaps we should stick to thinking up the design objectives first, using of course, a requirement tree to help us.

An automatic machine to make shoes look good.

This is the top level requirement. I suggested this as a reasonable starting point, but there was considerable debate on other possibilities. Some suggested '....to make shoes clean', but this was considered too restrictive.

Figure 5.3   The TLR for the shoe cleaning problem

I gave this problem to a group of students, and the following sequence of diagrams shows how **their** tree developed. There is annotation to outline the reasons why and how the group arrived at their conclusions about each level of the tree. Figure 5.3 shows the TLR that the students started with.

Choosing the correct statement for the TLR can be critical in ensuring that the tree develops in a satisfactory way. The TLR identified in Figure 5.3 **might** lead to good looking shoes that are not necessarily clean. Such a machine might coat the shoes with a high gloss lacquer. If the TLR was changed to read '. . . . to make shoes clean', the resulting machine might brush the dirt off but do nothing to provide a good shine. If you find that the TLR does not allow you to include necessary objectives by using the 'why' and 'what' questions, then modify it until it does. TLR changes are a part of the process of thinking about objectives.

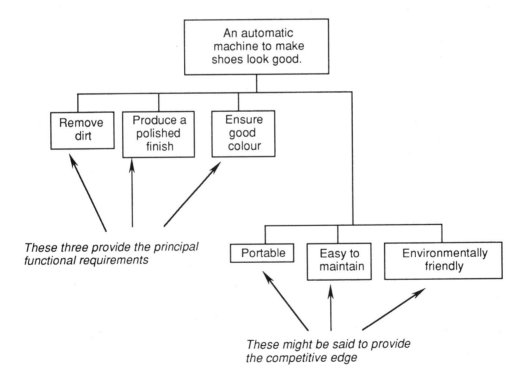

Figure 5.4   The shoe cleaning tree developed to the second level

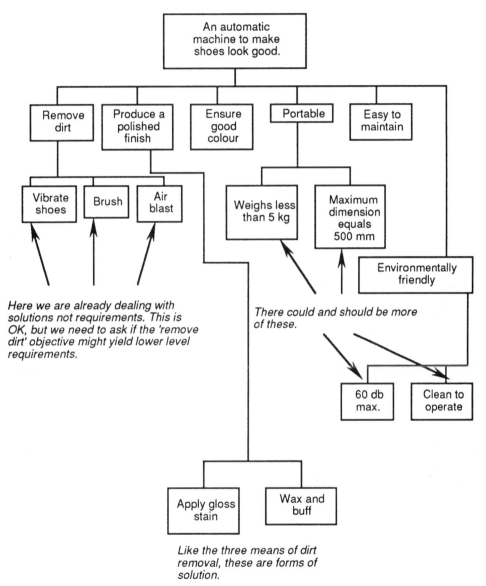

Figure 5.5 The shoe cleaning tree developed to the third level

Figure 5.4 shows the TLR and second level requirements developed by the group. If you tried your hand at developing this tree, it is practically certain that your second level requirements would be different to those developed by the student group. In fact, there could be many more second level requirements than those shown. Perhaps the group should have had requirements relating to the 'automatic' aspect of the device, the type of shoes for which it is to be used etc. Most of the second level requirements can be developed by asking the question 'what do we mean by that' of the TLR. However, the three on the right do not come out of the question quite as directly as the three on the left. And if (for example) we ask 'why do we want the machine to be portable' the direct answer is **not** 'an

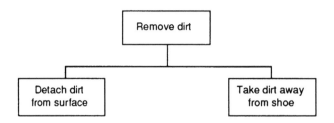

Figure 5.6 Possible developments from the 'remove dirt' objective

automatic machine to make shoes look good'! However, we could put this right by improving the TLR so that it recognises the need for broad market appeal. Perhaps we could have said 'a marketable automatic machine to make . . .' or, 'a commercially viable automatic . . .' etc. The main thing is that the tree makes you think about the requirements, and forms a focus for team discussions and eventual agreement.

Next the group added some third level objectives as shown in Figure 5.5

Now this is interesting. When the group looked at the second level requirement 'remove dirt', they found it impossible to come up with sub-requirements to it. As a result, they decided to put down several ways that the second level requirement could be achieved. I'm not saying that I agree with this. For instance, I might have added the sub-requirements shown in Figure 5.6.

A tree that starts by considering requirements and finishes off by including means of solution is called a 'requirement/means' tree. Such trees take the designer from the 'understanding the problem' phase to the commencement of the concept solution phase. This process is useful but try to put off the means development as long as possible. Always make absolutely sure that you have taken the development of requirements to the very limit before you go to the next stage. The group produced means from the 'produce a polished finish' requirement, but developed third level objectives elsewhere.

Definition:

means *n.* the medium, method, or instrument used to obtain a result or achieve an end.

An interesting feature of the tree shown in Figure 5.5 is the way that 'portable' leads to two quantified requirements. By our definition, these are no longer objectives but constraints. We will consider constraints again later, but for the time being it is sufficient to say a requirement tree's ability to encourage us to develop constraints is one of its most powerful attributes.

Now have a look at Figure 5.7 to see how the fourth and fifth level objectives were developed by the students. The fourth level objectives are developed from 'clean to operate' and comply with the 'what' and 'why' or 'downwards' and 'upwards' logic requirements.

When trying to develop the 'clean to operate' requirement, the group could only think of one sub-requirement at each of the next two levels (Figure 5.8). You should always attempt to develop as many sub-requirements as you can from the parent objective by

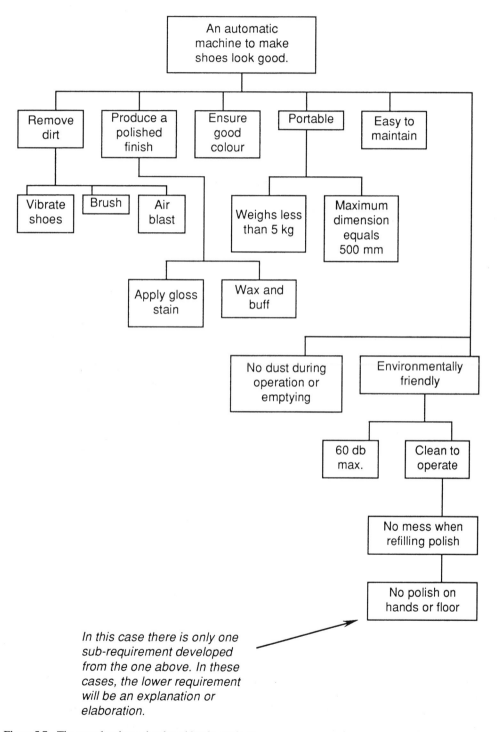

Figure 5.7 The completed tree developed by the students

Figure 5.8   Single sub-requirements clarify their parent

interrogating it with the 'what do we mean by this' question. However, in some cases, no matter how hard you try, you will only get a single sub-requirement out of it. What does this mean? Well, invariably, the single sub-requirement will be a refinement or clarification of its parent.

Let us continue by taking a look at a more involved requirement tree. The tree shown in Figure 5.9 was constructed by engineers at Rolls Royce. Fan blades in jet engines are assembled into a disc where they are clamped into position. However, the airflow between the blades is adversely disturbed by the irregularities in the disc, and a smaller 'filler' is required to fit in the gap between the base of each pair of adjacent blades. The filler provides a smooth surface over which the air can flow, thereby improving the efficiency of the engine.

Rolls Royce engineers wanted to consider alternative means of overcoming the airflow problem and, regardless of their familiarity with the problem (or even **because** of their familiarity with the problem) they decided to evaluate thoroughly what it was that they were trying to do. A requirement tree, developed by members of the design team was an ideal way of doing this. Note that (allowing for the use of abbreviated requirements) the upwards and downwards logic in Figure 5.9 always holds true. It is also interesting to note that the tree splits into major functional and 'competitive edge' requirements at the second level. This is a common feature of many trees.

All requirements that cannot be developed further are called 'bottom level' requirement. As many of these as possible should be quantified and expressed as constraints. This was done by Rolls Royce engineers for the filler, but the constraint values are not shown here for commercial reasons.

Although the requirement trees shown in this book are typeset, in real life they are usually initially produced freehand. Sometimes the media used for their production is pen and paper, but in team working it is often most effective to use a large white board so that everyone can see what is going on and easily get involved. Team development of a requirement tree is normally a very dynamic event, with the tree structure being subjected to frequent additions and deletions. In many cases, trees are 'finished' only for one member of the team to identify that something important has been missed. If the omission cannot easily be incorporated, the entire tree may have to be scrapped so

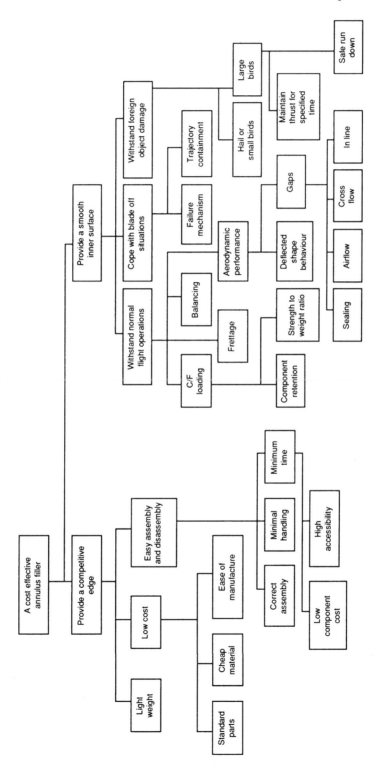

Figure 5.9 A requirement tree for an annulus filler

that a modified TLR can be identified that will allow the final structure to reflect all of the requirements and constraints.

Requirement trees can be a useful tool at all stages of the design process. Although traditionally they are most likely to be used during the initial problem-definition stage of a project, they are also valuable whenever engineers need to define or redefine the project requirements. This may occur when working on broad product aims, sub-assembly design, or detailed component design.

The logical structuring of a tree, together with its mixture of graphics and text, makes it an ideal method for supporting and controlling dynamic team interaction without stultifying free thinking. However, this strength also presents a problem because of the speed with which ideas can be developed and recorded. The space restrictions imposed by the need to work in the relatively small boxes on the tree often make it necessary to enter abbreviations for each requirement. The danger is that asking the 'what do we mean by this' question of an abbreviation can sometimes result in a sub-requirement that is not correctly stated. This can easily lead to the upward and downward logic of the tree breaking down. A simple solution to this problem is to provide a separate detailed description of each requirement to supplement the abbreviation. Then, the detailed requirement is used as the basis for developing sub-requirements, and so on.

When a tree has been completed, and members of the group are in agreement (or, more likely, have agreed to disagree) on its structure, the tree is usually redrawn using an appropriate computer-based graphics or word processing package. In this form, the tree provides a record of the decisions made by the group and, in some companies forms a part of the Quality documentation record.

COMMUNICATION AND DOCUMENTATION

The requirement tree method makes people think about what it is that they are trying to achieve, and to develop these requirements to a point where they can be formalised into the Product Design Specification discussed in Chapter 6. This thinking process provides the objectives for innovative design, and the constraints within which solutions must remain.

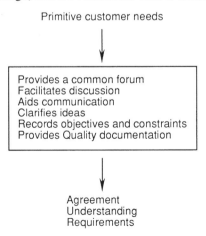

Figure 5.10 Inputs, outputs, and benefits of the requirement tree method

Many of the requirements will come directly from a knowledge of customer needs, whilst others (particularly constraints) will result from the commercial and technological limitations of the company. However, the 'processing' of these raw requirements into a form where they can be accepted by all of the people involved usually requires discussion, negotiation, and careful thinking if mistakes are not to be made and opportunities missed. Because of the differences in background, personal objectives, and loyalties of those concerned, the process of clarifying and agreeing requirements can be extremely difficult unless a structure can be imposed upon it. Requirement trees are a good tool for the imposition of such a structure because of their own inherent logic.

Figure 5.10 shows the requirement tree preparation activity, with the principal benefits of the transformation and the major inputs and outputs.

Frequently, a tree development session will end before the issues have been talked out. At this point, it is a good idea for someone to take the most recent version (or versions) of the tree and redraw it for circulation to all interested parties. This enables people to reflect on the discussion, and either prepare for the next meeting or engage in sub-group meetings to resolve contentious issues outside the larger forum.

When agreement on the requirements have finally been reached the tree will be formalised and signed off by the responsible manager. If combined with supporting documentation that explains the reasons for the decisions encapsulated in it, the tree can form a valuable source of accountability and traceability information.

RECAP

Requirement trees are a method that designers can use to encourage a structured investigation into the objectives and constraints of a project. They can be used by a designer working alone, but are more effective when worked on by a group.

The stages involved in the preparation of a requirement tree can be summarised as follows:

1. Define a top level requirement containing words that are descriptive of the total requirements of the design. This will enable you to develop a branch for each sub-requirement.
2. Check the tree logic all the way, develop the tree until no further qualitative objectives can be added. This can be slow work, but should be undertaken conscientiously.
3. If you discover that you want to add a requirement that does not fit in with the existing logic of the tree, it means that one of the higher requirements (or even the top level requirement) needs modifying. Do not hesitate to do this, it is a vital part of clarifying your thoughts about the problem.
4. When no more qualitative objectives are forthcoming, see if you can take each one and provide additional quantified constraints.
5. Throughout the whole process of development, use the tree as a basis for discussion with colleagues and representatives of the customer.
6. Formalise the agreed tree into a document that can be used for future reference.

ASSIGNMENTS

To develop the experience required to produce requirement trees, and to understand the problems involved, you should attempt to provide solutions for the two assignments that follow. Appendix 2 contains typical solutions to these assignments, but it is important to spend an hour or so developing **your** solutions **before** looking at them.

Assignment 5.1

Imagine that you are a consulting engineer who has been given a brief to undertake a feasibility study on the design of a machine to take loads of recently lifted carrots and prepare them ready for sale in high class retail outlets. A market survey has revealed that the customer wants the carrots to be prepacked in sealed 1 kg packs. Draw a requirement tree for the machine. Can you get down as far as fourth level objectives in all branches? At some stage during the preparation of the tree you may have to make some assumptions about the problem.

Assignment 5.2

You have made such a success of the carrot problem that you have been head hunted by a company that makes electrical domestic products. In your new capacity, you are working with the marketing department to specify the objectives for a new design of hair dryer to meet the needs of the 17 to 25 year old single male market. Making any assumptions that you want about the market, draw a requirement tree. Many of the objectives will be the same as for any other type of hairdryer, but include them in your tree just the same. Refer to the case study provided in Chapter 4 if you need more information about this particular product requirement.

SPECIFYING IMPORTANCE

The first part of this chapter has been concerned with determining the objectives and constraints that apply to a design problem. In some cases, the establishment of these criteria will be a sufficient definition of the problem for the designer to seek a solution. However, in many cases it will be found that some of the objectives and constraints are in conflict with each other, and this will require further thought to be given to the relationships between them.

As an example of the type of conflict that can occur between requirements, consider the trade-off that frequently has to be made between weight, durability, and cost. In the design of a high specification mountain bicycle, all of these factors are important. The weight must be kept low to minimise the effort required in moving the mass of the bike uphill or during stages where it must be carried. At the same time, the structure of the bike must be capable of withstanding the static and dynamic forces to which it will be subjected. Finally, the bike must be set at a price that the prospective purchaser will be prepared to pay. The potential for conflict between the three factors is obvious. For a given material, a reduction in weight can only be achieved by reducing the amount of material in the structure. Although less material might imply a saving in weight and cost, it might also reduce strength. Alternatively, it may be possible to choose a material with a higher mechanical specification, thereby enabling the structure to be lightened without losing strength. Here, the problem would probably be that the higher grade material would cost more than the original, and may have the added disadvantage of higher processing costs.

Such conflicts are commonplace in design, and experienced designers can frequently deal with them on an intuitive basis. Nevertheless, there is a risk that the tactical decisions made as a part of the trade-off process will be made without adequate consideration of their effect on the marketability of the product.

A well specified design problem will incorporate constraints on important design parameters. Hence, the initial specification for the bike would provide market constraints for weight, strength, and cost. In all probability, weight and cost would be provided with a maximum constraint, whilst strength would be assigned a minimum constraint as shown below.

$$\text{Weight} \leq W_{max}$$
$$\text{Cost} \leq C_{max}$$
$$\text{Strength} \geq S_{min}$$

If these constraints and the other requirements can be met by one or more of the designs under consideration then a solution to the problem is clearly possible, and the only remaining question might be how to evaluate a number of possible alternatives, all of which have parameter values falling within the original constraints. Frequently, this choice can be made by 'revisiting' the constraints to see if a product with improved marketability or profitability could be identified by changing one or more of them.

In cases where modifying the constraints does not help trade-off considerations, the next stage is to involve the unquantified objectives in the evaluation process. The problem with this is that objectives are difficult to use for this purpose.

Chapter 8, looks in detail at some methods that can be employed to help designers choose the best ideas to develop. A pre-requisite to using these evaluation methods is assessing the relative importance of objectives, and this is something that we need to consider whilst requirement trees are fresh in our minds.

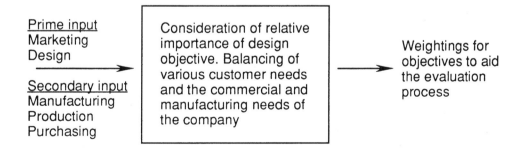

Figure 5.11   Inputs, outputs, and actions in the Weightings method

Remember that all objectives and constraints that influence customer perception can only be determined by reference to the customer. The same applies to the determination of the degree of importance or 'weightings' that are placed on the objectives. We need to know how to manipulate and present the weightings in a way that will assist in the evaluation of concepts. Of course, not all design objectives are purely concerned with directly satisfying the customer. The company will also have its non-quantifiable requirements associated with manufacturing capacity, purchasing strategy, production scheduling etc., and these will also need to be considered. Assigning weightings to objectives is a team effort, with input from a wide range of company functions in addition to marketing and design as shown in Figure 5.11. However, maximising customer satisfaction should be seen as a key aim for this activity.

The bottom-up approach

The first stage of the weighting process is to list the objectives. The requirement tree is likely to be a prime source for these, although others will almost certainly be identified from internal company sources. The second stage is to rank the objectives in order of importance.

Let us take the objectives from the 'shoe-cleaning' requirements tree as an example. If you look at the tree produced earlier in this chapter, you will see that the requirement for low noise and portability were fully constrained. There is no point in weighting these requirements because a particular design solution will either succeed or fail to satisfy them; there can be no intermediate position. The bottom level unquantified requirements, or objectives are listed below:

- Remove dirt.
- Produce a polished finish.
- Ensure a good colour.
- Easy to maintain.
- No dust during operation.
- No polish on hands or floor.

Because it is much easier to deal with constraints than objectives, now is a good time to take a second look at these and see if we can prescribe numerical limits of satisfaction for them, i.e. to see if we can convert them into easy-to-use constraints. For example, we might be able to remove 'easy to maintain' out of the objectives list by re-stating it as several constraints, e.g., maintenance required at a minimum of 100 operational hours, each maintenance operation to last a maximum of 10 minutes, all maintenance operations achievable with a screwdriver etc. Regardless of this, let us take the list as it stands and move to stage two.

In this case, all the objectives are concerned with performance features that will be of concern to the purchaser and/or user. How then do we find out what the correct order of importance of the objectives is to the customer? Easy: ask the customer of course.

In the case of the shoe-cleaning problem a questionnaire was given to a sample group of people. The questionnaire asked them to rank the six objectives in the order that they would be influenced by them if they were purchasing a shoe cleaning machine. Each person's returned questionnaire was collated, and a 6 assigned to their most important objective, a 5 to the second etc. After doing this for all of the returns the points allocated to each of the objectives were added up, which gave the following ranking:

Objective	Points
Remove dirt	1142
Produce a polished finish	971
No dust during operation	911
No polish on hands or floor	475
Ensure a good colour	395
Easy maintenance	306

Of course, the advantage of using a method like this is that it gives you a basis for assessing relative importance and not merely the order. For example, from the list we might come to the conclusion that 'remove dirt' is approximately four times more important than 'easy to maintain'. Conclusions like these need to be treated with care because they might be ignoring important factors that have influenced the way that customers have responded.

A trained mechanic answering the questionnaire will have a totally different perception of 'easy to maintain' than someone who has no mechanical expertise. Similarly, respondents will have different perceptions in regard to 'good colour' and 'polished finish'. Some people might see these statements as being very different ways of saying the same thing, in which case an alternative to these two such as 'produce bright colour' might have scored more than 'remove dirt'.

In the example that we have just considered, we used a 'bottom-up' approach. That is, we started with bottom level (the most detailed) objectives and worked directly on these to determine their importance. This approach frequently works well, but there are times where a top-down method provides a more disciplined approach. The top-down method can be particularly useful when a team of people are attempting to reach agreement on the relative importance of objectives that include company as well as customer requirements.

The top-down approach

Starting at the top of the tree, we assign a unitary weighting to the TLR, then proceeding down each branch of the tree in turn, allocate the portions of the unitary weighting to each sub-objective as we come to it. Here are two examples, the first with a generic tree, and the second with the Rolls Royce annulus filler tree.

Figure 5.12 represents a small but complete requirements tree. The broadest statement of requirement is the TLR from which sub-objectives 1 and 2 are developed. Sub-objective 1 yields two further sub-objectives (1.1 and 1.2) and, in turn, 1.1 yields three sub-objectives (1.1.1, 1.1.2 and 1.1.3). Sub-objectives 2 yields 2.1 and 2.2. The bottom level objectives that we require rankings for are: 1.1.1, 1.1.2, 1.1.3, 1.2, 2.1, and 2.2. We will assume that this tree did not yield any constraints, or that they have been previously removed.

The first stage of the top-down process is to assign a weighting of 1 to the TLR, and then divide this between the sub-objectives at the next lower level. The way that the TLR weighting is shared between sub-objectives 1 and 2 will depend upon the nature of the tree and will be the subject of consideration and negotiation between those involved. As always, the **process** of decision making is at least as important as the result. Let's say that, in this

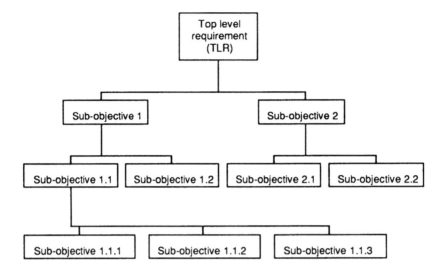

Figure 5.12 A generic requirement tree

example, the decision was taken that sub-objective 1 was three times more important than objective 2. Figure 5.13 shows how this would be indicated on the tree.

The boxes drawn under each objective contain the weightings that have been assigned. The TLR has been assigned a value of 1 and this has been divided between sub-objectives 1 and 2 in the ratio 0.75:0.25. Note that by adding together the weightings for sub-objectives 1 and 2, the weighting for the higher level objective can be derived. This is a good way of checking that all of the available weighting has being allocated.

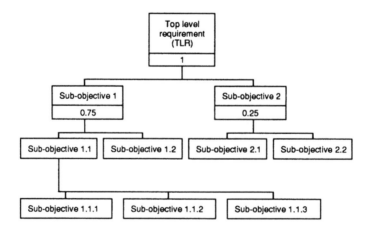

Figure 5.13 Weightings assigned at level 2

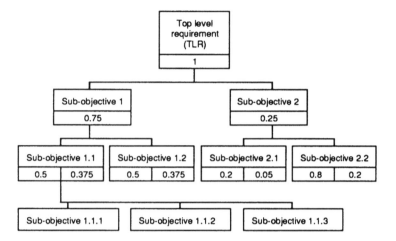

Figure 5.14 Weightings assigned at level 3

We now need to divide the weighting allocated to sub-objectives 1 between 1.1 and 1.2. In this case, say that the design team considered sub-objectives 1.1 and 1.2 equally important. Here, of the 0.75 weighting assigned to sub-objective 1, 0.375 would need to be assigned to each of sub-objectives 1.1 and 1.2.

Let us also say that the team decided that sub-objective 2.2 was four times more important than 2.1. Figure 5.14 shows how the requirement tree would look after the addition of the decisions made so far.

At the third level down there is a second box below each objective. In the case of each objective, the box on the left contains the multiplication factor representing the comparative importance of the objective in relation to others at the same level in the same branch. Hence, 1.1 and 1.2 are each to receive 0.5 of the weighting assigned to sub-objective 1. This is equal to a half of 0.75, i.e., 0.375. Sub-objectives 2.1 and 2.2 are to receive 0.2 and 0.8 of the sub-objective 2 weighting respectively. Hence, 2.1 receives $0.2 \times 0.25 = 0.05$

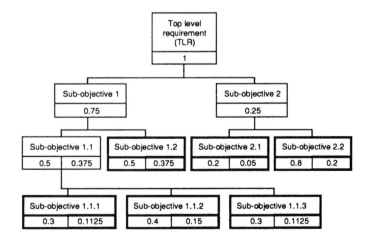

Figure 5.15 Weightings assigned at level 4

Note again how the sum of the weightings assigned to 1.1 and 1.2 equal that assigned to sub-objective 1, and the sum of the weightings assigned to 2.1 and 2.2 produces that assigned to sub-objective 2. Finally, the weighting assigned to 1.1 needs distributing between 1.1.1, 1.1.2, and 1.1.3. If the decision were to allocate these in the ratio 0.3:0.4:0.3, the final tree would appear as shown in Figure 5.15.

As a final check on the mathematics, the sum of the weightings made to each bottom level objective (represented in bold outline in Figure 5.15) should be 1.

Hence: $0.1125 + 0.15 + 0.1125 + 0.375 + 0.05 + 0.2 = 1\checkmark$.

The initial decision to allocate a value of 1 to the TLR does not need to be adhered to. Indeed, one of the drawbacks of using unity is that bottom level objectives can end up with weightings that are exceedingly small. In practice, this is of no consequence because we are only concerned with relative importance. However, if you do not like having a weighting of 0.1125 try starting with a TLR weighting of 100 rather than 1. All other things being equal, you would then end up with a weighting of 11.25 for the sub-objective 1.1.1.

Having considered a general case, lets look at how the Rolls Royce engineers assigned weightings to the annulus filler tree. This tree and its weightings was produced during a brainstorming session (Chapter 7) in which engineers were trying to establish the problem areas and the difficulties that lay ahead. Because the tree is so extensive, only half of it is reproduced in Figure 5.16. Even though they knew that many of the objectives would be converted to constraints in the near future, they used the weighting method as a means of encouraging discussion on the details of the problem. They decided to use the 'top down' approach because of the greater discipline that it demands in considering the relationship between objectives at all levels. It was not appropriate to involve the end-user (the airline) in deciding what the weightings should be because, in this case, the customers were other engineers within the company. The annulus filler project team were acutely aware of the need to find a solution that would provide all of the attributes identified in Figure 5.9. However, to make sure that their final solution satisfied the wider requirements for engine performance, safety, maintenance, etc., they involved staff from these areas in the weighting process. Because cross-functional teams and matrix organisation are a normal way of working at Rolls Royce, some representatives from the 'customer' functions were already members of the annulus filler team.

In addition to providing a means of expressing the relative importance of objectives, the requirement tree method also encourages designers to consider the problems that lie ahead. It is difficult to engage in detailed discussion about the importance of achieving some product attribute without evaluating how difficult it will be to achieve. This aspect of requirement trees makes them useful in making preliminary decisions about what resources (staff, computers, test facilities, research, time, etc.) might be required. Of course, the resources picture will not become clear until concept solutions have been generated, evaluated, and selected; nevertheless careful consideration of objectives frequently enables initial predictions to be made. This benefit was certainly in the mind of the Rolls Royce engineers when they started to consider the annulus filler objectives.

Figure 5.16 shows weightings applied to the 'provide a smooth inner surface' branch of the tree. This second level objective was allocated a half of the weighting available, the other half being allocated to 'provide a competitive edge'. The mathematics of the tree can be checked by adding together the weightings allocated to all of the bottom level objectives.

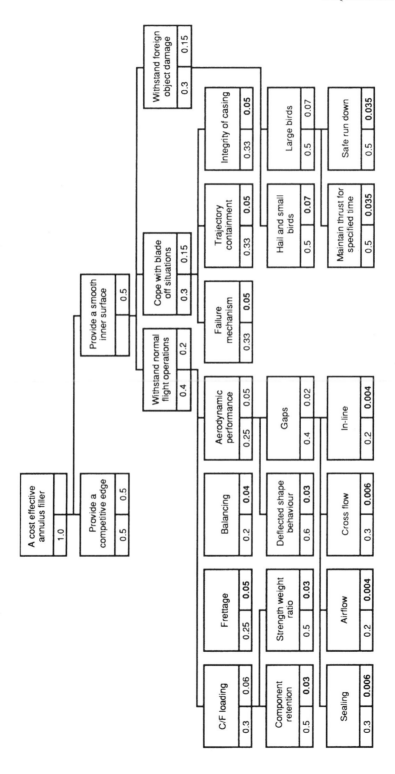

Figure 5.16 The weighted tree for the annulus filler

Because these are all sub-objectives of 'provide a smooth inner surface', their sum is equal to 0.5.

COMMUNICATION AND DOCUMENTATION

The weighting method involves people from various company functions in the process of making decisions about the importance of project objectives. In some cases, the discussions will also involve the customer and/or the marketing function.

As in the case of other methods, the weighting activity can be represented by the input, transformation, and output of information. Figure 5.17 represents this in block diagram form.

The information brought to the method relates to perceptions of importance held by the various parties involved. The need to reach agreement before weightings can be assigned to the tree is a catalyst to careful evaluation of an individual's own position as well as the position of others. An important aspect of this accommodation of opinions is the need to make trade-offs between conflicting views of importance. Provided that there are no outstanding disagreements of a substantial nature at the end of the process, the principal benefit of using the method will result from the negotiation process, and the final weighted tree will be a record of the consensus view.

Most of the information required to make the weighting method work will come from the perceptions held by individuals, although customer or marketing function briefs may also provide input. Output from the method will be used in the preparation of a product design specification and at a later stage in the evaluation of concept design solutions. Figure 5.18 shows the relationship between these elements, and shows the need for additional documentation. Although the tree will be a record of the final decisions reached, it will be necessary to record what influenced the process so that decisions can be traced, validated, and attributed at a later date.

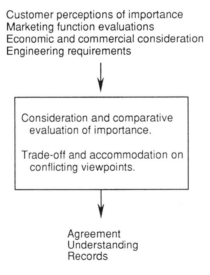

Customer perceptions of importance
Marketing function evaluations
Economic and commercial consideration
Engineering requirements

Consideration and comparative
evaluation of importance.

Trade-off and accommodation on
conflicting viewpoints.

Agreement
Understanding
Records

Figure 5.17 Inputs, transformation, and outputs of the weighting method

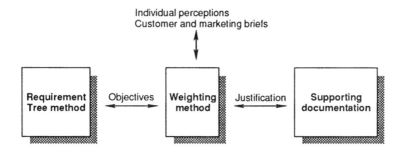

Figure 5.18 Links with other methods

RECAP

In general, every attempt should be made to quantify design requirements, because this makes it much easier to evaluate concepts. In the case of the remaining unquantified requirements, it frequently helps the concept development process if agreement can be reached on the relative importance of these objectives. This is particularly the case when there is a conflict between objectives.

The weighting method can help cross-functional teams to concentrate attention on objectives in an attempt to reach accommodation between individuals who may have very differing views on what is important.

The weightings can be developed using either a bottom-up or top-down method. The former tends to be more useful when the customer is directly involved, whilst the second can offer advantages when the process is carried out entirely or substantially within the company.

To provide a full set of documentation, the weighted tree will need to be supplemented by records of the information that was considered, why particular decisions were made, and what alternatives were examined prior to rejection.

ASSIGNMENTS

Assignment 5.3

Using either the requirement tree that you produced for Assignment 5.2, or my hairdryer tree in Appendix 2, develop weightings for all of the bottom level objectives. Use the top-down approach, working alone or (preferably) with two or three colleagues. Remember to make a record of why each decision was taken, paying particular attention to unresolved conflicts where you agreed to disagree.

Assignment 5.4

Make a list of the bottom level objectives from Assignment 5.2 and assign weightings to them using the bottom-up approach. Ask at least six of your colleagues to rate each objective on a scale from 1 (not important) to 5 (vitally important) as was done earlier in this chapter with the shoe cleaning problem. Are the weightings obtained by the two methods different, and what may be the reason for this?

SIX

PRODUCT DESIGN SPECIFICATIONS

OVERVIEW

Chapter 5 was concerned with the use of requirement trees to encourage thinking and communication relating to the market requirements for a product. These requirements are defined by objectives and constraints.

This chapter is concerned with the means by which requirements are drawn together into a document called the **product design specification** (PDS). The PDS is vitally important to the success of the design process. In effect, it can provide the 'legal' basis to which customer and designer can refer in arguments about whether the designer has achieved what the customer requested. However, in most companies, there will be many PDSs all relating to different parts of the same product. In addition to the overall PDS which lays down the requirements of the product from a customer or market point of view, there will be 'internal' company PDSs that specify the requirements of sub-assemblies and components. Each PDS describes the objectives to be met and the constraints to be worked within, and thereby provides a framework for innovation and a means of assessing the outcomes of the innovation process.

Because the PDS is so influential in describing the requirements of the final product, it is important that a great deal of attention is given to its compilation. This chapter examines the important issues that need to be considered when producing a PDS, and looks at the advantages and disadvantages of various ways of writing them.

Definition:

specification *n.* **1.** the act or an instance of specifying. **2.** (in patent law) a written statement accompanying an application for a patent that describes the nature of an invention. **3.** a detailed description of the criteria for the constituents, construction, appearance, performance, etc., of a material, apparatus etc., or of the standard of workmanship required in its manufacture.

performance *n.* **1.** manner or quality of functioning.

OBJECTIVES

When you have finished studying this chapter, you will be able to:

- convert product requirements into a formal PDS;
- evaluate the alternative ways of writing a PDS and choose the one most appropriate to your needs;
- write a specification in a way that minimises the opportunities for error and ambiguity.

ALTERNATIVES, TYPES, AND FEATURES

Because the PDS states the objectives and constraints for a product solution, it is important that it does so in a way that enables the designer to reach a functionally and commercially acceptable solution in an appropriate period of time. To achieve this, thought has to be given to the level of generality of the PDS, to make sure that time is not wasted or potentially good solutions excluded. For example, if a decision had been made to design a moving walkway to transport foot passengers around a theme park, it would be a waste of effort to have a PDS that merely stated the requirement to be a rapid transit system. A designer working with such a PDS could spend long periods considering unacceptable alternatives such as monorail systems, trains, and buses, only to be told in the end that he or she should have concentrated on walkways. Of course, if the aim was to evaluate **all** possible forms of rapid transit, the PDS would have to reflect this state of affairs.

Generally, it is convenient to identify three levels of generality in which a PDS may be written. These are:

- product alternatives;
- product types;
- product features;

The highest level of generality (i.e., the 'alternatives' level) is when the PDS allows the designer to look at all or several broad alternative methods of producing a solution. In the theme park example, the designer would work to a PDS that described the overall requirements for the system (e.g., number of passengers to be carried in unit time, speed of transit) but would not contain objectives or constraints that limited the designer to only one type of solution. At the next level lower (the 'type' level) the PDS would limit the designer to a particular solution-type by means of appropriate wording of the objectives and constraints. A 'feature' level PDS is the lowest in generality. Such a PDS is concerned with specifying the functional and commercial requirements of some feature (possibly a sub-assembly or component) in the product. It is **always** important for the designer to establish how much freedom is to be allowed. The need to discuss and decide upon the appropriate PDS level is most appropriate when the designer and the customer are in direct negotiation, and is much less likely to be a key issue when the designer is responsible to a manager who acts as an intermediary to the customer. The majority of design engineers are presented with a PDS as a *fait accompli* and are expected to have little to say about its suitability. This may be reasonable, particularly if the PDS relates to a small part of a larger system that has been specified at a higher management level within the company. However, if the designer is to be held responsible for the outcome, then it is totally reasonable that he or she should be able to evaluate and question the implications of the instructions contained in the PDS.

In many design projects, several versions of PDS will be written as the design develops. At the start of the project, when the overall requirements of the market have been established, but before there are clear ideas of how the requirements can be met, the PDS will be at the alternatives level. When work has been completed on the development of the alternatives and one or more have been chosen for detailed design evaluation, new PDSs will be required at the types level. In addition to stating the broad requirements common to all types, these will contain requirements that are only attributable to the product type with which they are concerned. If moving passenger walkways and monorail systems were selected for further consideration, each would have characteristics that would require different PDSs. For example, the monorail system would require its PDS to lay down requirements for queuing time, whilst the walkway PDS might contain requirements for bad weather protection and the degree of inconvenience that was acceptable to other pedestrians not using the system. In the case of complex engineering systems, it is not unusual for a PDS to go through 5, 10, 20 or more revisions by the time the design gets to the production prototype stage.

There is another reason why a PDS is a dynamic rather than a static document. At first, it seems strange that the customer, or the customer's representative in the form of the marketing department, would not be able to produce a definitive PDS. In practice, this is often the case. Although the need for a particular product function might be known, customers will often lack the technical or design expertise to propose or envisage the form of solution. Because of this, the ability of the available technology to provide the desired solution may not be taken fully into account in the earliest version of the PDS. This early description of the requirements is often called the 'brief' to distinguish it from the subsequent descriptions that can truly be defined as Product Design Specifications.

As alternative solutions to the market requirement are conceived, evaluated, selected, and developed, the PDS will also develop in parallel. In the end, certain aspects of the PDS are likely to be quite specific to the chosen solution. It is probable that the original brief or early versions of the PDS will still apply in general terms, but the later versions will be more specific. The last version of the PDS may actually approximate what civil engineers simply call a 'specification' which is a detailed description of the finished product or system.

One of the greatest dangers in writing a PDS is that it becomes a repository for preconceived ideas that are based upon assumption and prejudice rather than real requirements. It is the designer's duty to question the validity of the PDS to ensure that its constraints are accurate reflections of requirements, and are not unnecessarily restrictive. Such restrictions may prevent the designer from achieving the best solution and, at the very least are likely to add cost. A good PDS will set requirements without unnecessarily implying what the form of the product will be. This definition is a good test for the integrity of a PDS, and should be applied by the designer to evaluate its quality.

OBJECTIVES AND CONSTRAINTS

A PDS is a formal listing of the objectives and constraints that apply to the attributes of the product being designed. These objectives and constraints might have been established with the help of requirement trees or any other appropriate method. At this stage, before we take a look at an example of a PDS, it is appropriate to give some thought to the different implications of objectives and constraints. Chapter 5 identified a constraint as being a quantified objective, and gave an example in Figure 5.1 of some objectives and constraints that might be applied to the design of a new domestic food-mixer.

Looking at these requirements, an important difference between objectives and constraints can readily be seen. This difference is not in the nature of the requirements themselves, but in the way that a designer is able to utilise them during the design process. In the case of constraints, it is relatively easy to assess whether a design proposal satisfactorily meets their requirement. This attribute of constraints is particularly valuable because it means that everyone involved in the design process (engineers, marketing staff, customer etc.) can readily agree on how successful the proposal is. On the other hand, the extent to which a proposal meets an objective will always be open to personal opinion and different interpretation. It is precisely for this reason that Chapter 5 encourages the conversion of objectives into constraints whenever possible. In some cases, this conversion is achieved by considering the **consequences** of meeting the objective rather than by using the objective itself. In the case of the food-mixer, it may initially seem impossible to convert requirement 1 (that it should be 'aesthetically pleasing') into a constraint. However, the purpose of this requirement is to ensure that the potential purchasers of the product will find it aesthetically pleasing, not in some absolute sense, but in comparison with other similar products in the market. It is this comparative nature of some objectives that holds the key to quantification. In this case we might turn the objective into a constraint by saying that the aesthetics of the new mixer must be preferred in comparison to named competitor products by over 50% of a representative sample of potential purchasers. If the constraint also ties down the definition of 'representative sample', it is approaching the point where ambiguity would be avoided in the evaluation of design proposals.

Here is a case study which illustrates some of the issues that have been introduced. To reflect what may happen during the process of product design, the case study starts off with an outline brief of the type that a customer might be expected to present. This is developed into a requirements tree, and finally a PDS is produced. This study is based upon a design project involving surgical equipment manufacturers, medical staff, and staff from Loughborough University's Engineering Design Institute. The product in question is an instrument used by surgeons during certain operating procedures. It may be best to wait until after your meal before reading further.

CASE STUDY 6.1

There are a number of medical conditions where it is necessary for a surgeon to remove a length of the intestine, and then join the remaining ends together. This technique is called 're-sectioning'. Several alternative procedures are available to the surgeon for fastening the ends together, but there are advantages in using stainless steel or titanium staples for this purpose.

There was a need for surgeons to have a device that could staple intestine using keyhole surgery techniques, and for this a radical redesign of existing instruments was necessary. The surgeon's design brief, requirements, and PDS are the subject of this case study. All of the details presented here are taken directly from the project records, although some data has been omitted to keep the case study within reasonable space limits.

The following product brief was presented to design staff by surgeons.

INTESTINE STAPLER FOR KEY-HOLE SURGERY. FIRST BRIEF

The stapler must:
 Be operable through a key-hole port in the abdomen
 Be steerable within the abdomen
 Provide a leak-proof joint where the intestine is stapled
 Not exert excessive stapling force on the tissue
 Be easy to use under theatre conditions
 Provide repeatable results
 Meet sterility conditions

This first brief is typical of a product requirement definition initially received from a customer. Although all of the requirements are reasonable, none of them are quantified in a form that is directly useful to the engineer.

Frequently, the problem with customer briefs is that they omit important detail. This is not because the customer wishes to mislead, but because familiarity with the problem leads to the belief that certain aspects of the requirements are 'common knowledge'. Such assumptions on the part of the customer, and unquestioning acceptance of the brief by the designer, can lead to horrendous mistakes in the contents of the PDS. To minimise these risks, the design team held a series of meetings with surgeons and representatives of surgical instrument manufacturing companies. The principal aim of these meetings was to develop and understand fully all of the objectives for the project, and to gain agreement on these with the interested parties.

The construction of requirement trees played an important role in the development of the brief. The way in which these were used followed the description given in Chapter 5. Figure 6.1 shows part of the requirement tree that was developed out of the meetings. There are three second level requirements which reflect the basic attributes that will be needed in the product. The 'provide commercial edge' requirement was used to develop needs relating to cost effectiveness, mainly in comparison with products that could be identified as 'competitive'. The 'accept existing staple heads' requirement reflected an initial perception that one or two large manufacturers who manufactured staple cartridges were effectively controlling the market. The large quantities of staple cartridges made each year by these companies meant that their unit costs were very low, and that there were clear economic advantages in designing the new product to use these cartridges. As the project progressed, it became obvious that this objective was too restrictive, and it was finally abandoned.

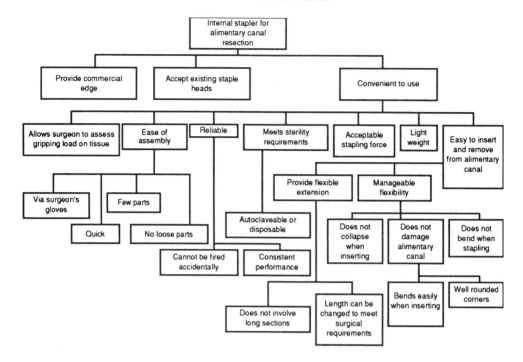

Figure 6.1   A requirements tree for the stapler problem

For the sake of brevity, Figure 6.1 does not show the development of sub-requirements from the two second level objectives that have so far been discussed. However, it does show the development of the 'convenient to use' requirement.

Discussions about the 'convenient to use' branch of the tree revealed a number of key requirements. One problem with existing devices was that they gave inadequate feedback to the surgeon about the forces that were being applied to the tissues. Improvement in this respect was felt to be an important requirement for the new product. Unfortunately, there were no research findings which provided quantifiable data on the range of force that was acceptable. Two requirements were concerned with the ergonomic performance of the instrument. To minimise the time taken for stapling, it was important that the preparation of the instrument was made as simple as possible. Because it is desirable to quote a specific maximum time for assembly rather than a vague statement, it was decided to record the time taken by surgeons to assemble the existing device and use this figure as a maximum for the new instrument. The second ergonomics related objective was low weight. Again, it was decided to turn this objective into a maximum constraint by using the weight of current devices.

One of the most important requirements in terms of its influence on the need for innovative thinking was related to the convenience of use under normal conditions. Because the most demanding of these conditions was associated with the constraints of keyhole surgery, many of the sub-requirements under this 'convenient to use' heading were targeted at the need to manoeuvre the stapling actuator into the correct position. Because some promising exploratory work had been undertaken by medical technicians, an early decision was taken to develop a design where a staple carrying cartridge and actuator were mounted on the end of a flexible and steerable extension shaft. The controls by which the surgeon was to operate the actuator were to be mounted at the other end of the shaft to the actuator, and would remain outside the body cavity. This decision had a marked influence on certain aspects of the 'easy to insert and remove' sub-requirements.

Because of the early decisions that were made about the form of the design, it is clear that the engineers involved with this project were not entirely free to propose other radical concepts for the solution of the problem. In other words, the PDS that would stem from the requirements would be at the 'type' rather than 'alternative' level. However, nothing in life is that simple. Although certain aspects of the design were agreed at the setting requirements stage, there were many design problems that were left wide open to creative thinking. For example, the means of providing the force to drive the staples through the tissue was not defined, and this aspect alone had many alternative solutions. For these reasons, the resulting PDS lies somewhere between the 'alternative' and 'type' levels.

When reading through the PDS, remember that it was completed at a very early stage of the design process, shortly after the completion of the first requirement tree. Some of the individual items within the PDS are difficult to evaluate without a detailed knowledge of the environment in which the product is to be used. Nevertheless, you have been given enough background information to evaluate the PDS critically. In particular, you might try listing your responses to the following questions:

- Do you feel that any of the items could be deleted because they are unnecessarily restrictive?
- Can you think of anything that should be included that has been omitted?
- Could (or 'should') any of the objectives be converted into constraints?

Product Design Specification

An intestinal stapler for key-hole surgery

1. *Performance*
1.1 To provide a stapled joint between two cut intestinal ends
1.2 To allow easy reach up to 120 cm from point of entry
1.3 Friction forces to be minimised, thus avoiding excessive loads
1.4 Extension should not buckle during entry
1.5 Easily negotiate anatomical bends
1.6 Extension should not deviate from its path during use
1.7 All staples must be fully formed
1.8 All closed staples should disengage from the device after closure
1.9 Joint to be leak-proof

2. *Environment*
2.1 Pressure range 1 atmos to max body pressure, or pressure during packing or transport
2.2 pH range 1–9
2.3 To be sterile prior to and during packing

3. *Life in service*
3.1 Disposable after one surgical procedure (10 hours max)

4. *Quantity*
4.1 10,000 per annum (partial European market)

5. *Size*
5.1 Extension length: > 120 cm
5.2 Staple cartridge diameter range: 26, 27, 28, 29 mm
     Cartridge length: < 44 mm (ideal length 25 mm)
5.3 Standard staple dimensions:
     Wire: 28 mm
     Crown: 4 mm
     Leg: 4.8 mm
     Closed height: 1 mm

6. *Weight*
6.1 Extension and head: 0.7 kg (maximum)

7. *Ergonomics*
7.1 Guideable end section should permit steering of the extension
7.2 Provide feedback to surgeon regarding staple status
7.3 Assembly of staple cartridge to extension prior to commencing surgery to take
     a maximum of 1 minute
7.4 Assembly procedures after the commencement not to exceed 30 seconds
7.5 Safety mechanisms to be operable single handedly
7.6 Comfortable operating forces
7.7 Easy grip for 5th percentile man
7.8 All visual indicators to be visible in theatre light

8. *Safety*
8.1 Safety locks must prevent accidental operation
8.2 Incapable of misfiring
8.3 Present no danger of biochemical adversity
8.4 All excised tissue must be removed
8.5 Final staple form must ensure:
     excellent haemostasis
     no tissue necrosis
     no post-operative stricture
     no inter-staple tissue tension
     no tissue trauma
8.6 Acceptable tissue damage during entry and removal

9. *Cost*
9.1 Disposable staple cartridge £50 manufacturing cost
9.2 Re-usable extension £350 manufacturing cost

Some of the elements of this PDS tend to be present in many other PDSs. First, the PDS is broken down into individual items that are numbered 1.1, 1.2, etc. A numbering system like this is essential for cross referencing items from other documents within a company. By referencing item 8.3, materials engineers can relate the chemical properties of alternative material choices to the requirement of the PDS without the need to repeat the item in full each time it is referred to. Secondly, items are presented in groups. All of the items relating to size, ergonomics, and safety etc. are grouped together under appropriate headings. This makes the task of locating items much easier than would otherwise be the case.

Like most PDSs, this one is a mixture of objectives and constraints. It is normal for the first PDS that is produced for a particular project to have a preponderance of objectives. This PDS exhibits such a tendency because of the uncertainties that surrounded the project at the time that it was produced. Several items need further work to ensure that they present unambiguous requirements. In this category are: 1.3 (what does 'minimised' mean?), 1.5 (what bend radii are applicable?), and 7.2 (exactly what sort of feedback is required?); no doubt you can identify others.

Regardless of the above comments and reservations, the PDS is now something that the engineer can work with in the early conceptualisation phases of the design process. The document will provide a good basis for evaluation of ideas and communication between the people who are involved.

REASONS WHY A PDS IS A DYNAMIC DOCUMENT

One reason why specifications develop is that an early PDS may be too demanding. For example, the PDS for the surgical stapler sets some challenging constraints on weight, assembly time, and cost. What happens if the designers cannot find a solution that meets the PDS? Well, they **could** give in and go for a few beers, but it is more likely that a new PDS would be negotiated. For example, the required weight might not be achievable because the cost constraint prevents the use of a suitable but expensive material. By relaxing the cost constraint we might be able to meet the weight requirement. Alternatively, we could investigate the possibility of meeting the cost constraint by relaxing the maximum weight limit. The final decisions about this resetting of constraints will be made by discussions with the customer or marketing department. However, it will be the designer who recognises and acts upon the need for accommodation of requirements. By the time that the designer recognises the need for this, it is likely that there will be a growing understanding of what the final solution will look like.

Even if the constraints in the early PDS do **not** need changing, a developing understanding of possible solutions will certainly require the addition of additional objectives and constraints. The process of PDS modification and addition is always a feature of design work, but is more obvious with complex products and systems. A product with 'n' sub-systems will usually have a PDS for each sub-system. The overall product PDS, and each sub-system PDS, may each go through a series of versions as the design develops.

The section of a PDS shown in Figure 6.2 is a small part of the specification for a Rolls Royce aeroengine fan blade. The detail contained in the PDS illustrates that it has been

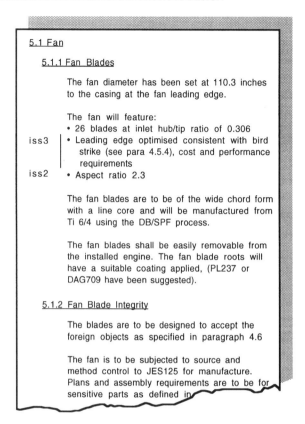

Figure 6.2 A PDS developed during the later stages of the design process

produced at an advanced phase of the design process. The PDS exhibits the attributes of item numbering and grouping that were discussed earlier, but there are some noticeable differences.

First, entries to the left of some items show that they have been changed several times as the project has proceeded. Secondly, some items are so closely defined that they determine a solution rather than an objective or open constraint. The PDS states that there **will** be 26 blades with an inlet hub/tip ratio of 0.306, and the aspect ratio **will** be 2.3. These requirements leave no room for manoeuvre on the part of the designer at this stage of the process.

We have seen how the market provides information for the first PDS or brief, and how the designer develops the details of the specification as understanding grows. However, there is another source of information that may strongly influence the process of PDS development, and this is basic research. The PDS for the turbine blade is a good example of this type of influence.

Frequently, a company will instigate a research programme to give it market advantage. In the case of aeroengine fan blades, a company like Rolls Royce will spend large amounts of money on the development of new materials and manufacturing processes. As benefits accrue from this basic research, the information will be passed to design engineers in the form of guidelines. In turn, these guidelines will be 'written-in' to a PDS to ensure that the latest technology is utilised.

DEMANDS AND WISHES

One approach to PDS writing that is occasionally used, is to express the requirements in terms of 'demands' or 'wishes'. Each item in the PDS is allocated to one of these two states by entering a letter D or W in a vertical column running alongside the items. The implication of assigning a letter is to indicate whether a particular item **must** be met if a concept is to be a contender for adoption, or whether it is only **preferable** that the item is complied with. Figure 6.3 shows part of an early PDS for a printer paper-feeder that incorporates the approach.

Great care needs to be taken when using the demand/wish approach. In accordance with our definitions of objective and constraint, a wish will be an objective and a demand will always be a constraint! To state a demand as an unquantifiable objective is nonsense because nobody can decide for certain if the demand has been met. Similarly, to call a constraint a wish merely shows that it is not really a constraint at all. Regardless of this, the uncertainty about technical feasibility and the trade-offs that are sometimes necessary between one part of the PDS and another frequently present problems for the PDS writer. The use of demands and wishes can sometimes be a way of coping with these uncertainties. For example, the specification of the target weight of the feeder might have been defined as 500 g with the following additions:

ITEM	SPECIFICATION	Demand or Wish
1	**Environment**	
1.1	Temp. range: 10 to 35 °C	D
1.2	Humidity: 20% to 70% non condensing	D
1.3	Resistance to household cleaning chemicals	W
.		
.		
2	**Aesthetics**	
2.1	Aesthetics must be sympathetic to printer	D
.		
.		
3	**Performance**	
3.1	The performance of the feeder must match that of the printer which operates at 10 sheets per minute at A4 and 6 sheets per minute A3.	D
.		

Figure 6.3 Demands and wishes may be assigned to draw attention to the relative importance of items

500 g (max)–400 g (max)   which is just another way of saying that 500 g (max) will do, but 400 g would be better; i.e. 500 g is the demand but 400 g is the wish

or 500 g$_{(1)}$–400 g$_{(3)}$ which says that achieving a 400 g mass is three times as desirable as a 500 g mass.

Of course, there is no point in assigning 'weightings' to objectives or constraints unless they provide a useful basis against which you can evaluate and choose alternative design concepts. We will deal with evaluation in Chapter 8. All we need to remember for the time being is that some objectives and constraints can be more important than others.

COMMUNICATION AND DOCUMENTATION

Product design specifications give a formal statement of product requirements in a manner that provides a useful definition for engineers to work to. It also provides the standard against which ideas may be assessed both absolutely and comparatively. The process of preparing the PDS is a vital activity which makes those involved think carefully about the objectives and constraints that are to be applied to the project. When complete, a PDS is a key document in the control of the attributes of the final product. Modification of the PDS as the project develops is inevitable, but the effective management of these change procedures is essential if product Quality is to be maintained. Figure 6.4 shows the PDS preparation activity, with the principal benefits of the transformation and the major inputs and outputs.

In most Quality systems, the PDS is an important document because of its central role in defining what the project objectives are. Either the PDS itself, or more probably supporting documentation, will make clear the reason for including each of the items that

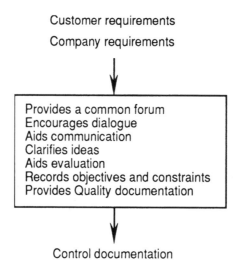

Figure 6.4   Inputs, outputs, and benefits of the PDS method

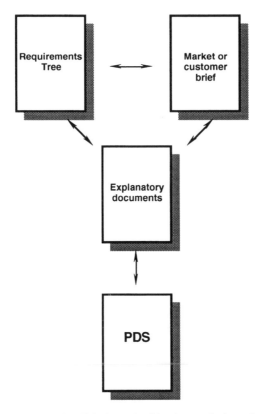

Figure 6.5 Documentation is required to link the PDS with other methods, and to record reasons for PDS revision

it contains. Similarly, the reason for modifications to the PDS must be made clear in documents that can be cross referenced from the PDS itself, see Figure 6.5. The original and subsequent revisions of the PDS must be agreed by relevant managers and be signed-off before issue. This is essential to ensure traceability, and assign responsibility for the decisions made.

The need to provide adequate documentation procedures, and documentation to control and record PDS development is particularly acute in the case of complex products. A product that is as complicated as a motor car will have many linked PDS documents. At any time, there will be PDSs referring to the overall requirements for the vehicle, the engine, the gearbox, the suspension, the body shell, etc. All of these will need to have been developed in parallel so that (for example) the suspension can be fitted within the body shell envelope, and the gearbox and engine can be assembled and provide the performance demanded by the overall vehicle specification. All of these interrelationships need to be considered when any one of the PDSs are modified. Will a modification to the engine PDS require changes to the gearbox or body shell PDS?

To minimise problems, it is necessary to provide cross reference information on a PDS to draw attention to items that interact with items on other associated PDSs. The identification of potential conflicts can then be negotiated to prevent downstream problems and expense.

RECAP

A Product Design Specification is a document that provides a formal definition of the objectives and constraints for a design project. It sets the rules for the innovative design process, and provides the basis by which concepts can be evaluated and chosen.

The process of PDS preparation can be summarised as follows:

1. Group the objectives and constraints under appropriate sub-headings.
2. List objectives and constraints as items under the sub-headings, and provide each with a unique identifying number.
3. In the case of associated PDSs, identify items that are linked and make a note of the nature of the link on all the relevant PDSs.

ASSIGNMENT

Assignment 6.1

In chapter 5 you did an assignment which entailed the construction of a requirement tree for a hairdryer. Use this requirement tree to produce a PDS. If you wish, you can use the sample tree in appendix 2, but it would be better if you developed your own. Remember to quantify as many items as possible and, in the case of those that you cannot quantify, think of ways that you might be able to resolve differences of opinion when assessing potential design solutions.

CREATIVITY METHODS

OVERVIEW

This chapter introduces methods that can aid the creative activities that form a part of the PDP. These methods can be applied by the individual designer, but are much more effective when working in a group. Their benefits arise from their effect upon people's willingness to volunteer ideas, and to associate the problems to be solved with their previous experiences. Above all, they encourage members of the design team to contribute ideas to a 'common pool', and to build upon ideas put forward by others. All designers, whether from an engineering or industrial design background can benefit from a working knowledge of the methods introduced in this chapter. The methods are also useful in encouraging team members from different backgrounds to work together.

OBJECTIVES

After completing this chapter you will be able to:

- understand some of the factors predisposing to creative effort;
- apply the following creativity methods;
    - —brainstorming
    - —gallery technique
    - —problem decomposition
    - —morphology.

FACTORS PREDISPOSING TO CREATIVITY

Throughout the PDP the designer is faced with a wide variety of tasks. Some of these tasks demand imagination and ingenuity, whilst others seem to be mechanistic and relatively mundane. If creativity means being inventive or imaginative then there seems little creativity in tasks like calculating the stresses in a component, assigning tolerances to dimensions, and specifying the material for a component. And yet much of what the designer does is seldom removed from the need to propose solutions to problems and evaluate their suitability. Establishing the characteristics of a product or sub-system by mathematical modelling is carried out for the purpose of assessment or development. Tolerance selection may involve choosing the balance between the conflicting attributes of cost and precision; and material selection may involve difficult decisions relating to the consequences for manufacturing process, cost, and strength. None of these tasks are mechanistic and, unless the designer has previously solved an identical problem, creative thought will be required to envisage what the solution may be.

definition

create, *v.t.* to bring into being by force of imagination. . . .

It is simply not the case that creativity is only, or even predominantly, called for during the initial concept generation stage of the PDP. The design process model proposed by Acar (1996) that was represented in Figure 1.10, showed that there is a continuing need to propose new ideas throughout the PDP. In the design of some products, the most difficult conceptual problems are associated with the layout or detail stages, and a great deal of imagination and ingenuity are required. It was this ongoing demand for creative effort that gave rise to our present day word 'engineer' which is derived from the French '*ingénieur*' which has the same root as '*ingénieux*' meaning 'ingenious' or 'clever'.

The ability to be creative is an essential attribute for a good designer. Paradoxically, many engineers feel that their strengths lie in analysis rather than problem synthesis. To a certain extent, this perception develops from the educational process that all professional engineers follow, which concentrates on the vital analytical foundation in subjects like dynamics, stress and strain, and thermodynamics. There are also widely accepted theories that propose that a person is born with tendencies towards creative or analytical thought, and that we tend to gravitate toward careers that make the most of our inherent tendencies. Of course, even if we accept the hypotheses of conditioned and inherited behaviour, everyone exhibits analytical **and** creative talent to some extent, and our aim should be to adopt techniques to improve our overall performance.

Regardless of the nature of the problem, there are several factors that are generally agreed to improve the effectiveness of the creative effort. These are:

- team working;
- broad knowledge of the problem;
- a conducive environment.

Team Working

Chapter 3 described the use of teams in a matrix organisation. In such a company structure, the teams provide a mechanism by which information can be communicated across functional boundaries. Another very important benefit of team work is their synergistic effect brought about by the sharing of ideas. The output from the team does not merely represent a compilation of the previously held views and ideas of its members. Instead, it is a compilation of some of those ideas together with others generated because of the stimulation of individual team members through listening to and conversing with others. It is important to remember that creative ideas are proposed by individuals within the team, but that the activities within the team can contribute to the thought processes that give rise to the ideas.

Broad Knowledge of the Problem

An individual's previous experience provides a strong influence on behaviour when a similar experience occurs some time later. If a method of approach has led to failure to achieve a task, it is likely that the same approach would not be adopted for a similar task in the future. Conversely, an approach leading to success would probably be tried again if circumstances allowed it. There are many reasons for this type of human behaviour, but perhaps the most basic is that we prefer success to failure, and tend to adopt approaches that our experience shows is conducive to achieving this. This tendency to play safe is rooted deeply in the survival instinct, and plays a very important positive role in all aspects of our lives, including product design. Knowledge of a product, the problems associated with its development, and the successful and unsuccessful design solutions proposed can be a powerful aid to proposing derivatives without the need to revisit failures.

The downside of product knowledge is that familiarity breeds complacency, and a feeling that what we already have **must** form the basis of future developments or, even worse, that what we have cannot be improved. Whilst designers should be wary of change for change's sake, competitor companies may not be so blinkered by convention and might be able to introduce superior products based on completely new principles.

The best way to attack design problems is by mixing experience and freshness together, thereby contributing the best of both approaches. Although some individuals demonstrate open-minded creativity in areas where they have extensive experience, it is frequently helpful to provide the two elements by bringing appropriate people together; and that brings us back to teamwork.

The use of properly structured teams can provide a combination of the various elements of knowledge to facilitate effective creative effort. Such a team is usually constituted from a broad range of personnel bringing experience to all aspects of the problem. The team also demonstrates a spread of experience and background to prevent 'tramline' thinking.

A Conducive Environment

The working environment plays a powerful role in determining the effectiveness of creative thinking of individuals and teams. A noisy environment, lack of focus, and fear of criticism all have negative effects, whilst time pressure can be either negative or positive depending upon the individual and the situation.

In general, environments that provide the opportunity for teams to work on clearly formulated problems with a minimum of disruption for a pre-defined period of time are advantageous for creative thought processes. Clearly, a conducive environment is advantageous for making decisions about the every day problems that we are continually faced with in life. Having to rush, feeling under pressure, or having to put up with noise and distraction all increase the probability of making a wrong decision. If anything, this situation is exacerbated in team work because of the disruption that such circumstances can cause to inter-personnel communications.

BRAINSTORMING

Over the years, the term **brainstorming** has become synonymous with team methods that attempt to improve the environment for creative problem solving. There is no formal definition of brainstorming other that the dictionary definition, and this is not particularly helpful in defining a procedure for the technique.

definition

brainstorm, sudden disturbance of the mind; sudden inspiration. . . .

Any occurrence where a group of people are brought together to ponder a problem can be called brainstorming, although many of the potential benefits may be lost by such a casual approach. For the purpose of this section, brainstorming involves a conscious effort to provide a conducive environment for creative thought. Even with this as the stated objective, there are many views on alternative brainstorming techniques and their respective advantages and disadvantages. To illustrate the point, we will examine two different brainstorming techniques and try to identify what each has to offer. The first is the 'controlled input' method, the second the '6–3–5' method.

Both methods attempt to encourage creativity by introducing two important elements:

1. **Suspended judgement.** It was stated earlier that fear of criticism was a negative factor for creative thought. If an attempt to propose a new way of doing things is met with criticism from peers, there may be a reluctance to volunteer more ideas because of the possibility of exposure to further censure. This fear is even greater when there is fear of criticism from someone of superior rank like a manager. Individuals' thresholds to criticism vary, although none are completely immune to its effects. There is no evidence to show that the more introverted and reticent members of a team are they any less proficient at creative thinking than confident extroverts. Because of this, brainstorming attempts to remove the threat of criticism following the presentation of an idea. Conversely, it is imperative that imperfect ideas are taken on by other team members if they feel that they can improve it by modification.

2. **Multiple concept generation.** There is a saying which goes 'there is more than one way of skinning a cat'. As a cat lover, I feel uneasy about this advice, but the point made is that every problem can be solved in several ways. This applies strongly to the sort of problems that designers face, where there are many objectives, some of which will be in conflict with others, and constraints arising from the market, technology, and commercial issues. Eventually, it will be the designer's task to select the best of these ideas for development, but the first stage is to ensure that the concepts provided for evaluation contain ideas of appropriate merit. One way of working towards this is to generate as many ideas as possible in the hope that the 'best' is not missed. This can be a problem when the team is heavily populated by members who are steeped in a conservative approach brought about by their previous experiences with a similar product. Brainstorming attempts to minimise this effect by encouraging the generation of many ideas.

The Controlled Input Method

The **controlled input method** attempts to provide normal brainstorming advantages by suspending judgement and generating multiple concepts. The procedure to be adopted is as follows:

1. **Set up a diverse group of between 5 and 12 people.** Like most brainstorming techniques, this one requires all of the team members to contribute in sequence. Experience shows that members tend to loose concentration if they have to wait too long between contributions. An additional problem with very large groups is that so many ideas will be generated before an individual has the opportunity to contribute, that idea modification becomes almost impossible. However, the group needs to contain a sufficient number of people to represent all of the appropriate knowledge areas that the company has at its disposal. Choosing members to provide this diversity is important but depends upon the nature of the problem being considered. Typically, a group considering product concepts might have representatives from marketing, customer support, design, manufacturing, and commercial functions. A group faced with the task of solving a broad based engineering problem might contain electronic, mechanical, and manufacturing engineers.

2. **Ensure a non-hierarchical structure.** A brainstorming group with a strong hierarchical structure faces two problems. Firstly, there may be an increased fear of criticism from superiors, and secondly it may be assumed that the superiors are responsible for the generation of ideas. Both problems, real or perceived, can reduce the effectiveness of the group. In general, it is a good idea to make the hierarchical structure of a brainstorming group as flat as possible and, if this is impossible, then it is not advisable to select someone of a superior rank to act as group co-ordinator.

3. **Select a group co-ordinator.** Although a strong hierarchical structure is not advisable, the group will need guidance if it is to remain focused on its task. The co-ordinator needs to be familiar with the problem, its various facets, and the context in which it is set. It is important that the co-ordinator is not seen as the group manager or leader because this would introduce the undesirable hierarchical effect.

    It may be necessary for someone at the meeting to keep records of the ideas that are generated, although an audio or video tape of the proceedings may delay the need for this to be prepared. If note taking is deemed desirable, this could be a second function for the co-ordinator even though this may reduce their capability to contribute to the interactions that take place. If this is a problem, note taking can be delegated to secretarial support.

4. **Provide a suitable working environment.** Although a suitable environment includes the provision of a previously defined time slot, a quiet location, an absence of possible irritations (like telephones, particularly mobiles), and the provision of creative necessities like tea and coffee, this is not sufficient. In this sense, 'environment' also includes the establishment of a suitable attitude by group members as they enter the meeting. Members should have been informed previously about the need for the meeting, what the problem is, and what the desired results will be in terms of the effect of an ideal outcome. Members should also be informed that they are expected to have thought

about the problem **before** entering the meeting. A room containing a flip chart, white board and/or overhead projector can be beneficial to the working of the group.

5. **Introduce the problem to the group.** Even though the group will have been primed about the objectives of the session, it is good policy to introduce the problem formally and invite discussion. This makes sure that everyone is working towards the same objective, and helps to achieve group focus. The co-ordinator should also reiterate the rules that are to be applied during the session, and the follow-up procedures that will be used. Finally, the co-ordinator identifies the person who will start the session by making the first proposal for a solution to the problem.

6. **Propose solutions.** The first proposer suggests a solution to the problem being discussed. The maximum time allowed for this proposal is defined in the rules for the session, but should be no longer than 3 minutes. During this time, no comments are permitted from other team members. The proposer may use sketches to support the idea, and these sketches may be drawn at the session or have been produced before it commenced. At the end of the presentation, a five minute period is allowed during which team members may ask and receive clarification about the proposal. No criticism, implicit or explicit is permitted at this point, and it is the job of the co-ordinator to ensure that this rule is adhered to.

    Various methods can be used for the proposal of solutions within the rules of interaction. Sketches of ideas can be made on sheets of paper provided for that purpose, or on wall mounted white boards. White boards have the advantage that team members can arrange themselves so that they can see all of the sketches easily. The disadvantage is that the ideas need to be copied with risk of inaccuracies for subsequent circulation. Electronic white boards provide a way round this problem in that paper copies can be taken as required.

7. **Consolidate ideas.** A period of three minutes is then allocated, during which time team members may make notes and think about the implications and possibilities that arise from the proposal.

8. **Make subsequent proposals.** Steps 6 and 7 are repeated for each team member around the table. Proposals may be related to developments of ideas previously presented to the group, or be completely new concepts unrelated to what has gone before. If a team member declares nothing to propose, the next person is invited to contribute until no more proposals are received or the allotted time has run out.

9. **Conclude the activity.** The controlled input method provides a highly formalised environment for the proposal and development of solutions to a stated problem. To achieve the advantages stated earlier, normal rules of interaction are suspended and, as a result, return to normality brings a desire for interrogative questioning of the type that would normally take place. Whilst the co-ordinator should continue to rule out criticism, it is often beneficial to allow a certain amount of free discussion during a closing period of 10 to 15 minutes.

10. **Follow-up.** It should be the task of the co-ordinator and/or secretarial support to provide minutes of the meeting. As soon as possible, members should be circulated with a list of the ideas generated and the comments that they attracted. It is important that the minutes are complete, factual, neutral, and not judgemental.

A follow-up meeting should be planned to take place within a short time of the provision of minutes, and it is the task of this meeting to evaluate the generated ideas and propose an appropriate course of action. Possible courses of action including holding further brainstorming sessions on sub-sets of the problem, or carrying out further evaluation of some of the proposals.

Because the controlled input method is very formal, some designers find that it inhibits creative thought. To a large extent, this drawback decreases as team members become more familiar and relaxed with the technique. All brainstorming methods impose some structure on verbal interaction to secure benefits, and the associated rules are usually seen as an intrusion. Making a decision to use brainstorming for the first time on an urgent and critical problem is almost certain to lead to failure and a decision never to use the technique again. The correct way is to practise applying the brainstorming rules on real, but non-critical problems. In this situation there will be much less pressure to succeed, and the team will be more prepared to accept the restrictions.

As team members grow accustomed to the method, they can agree to try modifications to the rules if they feel that this will lead to beneficial effects. The 'best' method is simply the one that works successfully for the group, and identifying this needs patience and effort. Maybe the team will find that they need to change the length of time allocated to the presentation and clarification aspects of steps 6 or 7. An experienced co-ordinator will tend to do this automatically throughout a brainstorming session in response to the changing requirements of the team.

An interesting variation on the method was used by a team of engineers at Lucas Engineering. Here, one team member was assigned the role of 'devil's advocate'. His only participation was to criticise each idea after it had been presented and clarified. At first sight, this may seem contrary to the main rules of brainstorming engagement, but because his role was to criticise **every** idea the theory was that no one could be personally offended. The technique also introduced a little humour into the proceedings.

If, after several practice sessions, the group still find the method unhelpful, the 6–3–5 method might be found to be more to their liking.

The 6–3–5 Method

A criticism of the controlled input method is that the normal rules of engagement for conversation between individuals are so deeply entrenched in our consciousness that imposing 'unnatural' constraints leads to discomfort. In the 6–3–5 method verbal communication plays no part, and some people find this easier to handle.

The method was proposed by the Bernd Rohrbach in the 1960s. The name given to the method was descriptive of the technique itself, in that a team of six people were required to generate three ideas in a succession of five minute periods. The procedure that was proposed is shown below:

1. **Prepare the group.** Essentially, this is the same as stage 1 of the controlled input method. All members of the team need to know about the problem in advance of the meeting, and the rules that will be adopted. Because the method forbids verbal communication, there is less of a perceived threat of criticism. Therefore, the provision of a non-hierarchical structure is not as important.

A co-ordinator is still required, but the role is less demanding than with controlled input. Here the involvement is limited to opening the meeting, calling time on the different stages, drawing the meeting to a close, summarising, and perhaps collating ideas for circulation.

2. **Generation of ideas.** Working in complete silence, each member of the team collects an 'idea sheet' from the table. This sheet, an example of which is shown in Figure 7.1, carries a matrix of boxes. The layout is three columns and six rows. Each person is allocated a number which defines the row into which their ideas will be entered on the sheets. The person assigned the number 2 will always enter their ideas in the boxes on the second row of the chart. Each person attempts to think of three solutions to the problem and enters these into their boxes. Ideas may be represented by words and/or diagrams. Five minutes is allowed for this task. At the end of the five minutes, each person passes the form to the person on their right. Another five minute period is allocated to the generation of a further three ideas which are entered into the appropriate row. This process is repeated until each form has been worked on by all team members.

   As the form circulates, participants see the contributions of other people as they receive another sheet. At each change over, the number of ideas displayed will grow, and these may stimulate additions or completely new ideas.

3. **Concluding the session.** By the time that the session is brought to a close, there will be a need for open discussion to evaluate what has been put forward and decide upon an appropriate course of action. This discussion can take place immediately following the formal session, or after the output has been collated and circulated.

	IDEA 1	IDEA 2	IDEA 3
Team member 1			
Team member 2			
Team member 3			
Team member 4			
Team member 5			
Team member 6			

Figure 7.1 A 6–3–5 idea sheet

You can vary the 6–3–5 method to fit the circumstances. There is no particular reason why you cannot have 15 people, each generating six ideas in ten minute periods, other than for the slight problem that the session would take two and a half hours to complete. At the other end of the scale, I have seen desperate students organise very successful 3–2–2 sessions in an attempt to overcome a troublesome problem in their group design project.

An experienced co-ordinator will keep a watchful eye on the progress being made and will allow more or less time for idea generation depending on group needs. This sort of flexible group management is good because it reduces the risk of frustration and boredom arising.

The 6–3–5 method is particularly adaptable to use on computer networks. Ideas can be entered into word processor versions of the 6–3–5 sheet, and be posted to colleagues using e-mail. The risk here is that the absence of a local co-ordinator sometimes means that people delay sending their mail until they have given their ideas more thought. The result is that recipients tend to drift off into doing other things and the spontaneity of the session is lost. It helps if members of the team use system clocks to give them a warning at (say) five minute intervals to ensure that things are kept on the move.

A variation of the 6–3–5 method is the brainwriting pool where, instead of passing the idea sheet to the adjacent person, it is placed back into the centre of the table for anyone to pick up and work on. Usually, although the brainwriting session will have an overall set time duration, no time limit is set during which an individual may work on a single sheet. The method works better if there are more sheets for circulation than there are people in the group, and it helps if the co-ordinator can provide several starter ideas to supplement those initially produced by the members. Brainwriting can also be achieved using e-mail. The difference is that whilst the 6–3–5 method calls for an ideas sheet to be sent to the same individual every time, a brainwriting sheet is e-mailed simultaneously to everyone taking part. If team members have access to World Wide Web pages, these provide a good alternative to interaction by e-mail.

Several computer based brainstorming programmes are now available as a result of growing research interest. Useful sources of information on these developments are provided in papers by Holt (1993 and 1995), Gallup (1991), Trost (1993), and Geschka, Kirchoff & Fluvius (1993).

MINDMAPPING

The term 'mindmapping' was coined by Tony Buzan in the 1970s, and is described in his book *Use Both Sides of Your Brain* published in 1983. The technique attempts to provide a means of rapidly externalising the ideas generated in the brain. Mindmaps are always produced freehand because rapid and uncritical recording is a necessity for effective progress. The resulting map can be 'tided-up' later. Mind maps can be produced by individuals or by groups, but in both cases speed is important. In the case of group work, it is possible for one person to take the role of 'scribe' although it is often better to let everyone have a pen so that they are able to get their own thoughts onto the diagram without having to wait and explain. Like many creativity techniques, mindmapping frequently works best when the team alternates between individual and group activity.

The stages of producing a mindmap are described below:

1. Take a large sheet of paper and write a brief description of the topic or problem to be addressed in the centre. As with all stages of producing the mindmap it is best if the description can be kept to a single word or at most a very brief statement. Draw a circle around the topic.

2. Write down around the topic the consequences, sub-problems, ideas, or sub-areas that are directly related to it and need investigation. Circle these and connect them to the central topic.

3. Taking each one of the sub-areas in turn, identify the issues that relate to it and represent them on the map by words, brief phrases, or pictographs. Frequently, you will have ideas that do not seem to stem directly from any of the sub-areas. In these cases either add a new sub-area or construct a small area of map unconnected to the main map. There will be plenty of time later to consider how your thoughts relate to the central topic. Spend 10 to 15 minutes doing this or until you start to find it difficult to make the map grow.

   If the map development is going well, you soon find that you are rapidly adding ideas in a seemingly *ad-hoc* manner to each of the sub-areas. This is good because it means that you have established good communication with your subconscious.

4. Organise the map by looking for connections between the various parts of it. If there are logical links between ideas or groups of ideas in different sub-areas, record these links by connecting them with lines. See whether you can introduce a more logical structure by adding or by combining some sub-areas. Redraw the map in a form which satisfies you and/or the team.

5. Conclude the activity by writing a report on the structure with sub-heading for each of the sub-areas. The map and report provide a valuable document on which to base future decisions.

Figure 7.2 shows a mindmap produced by Rolls Royce engineers when they were considering the design implications of redesigning the structures at the front end of the Trent 800 series engine. The result is a good example of how the technique should be used. The central 'topic' is expressed as a diagram that identifies those parts of the structure being considered. Although diagrams are not used elsewhere, ideas are expressed concisely. In addition to the central topic, sub-areas and their critical offshoots are circled to make them stand out. As well as identifying the issues to be dealt with, the map also records questions that the team needed to address before progress could be made. Of course, some of the issues recorded on the map are written in the shorthand of engineers who are familiar with engine design. This, providing that everyone involved understands, is as it should be because it enables the issues to be recorded quickly.

THE GALLERY METHOD

The gallery method can be considered as an idea in its own right or as an adjunct to various brainstorming techniques. The procedures adopted in the controlled input and 6–3–5 methods prevent participants from seeing all of the proposed ideas simultaneously. While this is acceptable in the context of these methods, it is sometimes advantageous to let a

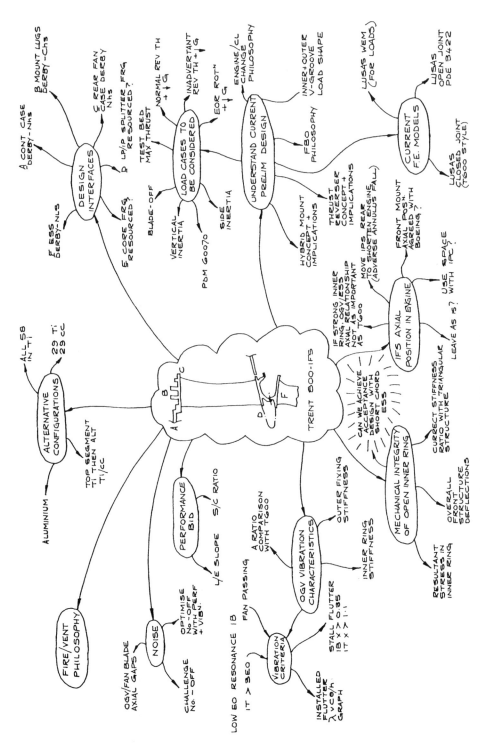

Figure 7.2 A mindmap produced by Rolls Royce engineers for the Trent 800 series engine

team of people have simultaneous access to all of the proposed ideas so that they can more easily make comparisons, produce hybrids, and occasionally generate mutant solutions. The gallery method involves providing all of the previously generated ideas in a format where they can be seen by everyone attending the session. The ideas in the form of diagrams or a mixture of diagrams and text can be photocopied onto A4 or A3 sheets with everyone being provided with a copy. Additional ideas that are generated at the meeting are best proposed in a larger format on a white board or wall mounted sheets of paper. However, it can help if even the original ideas are prepared in large format for wall mounting, so that participants can walk round the offerings and sketching modifications and completely new ideas as the meeting proceeds. The wall mounting of many ideas gives rise to the descriptive term 'gallery' method.

Frequently, the gallery method is run as a 'free format' meeting, with no rules of engagement and an understanding that everyone will contribute appropriately. A certain amount of formality can be introduced by electing a co-ordinator to ensure that everyone is given a reasonable opportunity to contribute and that all of the ideas are given some attention. Hellfritz (1978), who first defined the gallery method, proposed the following sequence of steps as a formal procedure:

1. **Problem introduction.** The co-ordinator introduces the problem to the design team. This can be done at the commencement of the meeting, but it is usually more effective to provide advanced notification so that any preparation or reading can be completed in advance.

2. **Idea generation stage 1.** Members of the team work on their own for 15 to 20 minutes to generate solutions to the set problem. During this stage, team members are largely unaware of what others are doing, and there is no opportunity for discussion or criticism. Ideas are externalised as text and/or diagrams on paper.

3. **Association of ideas stage.** All ideas from all of the team members are displayed. Ideas may be spread over a large table or preferably wall mounted for easy viewing. The team spends 15 to 20 minutes discussing the ideas, seeking promising combinations or alternatives. At the end of this stage, the decision might be that time must be spent on generating totally new concepts, or that the team will concentrate on developing one or several of the ideas already proposed.

4. **Idea generation stage 2.** Team members again work on their own to develop new or existing ideas stemming from the interactions of the association stage.

   Stages 3 and 4 can now be repeated if necessary until either the time allocated has run out or a successful conclusion has been reached.

5. **Idea selection.** Promising ideas are selected for further development. Chapter 8 will deal with some of the methods that may be used to do this.

If the team can allocate space, it sometimes helps if the ideas can remain wall mounted until after the concept development stage has been concluded. This enables sub-groups that are working on particular aspects of the problem to call impromptu meetings in the place where the concept material is already on display. Groups working on separate but interacting aspects of the same problem can readily call joint meetings to discuss interface problems with opportunities to review current thinking and propose new approaches.

It is interesting to note that police incident teams usually use a type of gallery method to display information about a crime and suspects. Photographs of the crime scene, statements from witnesses, transcripts of interviews etc., are displayed on a wall. This makes it easier for officers to establish logical links between items of evidence and to propose appropriate investigative measures.

PROBLEM DECOMPOSITION

Problem decomposition is a fundamental method by which humans develop solutions to problems. If you decide to go on a climbing holiday, one of the first problems that you have is how to get there. In reality, this single problem consists of several sub-problems all of which need solving in a way that makes them fit together. Some of the sub-problems are likely to be: (1) where to go, (2) how to raise the money, (3) how to travel, (4) how much to take in terms of equipment and provisions, (5) how to carry the equipment and provisions, and (6) how long to stay. If an answer cannot be found to any one of these problems, the project will probably be doomed to failure. At the same time, the decisions made in regard to any individual problem affect the answers to at least one of the other problems. Deciding where to go and how long to stay influences how much money needs to be raised. The amount of equipment and provisions affects the means by which it must be carried or transported.

Recognising that an overall problem or task is made up of a number of sub-problems is commonplace, and something that we generally deal with very effectively. The method is also used when solving design problems as is indicated in the VDI model of the design process shown in Figure 1.7. The main difference between many design problems and every day problems is one of complexity brought about by the need to combine numerous sub-systems into a coherent product. The overall functionality of products like automobiles and aircraft can be expressed quite simply in terms of the attributes that they offer to customers and users, like high speed transportation, comfort, and economy. However, the problem of providing these attributes can only be overcome when designers can solve the multitude of sub-problems that stand between the need and the solution. Complex problems sometimes require the use of formal decomposition procedures. These procedures are particularly valuable when there is a need to involve staff with specialist skills for the solution of different sub-problems, or where the overall problem is so extensive that it becomes easy to lose track of what the requirements are. Used at the concept generation stage, problem decomposition provides a means of encouraging creative thinking about possible solutions.

Problem Diagrams as an Aid to Decomposition

Problem diagrams are a well established method for depicting sub-problems and sub-systems within a design. The method uses a combination of graphical and text based description in a diagrammatic framework. The method may be used as an adjunct to brainstorming, and the resulting diagrams can be used to communicate ideas to other people.

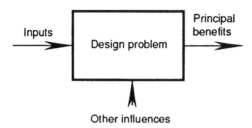

Figure 7.3 The design problem is represented as a black box with inputs and outputs, and a recognition that the eventual solution must provide functions to link the two

The method starts by representing the overall design problem in 'black box' style as illustrated in Figure 7.3 with inputs and desired outputs. This leads to the development of expanded diagrams showing the required functions, their connections, the need for information flow, and material supply and disposal. The following case study illustrates the way that the method can be applied.

CASE STUDY 7.1

Figure 7.4 shows an overall problem diagram for a device to lower gas cylinders into the cellars of public houses. Over 65% of public houses in the United Kingdom keep their beer and ancillary supplies in cellars below ground level. The ancillary supplies include cylinders of compressed carbon dioxide and nitrogen that are used to pressurise the beer in metal containers. Several years ago, the beer and the gas cylinders were delivered by the brewers in lorries that had a two-man crew. Beer containers were, and still are, rolled into the cellar down ramps which are accessed by opening doors in the floor outside the public house. Most gas cylinders were passed by hand from the first crewman stood at ground floor level, to a second crewman stood in the cellar. Over recent years, the delivery of many gas cylinders have been taken over by the gas producers who operate lorries with a one-man crew. Gas cylinders can weigh up to 43 kg, and this has given rise to handling problems for the delivery staff. Transporting the cylinders down internal stairs is difficult even when they are wide enough to take a trolley, and attempting to roll cylinders down the beer ramps is not feasible because of the danger of damaging the valve and releasing large amounts of gas. The only other alternative is to request the assistance of staff from the public house, and this is considered unacceptable because of the implications of legal redress if an injury occurs.

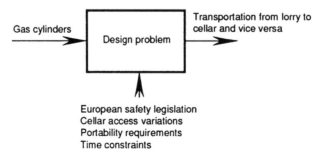

Figure 7.4 The beer gas transportation problem

The product design specification for this problem might be set at either the alternative or type level as described in Chapter 6. If the decision is made to retain the lorry delivery system and cylinders in essentially the same form as at present, the problem and its possible solutions are restricted to the 'type' level. An important task for the design team is to break down the overall problem into sub-problems. Care needs to be taken when doing this because the result will almost certainly be influenced by perceptions of what the solution might be. This is acceptable provided that the risk is recognised, an effort made to identify these perceptions, and alternative ways of problem decomposition sought. By a combination of thinking about the overall problem and, in this case by watching the delivery staff at work, the following sub-problems can be identified:

- Moving the full cylinder from the lorry to ground level.
- Transporting the full cylinder to the cellar opening – this can be a distance of 20 m or 30 m if the lorry cannot park near the public house.
- Lowering the full cylinder into the cellar.
- Moving the full cylinder to the correct location in the cellar.

Delivery staff also need to retrieve empty cylinders so that they can be recharged. This task is effectively the reverse of that required for the full cylinders.

- Moving the empty cylinder to a position under the cellar door opening.
- Raising the empty cylinder to ground level.
- Transporting the cylinder to the lorry.
- Placing the cylinder on the lorry.

The expanded problem diagrams shown in Figure 7.5 show how the overall problem can now be represented.

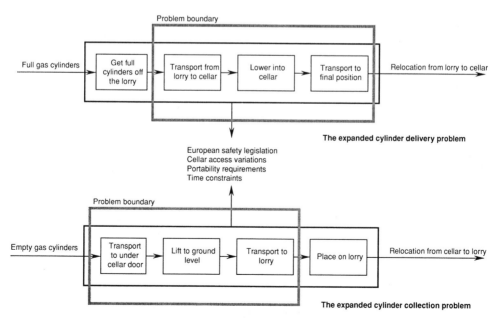

Figure 7.5 Expanded problem diagrams for the cylinder handling problem

This first attempt at expanding the problem shows several features of the method. The boxes contain all aspects of the operation that have been described. However, getting full cylinders off the lorry and placing empty cylinders on the lorry are not seen as major problems. This is because lorries are fitted with an electric lifting platform at the rear onto which cylinders can be rolled. The central problems are associated with transfer to and from the lorry and the cellar door, and lowering and raising the cylinders. These are the problems that need to be addressed, and the diagrams identify this by placing them within a 'problem boundary' box. Both the delivery and collection problems are influenced by legislation, access constraints, portability requirements and the time constraints under which the operators are working. These influences are recorded on the diagram.

As soon as ideas are put forward for the solution of one or more of the problems, the diagrams will change to reflect the new sub-problems that will inevitably arise. One solution that was proposed was a multi-function sack-trolley that the operator could use to transport up to three cylinders to and from the lorry and cellar opening. Although a simple sack-trolley was adequate for transportation over ground, it did nothing to alleviate the problems associated with lifting and lowering the cylinders from and into the cellar. Therefore, the proposal was to incorporate a lifting device into the trolley as well as a means by which it could be securely fixed at the cellar opening.

Whilst this proposal presented several interesting possibilities, it also generated additional problems that needed consideration. In addition to the need to investigate means of securing the trolley securely above the cellar opening, the proposal gave rise to important safety considerations. If the trolley was being used to lift empty cylinders out of the cellar, would there be a danger of members of the public falling down the cellar opening whilst the operator was working below? Figure 7.6 shows how the problem diagram was expanded to break down the problem areas for the idea. The diagram also shows how logical links between problem areas can be identified. In this case, a link represented by a broken line is shown between the 'weigh cylinders' and 'activate lifting

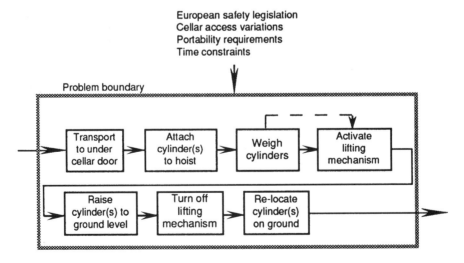

Figure 7.6 The problem diagram for one particular conceptual approach

mechanism' problems. This is a recognition that there may be a need to ensure that the lifting device is not overloaded, and that excessive weight should prevent the lifting mechanism from functioning. Such logical links are often converted into the functionality of the product. In this case, a sensor might provide a control signal to either prevent the lifting mechanism from working and/or provide a warning for the operator.

CASE STUDY 7.2

The previous case study shows that problem diagrams, like requirement trees, can start off defining the problem, and end up illustrating solutions. When they are used to identify the various functions that need to be provided in a design solution, they are usually called 'function diagrams'.

Problem diagrams and function diagrams are particularly useful when illustrating the elements of a process design problem. Figure 7.7 illustrates the technique applied to the definition of a process line to prepare carrots for the supermarket.

Carrots destined for the shelves of high quality retailers are frequently inspected for quality and uniformity prior to being bagged in pre-weighed lots. Figure 7.7 shows the requirements for such a process plant represented in problem diagram form. In this case, the prime requirements are to wash, inspect, sort on the basis of quality and uniformity, divide into lots on the basis of weight, and bag. The diagram shows the feed forward and feedback signals that are required for the weighing and bagging part of the process. When the weighing device senses that sufficient carrots have reached the weigh station, a signal is fed forward for the lot to be taken onto to the bagging station. Similarly, when the lot has been deposited in the bag, a signal is passed back to the weigh station to admit more carrots for the formation of the next lot. The diagram shows how quantities passing the system boundary should be identified. Although it may not be the problem of the process

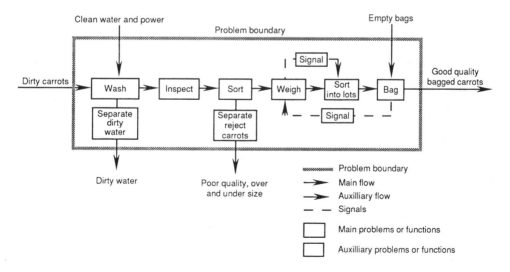

Figure 7.7 Problem diagram for a carrot processing plant

designers to deal with means of handling wash water and reject carrots, these elements exist and will certainly influence design decisions.

MORPHOLOGY

Morphology is concerned with the study of the structure or form of things.

> **definition**
>
> **morphology,** *n.*   (Biol.) study of the form of animals and plants; (philol.) study of the form of words.

Designers use a morphological approach when they consider all of the different ways that they can meet the various functional requirements of a design problem. The problem definition diagrams help the designer to identify these functional requirements, and creative methods like controlled input and the 6–3–5 method provide alternative ways of meeting the requirements. Some design problems have large numbers of functional requirements and, if each of these has a multitude of possible solutions, there can be problems in presenting these options so that further development can be made. This is where a morphological chart can be useful.

Figure 7.8 shows a morphological chart that was developed when considering alternative design solutions for a stretch-wrap palletizer. For transportation purposes goods are frequently loaded onto wooden pallets by fork-lift truck where they are wrapped in plastic film which is subsequently shrunk by the application of heat. The film provides structural integrity to the load, so that it can be transported without fear of slippage. A company that manufactures pallet handling equipment set about the design of a stretch-wrap palletizer to add to their range of equipment. First, they set out to determine the functions that the machine would have to provide. These functions were determined by analysing customer requirements and competitor machines, and representing the requirements in a product design specification. Because the machine had to provide an ordered sequence of operations with numerous safety mechanisms, the functions were represented in problem diagrams. Subsequently, because the machine had over 50 identifiable main and auxiliary functions, these were grouped into logical sets. These sets included drive systems, pallet clamping, film cutting, heating, and control systems.

In Figure 7.8, some of the functional requirements of the palletizer have been listed down the left hand side of the morphological chart. These functions are:

- the pallet support drive
- the pallet rotation drive
- pallet table support
- film clamp
- film gathering
- film cutting drive
- top clamping
- top clamp traversing

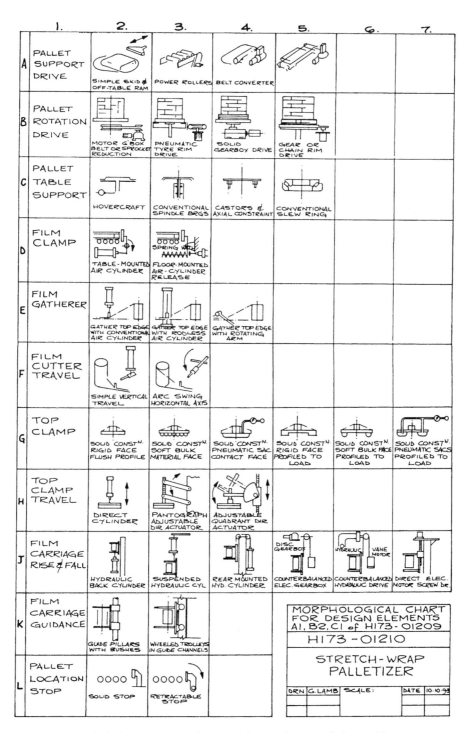

Figure 7.8 A morphological chart for some elements of the stretch-wrap palletizer problem

- film carrier traversing
- film carrier guidance
- pallet location

To the right of each function entered on the chart are possible means of providing solutions to the problem. Hence, the drive system used to rotate the pallet and its load on the machine might be provided by:

- a motor, gearbox and belt or chain drive to a central pulley or sprocket
- a motor and gearbox directly driving the table
- driving the rim of the table by friction
- driving the rim of the table via a gear or chain

At a glance, the morphological chart shows the functions that are being considered and the various means through which solutions may be provided. Figure 7.8 illustrates some of the alternatives considered for this machine, and you will probably be able to think of other solutions. In addition to being a good method to present and record options at various stages of the design process, the morphological chart can help the design team to progress their work. Frequently, presenting ideas in this way will lead to a recognition that there are shortcomings or that there are alternatives that have not so far been considered. Obviously, this can provide a spur to further creative thinking. An additional benefit of the morphological chart method is that it helps the design team to think about how the various ideas might fit together into a complete system. For example, a decision to use an air-cylinder for the film clamping problem would mean that the machine would have to be provided with a supply of compressed air. In this case it would be worth scanning the chart to see if other functions might use this facility instead of (say) a hydraulic power pack, thereby reducing the number of systems on the machine.

The representation of ideas on the morphological chart can be by means of drawings or pictographs, by a written description, or by a mixture of both. Figure 7.9 is a chart produced by a design team examining options for the segment M hairdryer introduced in Chapter 4. Like the chart for the palletizer problem, this was produced early in the design process whilst radical thinking about the problem was still possible. A mixture of pictographs and text have been used to describe the options being considered.

Morphological charts are a useful method of recording and presenting alternative solutions to the various functional requirements of a product. As such, they can be incorporated in reports and presentations where they provide a concise means of displaying the information. They also provide a forum for discussion when alternative combinations of solutions are being sought, or when the design team is trying to assess all of the marketing, technical, and commercial implications of the options. In all but the most simple product, the number of possible combinations of solutions is likely to be large, and the risk is that opportunities may be overlooked simply because they are not put before the design teams at the appropriate time. In the morphological chart shown in Figure 7.9, 11 functions have given rise to 38 possible solutions. Although these 11 functions represent only a part of those that the machine provides, the total number of possible combinations of ideas is 331,776. This is simply calculated by multiplying together the number of ideas in each row of the matrix.

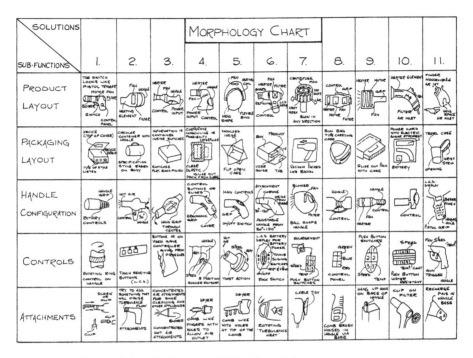

Figure 7.9   A morphological chart for the segment M hairdryer design

RECAP

Even though the creative abilities of people may differ, there is no doubt that the creative performance of individuals and groups can be improved substantially by the use of appropriate methods. These methods work in two ways. Firstly, they encourage inhibitions to be shelved by removing pressure on the individual, and providing environments where ideas may be generated and recorded quickly. Secondly, they provide a common forum for group work by exposing ideas to members of the team in a non-judgemental way.

Although creativity is a vital aspect of the PDP, it is one of the most difficult to manage and record. A secondary advantage of the methods is that they can provide means by which the workings of the creative phase of design can be recorded, thereby improving the traceability and accountability of design decisions at a later date.

ASSIGNMENTS

Because creativity methods are most effective when employed by groups, it is best if you work as a member of a team when attempting the following assignments. However, if this is not possible, and you need to work alone, the problems will allow you to gain some appreciation of the benefits that can accrue.

Remember that if you are inexperienced at team working, the outcome of your first efforts at using these techniques will be more of a reflection of this inexperience, rather than on the methods themselves.

Assignment 7.1

Rather than provide you with some problems to solve, I would like you to generate a list yourself. I call this sort of list a 'bug list', because the things that generally appear on them are problems that annoy or 'bug' us. Write down a list of annoying things that happen to you, concentrating on things where you think that it might be possible to find a solution. I sometimes give this task to my students so that we have a store of problems to apply the creativity techniques to. Ideally, you would try to find solutions to other people's problems rather than the ones that you had generated yourself, but obviously there are no rules about this. The following list is part of one that a small group of first year undergraduate students generated in less than 10 minutes. I have omitted those that might have prevented this book being published.

- doors that squeak
- doors that stick in damp weather
- glasses that 'mist-up'
- cold toilet seats
- toilets where the paper has run out
- big bunches of keys
- polishing shoes
- lecturers
- loose change
- pens that don't work
- etc.,

After you have generated your own list, select two problems that you would like to work on. Choose problems that you consider can be handled in a reasonable period of time; obviously this would tend to exclude things like 'travel to the moon on a number 2 bus' but, on the other hand it is better if the problem does not have a clear means of solution at the outset. The reason for this is that there is then a tendency to cling on to the obvious rather than generate novel ideas when the solutions to the problem are already known.

Take the first problem, and apply the 6–3–5 method in an attempt to generate solutions. Re-read the notes on the method carefully before starting. If you are working in a group of 'n' people, try to generate at least $2 \times n$ distinct ideas plus a similar number of hybrids. Of course, the number of ideas that you produce will depend upon the size of the problem, the experience and background of members of the team, and serendipity.

When you have finished, make some reasonably neat sketches of the ideas that came out of the sessions (you may need more than one), and provide a short paragraph for each idea describing its strengths and weaknesses.

Assignment 7.2

Take the second of the two ideas selected from the bug list of Assignment 7.1, and apply the controlled input method to its solution. Again, read the notes on the method carefully before proceeding, and complete the session with a written summary.

Which of the two methods do you prefer? Is this because of some basic advantage of one method over the other, because one method requires more practice than the other, or simply because one of the problems was more conducive to brainstorming? Whatever your conclusions, remember that all these techniques need a lot of practice before you can get the best out of them.

Assignment 7.3

Take one of the ideas generated during Assignments 7.1 or 7.2 and draw a mind map like the one shown in Figure 7.2 to explore the problems that will be involved in bringing it to completion.

Assignment 7.4

Using Figure 7.7 as an example, draw a problem diagram for an automatic system to change a tyre on a car wheel. Assume that the system is to be installed in one of the high-street retailers that you can go to for replacement tyres or exhausts. Remember that you do not need to think of detailed solutions to any parts of this problem; only what the events are, in what sequence they are required, what materials must be provided and disposed of, and if there are any information 'feed-back' or 'feed-forward' requirements. Get this one right and you may be able to retire earlier than you had thought.

Assignment 7.5

Construct a morphology chart, and enter the functions that were identified from the tyre problem that you worked on in Assignment 7.4. Use either the 6–3–5 or controlled input methods to generate several alternative solutions for each of the functions, and enter these onto the morphology chart.

Can you identify any logical linkages between solutions for the various functions; perhaps based on the type of power requirements or services? Identify two or three combinations of solutions that you consider to have potential for development. Which solutions do you feel might be the most difficult to fully develop? Based on the morphology chart, write a one-page report for the company's technical director outlining the options available.

EIGHT
EVALUATION AND SELECTION

OVERVIEW

This chapter describes a formal method for reaching agreement when evaluation and selection of alternative design concepts are required. The method is based upon the '**evaluation matrix**' which provides members of the design team with a common format for listing requirements (their own and/or the customers), the attributes of the available options, and appropriate assessment measures. The method can be used for evaluating alternative design options at the first concept or detail stages of the PDP. Evaluation matrices can also be used to evaluate the suitability of bought out products, and alternative materials.

OBJECTIVES

When you have finished studying this chapter, you will be able to:

- understand the importance of being able to evaluate design options;
- recognise appropriate criteria for concept evaluation and selection;
- select appropriate criteria by which different design attributes may be assessed;
- understand the strengths and limitations of different evaluation methods;
- employ methods by means of which design concepts can be assessed, compared, and chosen;
- present the results of concept evaluation in a concise but well supported manner.

THE NEED FOR EVALUATION

The ability to evaluate alternative design options is critical to the final outcome of the design process. Regardless of how much effort has gone into assessing customer needs, preparing a PDS, and generating conceptual solutions, all will be to no avail if the best concept is not selected for development.

Theoretically, the existence of a complete and well written PDS should make the task of concept evaluation easy. In addition to providing a written statement which links the design task with the customer, the PDS also provides a check list against which the attributes of the alternative design options can be tested. Therefore, the concept that provides the closest match to the requirements identified in the PDS is bound to be a strong contender for development into a product.

In reality, things are rarely quite so straightforward for a number of very good reasons. First, it is unusual for the PDS to be written in terms that are entirely unambiguous. This is not necessarily because of incompetence on the behalf of the authors of the PDS, but because PDS clauses are often generated at a time when understanding of the requirements and their implications is incomplete. Second, in the case of clauses that define objectives, there will be room for opinion to play a part in the evaluation of how well the concept meets the need, and this frequently leads to differences of opinion. Third, when requirements are defined as constraints, alternative concepts may satisfy the variables with different values within the acceptable range. In this case, comparison and evaluation will depend upon the design team's ability to define criteria by which relative importance can be assigned to different variable ranges.

Frequently, defining objectives and constraints which describe product attributes is the easiest part of defining the criteria for evaluation. On the other hand, factors that influence the profitability of the product, but which are not a part of its functional specification are important and much more difficult to assess at the concept stage. There are many such factors, and the following list identifies some of the most obvious and problematic:

- **Technical risk.** How much is known about the technology that will be necessary to bring the alternative concepts to market? Is it merely a matter of buying ready made and fully understood technology off the shelf, or is development work necessary? What are the chances of the development failing to come up with a satisfactory solution?
- **Development cost.** How much will it cost to develop each of the alternative concepts into a marketable product, and what are the implications of this on profitability?
- **Time to market.** If development work is required, how long will this take, and what are the implications of this on the marketability of the product? Is it likely that the delay will permit a competitor to gain advantage?
- **Personnel issues.** Does the company have access to personnel with the knowledge necessary to develop the concepts? The personnel might be found within the company or elsewhere.

Because design is a highly iterative process, with a continuous cycle of specification, conceptualisation, selection, and embodiment, the evaluation and selection part of the process will be repeated over and over again throughout the NPD process. Although the cycles in the latter stages of the process will be taking place at a time when product knowledge is relatively well developed, the problems and consequences of mistakes will be equally acute. A feature that is common to all of the evaluation/selection stages is the need to agree on the relative merits of the available choices. This agreement will be between the interested parties who should include representatives of the customer and/or marketing function, engineering, finance and commercial functions, etc. Agreement will be more forthcoming if a framework for assessment is adhered to, and the following section introduces several methods that can be used to this end.

ORDERING AND RANKING

A necessary first step towards selection is the arrangement of the available concepts in order of merit. The outcome of this step will depend upon the extent to which each of the available concepts meet the criteria laid down in the PDS. Although ordering is necessary, it is rarely sufficient to permit selection decisions to be made with confidence. If five concepts were being evaluated, a study of the benefits offered by each concept could lead to an observation that one was superior than the others. However, with this information alone, the design team might be unaware that there was a close contender in second place which, with some additional work might become the best option to choose. Placing the options in order of merit together with a measure of their relative suitability is called

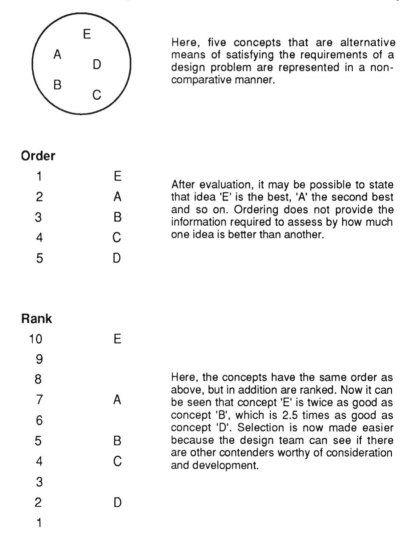

Here, five concepts that are alternative means of satisfying the requirements of a design problem are represented in a non-comparative manner.

Order

1	E
2	A
3	B
4	C
5	D

After evaluation, it may be possible to state that idea 'E' is the best, 'A' the second best and so on. Ordering does not provide the information required to assess by how much one idea is better than another.

Rank

10	E
9	
8	
7	A
6	
5	B
4	C
3	
2	D
1	

Here, the concepts have the same order as above, but in addition are ranked. Now it can be seen that concept 'E' is twice as good as concept 'B', which is 2.5 times as good as concept 'D'. Selection is now made easier because the design team can see if there are other contenders worthy of consideration and development.

Figure 8.1 Ordering and ranking of concepts are necessary for selection 'ranking' and this provides the design team with a more useful basis for decision making (Figure 8.1). In addition, the process of providing the ranking imposes a discipline on the team that would not otherwise be present. Ranking the concepts **makes** the team think about the relative importance of the various attributes available in the design options.

Because each of the concepts being considered will offer different attributes, the ability to rank will depend on the availability of assessment criteria. Whilst constraints provide numerical 'go' and 'no-go' criteria for assessment, objectives by their nature are more subjective. The need to deal with objectives in a rational manner is behind the weighted objectives method described in the case studies in Chapter 4, and the way that these weightings can be used at the evaluation stage are described in the following case study. The purpose of this study is to introduce the principles of evaluation matrices, and it is left to a subsequent example to look in detail at how the methods works in practice.

CASE STUDY 8.1

The design team working on the segment M hairdryer introduced in Chapter 4, used the market study to help them develop a weighted requirement tree. An abbreviated version of this tree is shown in Figure 8.2. The Tree contained many levels, and this attention to detail provided an extensive check list for the team at the later stages of the NPD process. However, during the development of initial concepts, the team needed a basic set of criteria against which to assess them, and decided that the requirements in level three of the tree were sufficient for this purpose. At level three, the level two requirements of safety, market competitiveness, performance, and ergonomics are subdivided in the following way:

- Safety
  —complies with relevant safety standards
  —low risk to users.
- Market competitiveness
  —aesthetically pleasing for the M segment
  —competitive warranty (guarantee) terms
  —low cost
  —portable
  —environmentally friendly.
- Performance
  —high quality
  —efficient
  —reliable
  —robust
- Ergonomics
  —single handed use
  —suitable controls for the M segment
  —use remote from mains socket
  —acceptable weight.

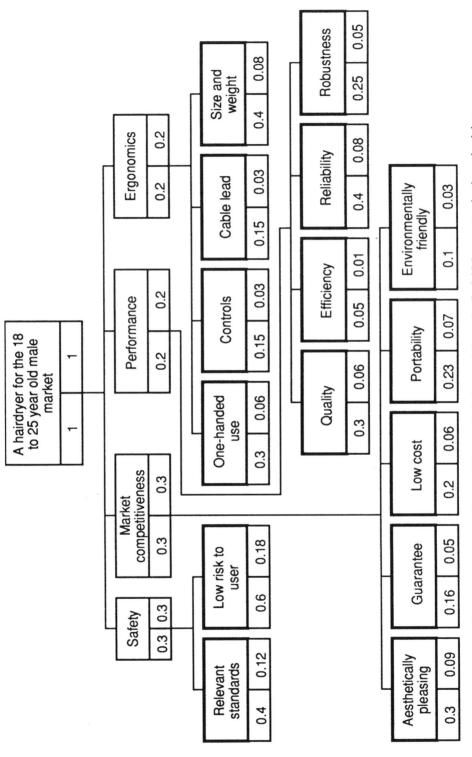

Figure 8.2 A weighted requirement tree for the hairdryer problem provided adequate information for initial concept evaluation at level three

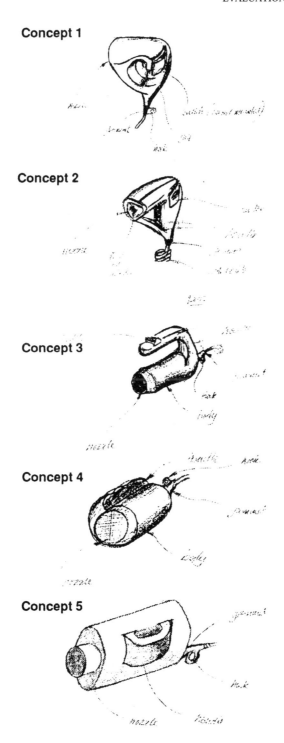

Figure 8.3 Five styling concepts for the segment M hairdryer

The team produced five basic concepts for the new hairdryer, which are shown in Figure 8.3. At this early stage of concept generation, the design team were concentrating on the development of styling aspects that might prove to be attractive to segment M. Nevertheless, even at this stage there were implications for attributes such as price, size and weight, and even reliability in so far as it was affected by component layout.

As a part of the process of generating alternative styling concepts, the engineering implications of control positioning, weight distribution, material choices, and manufacturing methods were taken into account. As an aid to evaluating the concepts, the design team set about producing an evaluation matrix. One of the primary purposes of the matrix is to force the team to evaluate each concept against all of the requirements, and to work towards a consensus decision on which concept or concepts to develop further. The need to develop a matrix and agree on its contents provides the framework within which evaluation issues can be discussed and agreed. As with all design methods, it is the work that goes into the discussions prior to production of the matrix rather than the matrix itself that provides the benefit. The finished matrix provides a succinct statement of the decisions that were made, and hence forms a useful document for recording the outcome and informing other people. Figure 8.4 shows the final version of the matrix for the hairdryer concepts, and we will use this as a basis for considering the methodology of producing such a document.

	CRITERIA	DATUM (BaByliss Chrome Salon Professional)	1	2	3	4	5
1	Safety						
	Relevant standards		S	S	S	S	S
	Low risk to user		S	S	S	S	S
2	Market competitiveness						
	Aesthetically pleasing		+	S	+	+	S
	Guarantee		S	S	S	S	S
	Low cost		+	+	+	+	+
	Portability		S	S	+	+	+
	Environmentally friendly		+	+	+	+	+
3	Performance						
	Quality		S	S	S	S	S
	Efficiency		S	S	S	S	S
	Reliability		S	S	S	S	S
	Robustness		–	–	S	+	+
4	Ergonomics						
	One-handed use		S	S	+	S	S
	Controls		+	S	+	S	S
	Cable lead		S	+	+	S	S
	Size / weight		S	S	S	+	+
		$\Sigma+$	4	3	7	6	5
		Σ	1	1	0	0	0
		ΣT	3	2	7	6	5

Figure 8.4 An evaluation matrix for concept solutions to the segment M hairdryer problem introduced in Chapter 4

The criteria against which the alternative design concepts are to be evaluated are listed in the left-hand column of the matrix. These criteria are taken straight from levels two and three of the requirement tree. The columns headed 1 to 5 each represent one of the concepts. The purpose of this type of evaluation is to compare each new concept against a datum product. If, as is the case here, there are already products on the market that are selling into the segment under consideration, it is usual to take one of these existing products as the datum or 'standard' against which the new designs are compared. In this matrix, the datum product is the BaByliss Chrome Salon Professional, which had proved to be the most popular design in the market survey. Obviously, any new product aimed specifically at segment M would have to compare favourably with this product.

The first, and most difficult task that the design team faces is to compare each of the concept designs with the datum product for each of the assessment criteria, and then to decide whether it meets each criteria equally, more effectively, or less effectively than the datum product. If a new concept promises a better match to customer requirements in terms of one of the criteria a + is placed in the appropriate box of the matrix. If it performs less well a – is entered, and if it promises the same match S is entered. Hence, from Figure 8.4, concept 1 has been deemed to be better than the datum product in terms of aesthetics, cost, environment friendliness, and control layout. There is a consensus that the design may not be as robust as the datum, and in all other aspects the concept and the datum are equally matched.

The matrix takes only a few minutes to assimilate, but may have taken many days or weeks of investigation and discussion to prepare. In some cases, a considerable amount of detailed investigation will need to be carried out before the decision to place +, –, or S in a particular box can be made. In the case of the hairdryer, decisions about 'aesthetics', 'one-handed use' and 'control positioning' will have to wait for the production of models and feedback from potential customers, whilst 'robustness' cannot be assessed until information is available on the effect of shape on casing strength and any styling implications for the choice and fixing of internal components. When all of the concept-criteria boxes have been filled with either +, –, or S, the design team will be able to use the information to help them make choices. The usual procedure is to summarise the information in each column by summing the + and – entries and recording them below. In the column associated with concept 1, there are four +, and one – symbols and these are recorded as $\Sigma +$ and $\Sigma -$. Summing the $\Sigma +$ and $\Sigma -$ totals (i.e., $4 + (- 1) = 3$) is then recorded as ΣT, and this provides a crude measure of the relative worth of the concepts against the datum. On this basis, the 'best' of the five concepts considered in Figure 8.4 is concept 3, which has a ΣT value of 7. This is followed by concepts 4, 5, 1, and 2 in descending order of suitability.

As stated earlier, the primary purpose of producing this matrix is to make the team think carefully about the extent to which each concept meets all of the requirements. As a result, team members should be able to defend or at least argue the case for each of the symbols placed on the matrix. Regardless of this, great care is necessary in coming to any conclusions about concept suitability from the numbers in the Σ rows at the bottom. In practice, the +, –, and S symbols do little more than identify problems, possibilities and opportunities in the concepts as they exist at the moment. If improvements can be made to the controls and reliability of concept 4 it may be possible to upgrade the S in these boxes to +, thereby giving it a higher ΣT value than concept 3, and the matrix helps the team to focus on such matters.

WEIGHTED EVALUATION

A problem with the type of evaluation matrix introduced in the previous section is that it provides no indication of the relative importance of criteria. In most cases, some criteria will be more important to the future success of the product than others, and this can strongly influence the choice of designs for further development. If the market study found that minimising weight was very important for the segment M hairdryer, it is conceivable that concept 5, which is superior to concept 3 in this respect, may have the greater potential for development, even though it has been deemed inferior in terms of other ergonomic attributes and aesthetics. If the team members are aware of the difference in importance of the criteria, and apply this knowledge during the selection process, then the type of matrix shown in Figure 8.4 is adequate. The only risk is that team members will be working with different perceptions of the relative importance of criteria even though they think that they are using a common basis for evaluation. Introducing the need to state the criteria weightings on the matrix provides a formal framework that forces agreement on the team, and makes them take proper account of the relative importance ratings (RIR).

RIR can be established using any method agreeable to the team as a whole, provided that all the criteria are considered and related back to customer requirements. The

	CRITERIA	RIR		1	2	3	4	5
1	Safety	**0.3**						
	Relevant standards	0.12		S	S	S	S	S
	Low risk to user	0.18		S	S	S	S	S
2	Market competitiveness	**0.3**						
	Aesthetically pleasing	0.09		+	S	+	+	S
	Guarantee	0.05		S	S	S	S	S
	Low cost	0.06		+	+	+	+	+
	Portability	0.07		S	S	+	+	+
	Environmentally friendly	0.03		+	+	+	+	+
3	Performance	**0.2**						
	Quality	0.06		S	S	S	S	S
	Efficiency	0.01		S	S	S	S	S
	Reliability	0.08		S	S	S	S	S
	Robustness	0.05		−	−	S	+	+
4	Ergonomics	**0.2**						
	One-handed use	0.06		S	S	+	S	S
	Controls	0.03		+	S	+	S	S
	Cable lead	0.03		S	+	+	S	S
	Size and weight	0.08		S	S	S	+	+
		Σ+		4	3	7	6	5
		Σ−		1	1	0	0	0
		ΣT		3	2	7	6	5
		ΣW		0.16	0.07	0.37	0.38	0.29

The RIR column has a vertical label: DATUM (BaByliss Chrome Salon Professional)

Figure 8.5 An evaluation matrix for concept solutions to the segment M hairdryer problem introduced in Chapter 4

	CRITERIA	RIR	DATUM (BaByliss Chrome Salon Professional)	1		2		3		4		5	
1	Safety	**0.3**											
	Relevant standards	0.12	0	0	0	0	0	0	0	0	0	0	0
	Low risk to user	0.18	0	0	0	0	0	0	0	0	0	0	0
2	Market competitiveness	**0.3**											
	Aesthetically pleasing	0.09	+1	+1	+0.09	0	0	+1	+0.09	+1	+0.09	0	0
	Guarantee	0.05	0	0	0	0	0	0	0	0	0	0	0
	Low cost	0.06	+1	+1	+0.06	+2	+0.12	+1	+0.06	+1	+0.06	+2	+0.12
	Portability	0.07	0	0	0	0	0	+1	+0.07	+1	+0.07	+2	+0.14
	Environmentally friendly	0.03	+1	+1	+0.03	+1	+0.03	+2	+0.06	+1	+0.03	+1	+0.03
3	Performance	**0.2**											
	Quality	0.06	0	0	0	0	0	0	0	0	0	0	0
	Efficiency	0.01	0	0	0	0	0	0	0	0	0	0	0
	Reliability	0.08	0	0	0	0	0	0	0	0	0	0	0
	Robustness	0.05	-1	-1	-0.05	-2	-0.1	0	0	+1	+0.05	+1	+0.05
4	Ergonomics	**0.2**											
	One-handed use	0.06	0	0	0	0	0	+1	+0.06	0	0	0	0
	Controls	0.03	+1	+1	+0.03	0	0	+1	+0.03	0	0	0	0
	Cable lead	0.03	0	0	0	+1	+0.03	+1	+0.03	0	0	0	0
	Size and weight	0.08	0	0	0	0	0	0	0	+1	+0.08	+2	+0.16
	ΣW				+0.16		+0.08		+0.40		+0.38		+0.50

Figure 8.6 A fully weighted evaluation matrix for the hairdryer concepts

Evaluation	Points
Far inferior to datum	−2
Somewhat inferior to datum	−1
Same as datum	0
Somewhat better than datum	+1
Far superior to datum	+2

Figure 8.7 Point scores for criteria compliance

requirement tree method introduced in Chapter 5 provides a means of comparing objectives to facilitate weighting assignment. These weightings can then be used directly as RIR in an evaluation matrix. Figure 8.5 shows the previous matrix modified to include RIR scores and a new ΣW row which contains the sum of the weightings assigned to each concept. For concept 1, the sum of the weightings for the criteria on which it performed better than the datum is $0.09 + 0.06 + 0.03 + 0.03 = 0.21$, whilst the weighting for the criterion on which it performed less well than the datum is 0.05. The overall score for that concept is $\Sigma W = 0.21 - 0.05 = 0.16$.

When criteria weighting is applied, concept 4 shows marginally stronger than concept 3; a reversal of the situation shown in Figure 8.4.

The matrix can be made to display the relative worth of the concepts even more accurately by including measures of how well each concept satisfies the criteria. In satisfying the heavily weighted size/weight criteria, concept 5 may be so superior to concept 3 and 4 that it becomes a leading contender for selection. Figure 8.6 shows a fully weighted evaluation matrix that illustrates this effect.

In the way that the criteria and RIR scores are presented, the matrix in Figure 8.6 is identical to that in Figure 8.5. The essential difference is that the degree to which the attributes of each concept meets the assessment criteria has been recorded using a 5-point Lickert scale. In this case, the scale points were defined as shown in Figure 8.7.

Utilising this points system means that all of the 'S' symbols in Figure 8.5 are replaced by a '0' in Figure 8.6, whilst all + symbols are replaced by a + 1 or + 2 depending on how well each criteria is met. Similarly, − symbols are replaced by either − 1 or − 2. Each RIR is then factored by the assigned points score and entered into the second column associated with each concept. The two columns associated with concept 2 in Figure 8.6 provide a good example of how this approach works. In respect to cost, concept 2 has been awarded a points score of + 2, which means that it performs particularly well in this respect. The RIR for cost is 0.06, so $0.06 \times (+ 2) = + 0.12$ is entered against low cost in the second of the concept 2 columns. From a robustness point of view, concept 2 performs particularly badly in comparison with the datum, and its point score of − 2 yields a total of − 0.1 in the second column. When similar consideration is given to the scores and RIR for environmentally friendliness and cable provision, the weighted totals can be summed against ΣW. The summed total of + 0.08 provides a measure of overall compliance of the concept with the evaluation criteria. Using this more developed approach, concept 5 emerges as the most promising contender because of its strong superiority in terms of heavily weighted criteria.

THE EFFECT OF UNCERTAINTY

As with all of the methods that are described in this book, there is no such thing as a correct or incorrect format for an evaluation matrix. What is important is that design team members are comfortable with the format chosen, and feel that the costs in time and effort are outweighed by the benefits. The essential role of the matrix is to make team members think about all of the alternative designs available, and to evaluate each design against all of the desirable attributes. The matrix forces this activity by imposing the requirement to produce an agreed document at the end of the process. At the early stages of the design process, when broad conceptual ideas are being put forward, the team members will be uncertain about many issues relating to the reasonableness of the desired attributes and the achievability of some aspects of the alternative designs. These uncertainties constitute risks that experienced designers try to remove as early as possible. Chapter 9 deals at some length with risk, but its influence can usually be seen in the format chosen by the design team for their evaluation matrices. When the team is uncertain about important aspects of the evaluation criteria and concepts, assigning weighting will be difficult and there may be a tendency to avoid the problem by opting for a non-weighted matrix which merely relies on subjective comparisons between the concepts and a datum. At early PDP stages this type of matrix of which Figure 8.4 is an example, can be valuable in highlighting these shortcomings in information or knowledge. However, the drive should always be towards a quantification of the reasons leading to decisions, even though a certain amount of uncertainty will almost always be present. If risk cannot be removed completely from the decision-making process then at least the source, nature, and scope of the risk should be determined so that appropriate action can be taken to minimise the consequences of risk turning into failure.

With the foregoing comments in mind, it is always good practice to attempt quantification of the match between concept attributes and evaluation criteria, and to record areas of uncertainty where this is not entirely possible. The following case study shows a variant that takes account of uncertainty.

CASE STUDY 8.2

Chapter 6 contained a description of the PDS for a device to staple intestinal tissue during surgery. At a subsequent stage in the development of this product the design team identified a problem and associated possibilities. The device was to work by squeezing two layers of tissue together and joining them together by a ring of small titanium staples. The squeezing force applied to the tissues turned out to be critical. If the force was too large, there was the possibility that the crimped staples would lock this force into the tissue, reducing blood flow and cause tissue death (necrosis). If the force was too small, the contents of the intestine might leak through the joint before healing took place, resulting in serious infection of the abdominal cavity. The team looked at several ways of controlling and/or assessing the squeezing force during use, but eventually decided to develop a device that could measure both the volume of blood and the oxygen content in the compressed tissue. After undertaking some theoretical and experimental investigations, the team identified four designs as contenders for development. The ideas used the properties of tissue that cause variations in the quantity of reflected laser light with variations in blood volume and oxygen content. Each of

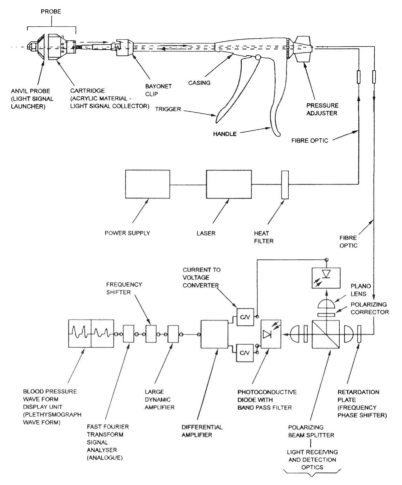

Figure 8.8 One of the design concepts for the blood monitoring function of a stapling device

the four methods differed in the means of analysing the reflected signal. Figure 8.8 provides a diagrammatic representation of one of the four designs.

In the evaluation matrix that follows, the point scores awarded to concept attributes are based upon a system recommended by the VDI 2221 guideline. The definitions for the point scores are different to those used in the preceding case study but serve a similar purpose. Figure 8.9 shows the scale.

Meaning	Points
Unsatisfactory	0
Just tolerable	1
Adequate	2
Good	3
Very good (ideal)	4

Figure 8.9 The 5-point VDI guideline for concept evaluation used in Figure 8.10

Attribute	No	Objective	Weight	Parameter	Concept A			Concept B		
					Magnitude	Score	Weight value	Magnitude	Score	Weight value
Function	1	Reliability of adjusting intensity of signal	0.002	Sensitive settings	Very low	0	0	Just tolerable	1	0.002
	2	Indicate normality and abnormality of blood flow	0.01	Techniques familiar to surgeon	Very familiar	4	0.04	Not very familiar	1	0.01
Working principle	3	Simple and clear functioning	0.01	Simple to monitor blood perfusion at different depths	Very simple	4	0.04	Adequate	2	0.02
	4	Clear response	0.002	Easy to interpret results	Very obvious	4	0.008	?	1	0.002
Safety	5	Does not puncture tissue	0.002	Probability of not puncturing tissue	Just tolerable	1 -	0.002	Just tolerable	1 +	0.002
Quality control	6	Modular sections that can be tested separately	0.003	Easy to test separate components	Just tolerable	1	0.003	Good	3	0.009

Figure 8.10 The evaluation matrix for the blood monitoring concepts

Fundamentally, the engineers who prepared the evaluation matrix shown in Figure 8.10 used the same technique as that demonstrated in Figure 8.6. Broad headings from the PDS are identified in column 1 together with their identification numbers in column 2. The third column contains an expansion of the column 1 requirements, and the RIR score (called 'weight') are taken from a requirement tree and listed in column 4. The next column, headed 'parameter' is merely a clarification of the basis upon which concept suitability will be judged. For each concept, there are three columns. The first contains a short written statement of how well each criterion is provided for by the concept. In general, these descriptions follow the meanings defined in Figure 8.9, although some are modified to better describe a particular parameter. The second of the concept columns contain the numerical point score associated with the entry in the previous column, whilst the third concept column contains the product of the score and the RIR. As before, the products for each concept can be summed to give an overall 'utility' value.

Some of the concept scores in Figure 8.10 have a + or − symbol appended. A + means that the score given to that criterion is thought to be a conservative evaluation and in all probability the concept will perform better in that respect. A − means that there is concern that the score may be high and difficult to achieve in practice. Usually, the + and − symbols mean that there has been a degree of disagreement between team members. In any case, further work is essential to reduce the risk of unpleasant surprises in the future.

COMMUNICATION AND DOCUMENTATION

Evaluation matrices can provide a valuable platform to facilitate communication and decision making at appropriate stages of the PDP. Because of the formalised structure of the matrix, team members are forced to communicate in a common language in order to take part in the negotiations and discussions leading to construction of the matrix. Because the matrix provides a link between concept attributes and customer and company requirements it is particularly useful in forcing the marketing and design functions to work together. In this respect, the matrix provides the marketing function with an overview of the problems and opportunities facing the design team and encourages marketing to examine the consequences of possible deviations from the original product brief. Figure 8.11 shows the input, outputs and benefits of the evaluation matrix method.

If a product's requirements have not been well thought out and recorded in either a PDS or requirement tree, the effective development of an evaluation matrix will be impossible. Indeed, many problems encountered in the construction of the matrix can be readily identified as having roots in woolly thinking about what the customer will buy, or in not thinking through the implications of the design ideas that have been put forward for evaluation. Problems in matrix development are always indicative of poor preparation, and should encourage the team to back-track in order to attain a thorough understanding of the factors involved.

Because the matrix only records the outcome and fundamental reasons of the evaluation process it is invariably necessary to provide supporting documentation to explain the reasons for assigning particular scores to concept attributes. Figure 8.12 shows the relationship between the matrix, PDS, objective tree, and supporting documentation.

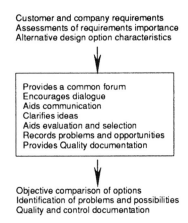

Figure 8.11 Inputs, outputs and benefits of the evaluation matrix method

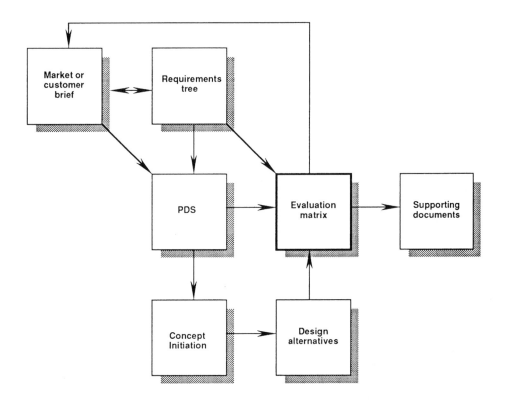

Figure 8.12 The evaluation matrix can play a pivotal role in linking product requirements with the attributes

OTHER APPLICATIONS

Evaluation matrices can be used in any situation where decisions have to be made regarding the evaluation and selection of alternatives. As well as being suitable for concept selection, they can be valuable when assessing the relative worth of bought-in products from suppliers, choice of materials for a particular component, or component manufacturing routes.

CASE STUDY 8.3

An example of matrix to evaluate material options is shown in Figure 8.13. The pump is representative of the type found in some drink vending machines. It is important that any risk of food contamination is avoided as far as possible. A good way to achieve this is to ensure that there is no ingress of contaminents along the impeller shaft. The impeller which transports the coffee, tea or mushroom soup (they usually taste the same) is turned round by means of in-built magnets and an external drive. This means that the spindle on which the impeller turns can be stationary, removing the need for seals in the housing. In the case shown, the decision had been made to manufacture the impeller out of food grade plastic, but the choice of spindle material had not been finalised. The two options most favoured were ceramic and stainless steel. As a preliminary stage in the process of selection the evaluation matrix shown in Figure 8.13 was produced. The eight factors considered to have relevance to the decision were listed down the left hand column of the matrix, whilst their relative importance rating (RIR) were listed in the second column. Each material was given a rating that expressed its ability to meet the requirements of the specification factors, and the weighted scores for each factor was

Specification Factor	RIR	Ceramic		Stainless steel	
		A	B	A	B
Strength	3	5	15	10	30
Hardness	1	10	10	8	8
Fatigue	2	5	10	8	16
Wear	8(2)	10	80	8	64
Rigidity	3	10	30	8	24
Temperature stability	5	10	50	8	40
Toxicity	10	10	100	10	100
Complexity	1	10	10	10	10
Σ			305		292

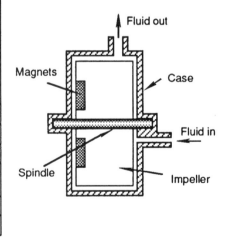

Figure 8.13 Material evaluation matrix for a vending machine pump problem

entered into the next column. Finally, the sum of the weighted scores were computed for each material. For this application, wear characteristics were of paramount importance. Firstly because of the possible consequences of wear particles in the foodstuff, and secondly because of the implications for pump life. The way that a component wears is dependent upon the properties of both rubbing surfaces, and cannot be determined with reference to only one component. In the Figure 8.13 matrix, this interrelationship of wear properties is noted by the number 2 in brackets following the RIR value of 8 for wear. This refers to component number 2 which is the impeller.

Because the pump components will cycle between room ambient temperature and near to boiling point, it is important that the geometry and material selection decisions take this into account. Thermal expansion is one aspect of this consideration and is important because clearances may be lost or become excessive as the temperature rises. Ceramic scores particularly well in this respect because of its low coefficient of thermal expansion.

CASE STUDY 8.4

The next example of an evaluation matrix is based upon a survey of answering machines carried out by *Which?* magazine. The survey provided more information than I am using here, but it is sufficient to illustrate what can be done. Figure 8.14 summarises the factual data provided by *Which?* on the machines that did not include a telephone.

This sort of information, like that provided in the product feature charts described in Chapter 4, is already in a convenient form for evaluation. Although *Which?* does an excellent job in pointing out the strengths and limitations of the products that they review, the best buys are based upon their perceptions of what people want, and this may not necessarily fit your requirements. To evaluate the products properly you must first specify **your** needs and, if possible give some sort of RIR to your various requirements. I purchased an answering machine of the type described here quite recently, and these were the issues that were important to me:

1. An ability to record a large number of messages when I am away from home for lengthy periods.
2. The facility to playback messages from a remote phone.
3. A capability that enables me to intercept calls from another extension when I have left the answerphone switched on.
4. A maximum cost of between £60 and £80.

It may seem strange that I set the maximum cost between two limits. After all the maximum should be just that; a single maximum figure beyond which I would not be prepared to go. In reality, this is rarely the case. I would **like** to pay as little as possible for the features that I consider important. I have some sort of feel for what such a machine might cost me, and I know how much my bank account can stand, but in the end I am prepared to be swayed between the limits of what I think is necessary and the maximum that I can afford. In other words, I very much hope that I can get what I want for £60, but might be persuaded to go to £80 if it means getting the most important of

★ best ★ ↑ ★ ↕ + ↓ ⊥ worst	Answercall Pace	Betacom Memo	BT Response 10	BT Response 1000 plus	Casio Phonemate 3800	Dialatron Designer 220	Geemarc Ansamac 50
Price (£)	35	60	40	130	40	23	30
Country of origin	China	China	China	Malaysia	Malaysia	China	China
Colours available	White	White, grey	White	Grey	Grey	Black	White, black
Recording system	Cassette	Digital	Cassette	Digital	Cassette	Cassette	Cassette
Max announcement time (min/sec)	2min 10 sec	1min	2min	20min	1min	2min 25sec	43sec
Max time per message (min/sec)	2min 30sec	3min	3min	3min	5min	2min 30sec	2min
Total message length (min)	15	10	15	20	15	15	15
Power failure protection	√	√		√	√	√	√
Logs time and day	√	√		√	√		
Toll saver	√	√	√		√	√	
Records conversation				√			
Remote announcement change	√	√		√		√	
Interrupt from extension		√	√	√	√		√
Wall mounting				√			√
Memo facility	√	√	√	√	√	√	
Call forwarding				√			
Quality of announcement	★	+	★	★	+	★	+
Quality of incoming messages	+	+	★	+	★	★	★
Ease of setting up	★	✱	★	★	★	★	★
General ease of use	★	✱	★	✱	★	★	+
Remote access ease of use	+	✱	★	✱	+	+	★
Remote access security	+	✱	+	✱	+	+	+

Figure 8.14 Summary data from the *Which?* survey of answering machines without telephones

my requirements. This means that I need to rank my requirements in some sort of way. Figure 8.15 shows the conclusion that I reached by distributing 10 points between the three non-cost objectives.

Whilst the product features chart is independent of customer needs, the RIR ratings given in Figure 8.15 are specific to me, and will be of vital importance in the way that the product attributes are evaluated.

Although other features may be of interest to me, the ones rated in Figure 8.14 are the ones that I feel will be the most influential in making the decision on which product to buy. Figure 8.16 shows how the RIR and product information can be combined into a single evaluation matrix.

Large number of messages	5
Intercept calls	4
Remote playback	1

Figure 8.15 RIR data for the answerphone

Legend:

✱	best
★★★	
★★	
↕	worst

	RIR	Answercall Pace	Weight	Betacom Memo	Weight	BT Response 10	Weight	BT Response 1000 plus	Weight	Casio Phonemate 3800	Weight	Dialatron Designer 220	Weight	Geemarc Ansamac 50	Weight
Price (£)	60-80	35	√	60	√	40	√	130	x	40	x	23	√	30	√
Country of origin	-	China	-	China	-	China	-	Malaysia	-	Malaysia	-	China	-	China	-
Colours available	-	White	-	White, grey	-	White	-	Grey	-	Grey	-	Black	-	White, black	-
Recording system	-	Cassette	-	Digital	-	Cassette	-	Digital	-	Cassette	-	Cassette	-	Cassette	-
Max announcement time (min/sec)	-	2min 10 sec	-	1min	-	2min	-	20min	-	1min	-	2min 25sec	-	43sec	-
Max time per message (min/sec)	-	2min 30sec	-	3min	-	3min	-	3min	-	5min	-	2min 30sec	-	2min	-
Total message length (min)	5	15	75	10	50	15	75	20	100	15	75	15	75	15	75
Power failure protection	-	√	-	√	-		-	√	-	√	-	√	-	√	-
Logs time and day	-	√	-	√	-		-	√	-	√	-	√	-	√	-
Toll saver	-	√	-	√	-	√	-	√	-	√	-	√	-		-
Records conversation	-		-		-		-		-		-		-		-
Remote announcement change	1	√	1	√	1	√	1	√	1		1	√	0	√	0
Interrupt from extension	4	√	0	√	4	√	4	√	4	√	4	√	4	√	4
Wall mounting	-		-	√	-		-	√	-		-		-		-
Memo facility	-	√	-	√	-	√	-	√	-	√	-	√	-	√	-
Call forwarding	-		-	√	-		-	√	-		-		-		-
Quality of announcement	-	★		✦		★		★		✦		★		✦	
Quality of incoming messages	-	✦		✦		✦		✦		✦		✦		★	
Ease of setting up	-	★		✱		★		★		★		★		★	
General ease of use	-	★		✱		★		✱		★		★		✦	
Remote access ease of use	-	✦		★		✦		✱		✦		✦		★	
Remote access security	-	✦		★		✦		✱		✦		✦		✦	

Figure 8.16 Evaluation matrix for the answering machine

There is no attempt here to compile a list of weightings that can be summed to provide an overall product rating. This would have been possible if I could have expressed preferences for the subjective measures like 'announcement quality' and 'ease of setting up' identified in the lower section of the matrix. In this case, I did not feel that these were important issues which meant that the evaluation centred around 'go and no-go' criteria like the presence or absence of a certain feature. Regardless of this, my requirement with the highest RIR was expressed quantitatively in the *Which?* chart, and this gave me the opportunity to provide a weighted assessment by multiplying the RIR and the total available message length. Although it would be nonsensical to add this to the other weightings, it did provide a quantitative measure of how well that particular attribute was provided for.

The first decision was to reject the BT Response 1000. At £130 it was well above my top limit on price, and it did not even provide all of my three requirements. Although the Betacom Memo was the *Which?* best buy, it fared badly against my top requirement for a long total message time. The Answercall Pace and the Dialatron Designer 220 were rejected because they did not provide the required interrupt facility. This left the BT Response 10, the Casio Phonemate 3800, and the Geemarc Ansamac 50. From the point of view of my previously stated requirements, all of these were equally suitable, although the Geemarc Ansamac 50 had the advantage of being £10 cheaper than the other two. However, I was now working well within my maximum price limit and decided to examine the more subjective attributes to see if they would help me to make up my mind. In the end, the higher overall evaluation given to features like "quality of announcement", "ease of setup", and "general ease of use" led me to choose the BT Response 10, and several months later I am still convinced that it was the right decision for **me**.

RECAP

It is pointless producing brilliant concept solutions to design problems if incorrect decisions are made in choosing the best idea to develop into a product. To ensure that the best available option is chosen, a structured approach to evaluation and selection must be adopted. To this end, the construction of an evaluation matrix forces the design team to seek agreement on the extent to which each concept meets all of the criteria. It is not the completion of the matrix itself that facilitates concept choice, but the discussion which precedes it. However, the completed matrix is a powerful tool to remind team members what was agreed and why particular choices were made. The matrix is also useful as a concise means of explaining and supporting the decisions to other company personnel and possibly the customer. The completed matrix, together with supporting explanatory documentation can also provide important documentation within the company's quality control system.

The stages of producing a basic weighted evaluation matrix are as follows:

1. Identify the criteria against which the concepts will be evaluated. These may be obtained from the PDS and/or the requirement tree.
2. List these criteria down the left hand column of a matrix.

3. Provide a second column containing the RIR of each criterion. These may be obtained from a weighted requirement tree or by any other method leading to a rational and agreed weighting.

4. For each concept, provide a broad column subdivided into two further columns.

5. Associate each concept column with a particular concept that is to be evaluated.

6. In the first of each pair of concept columns enter a score that describes the degree to which the concept satisfies each criterion.

7. In the second of the pair of concept columns enter the product of the RIR and concept scores.

8. Provide an overall utility score for each concept by summing the individual entries in the second concept columns.

9. Rank the concepts on the basis of the utility scores.

Although evaluation matrices are a useful tool in comparing concepts against assessment criteria, they are also an encouragement to further design improvements. Each entry in the matrix requires intelligent and critical appraisal to see whether a concept's performance can be improved by making alterations or additions to certain aspects of the design. In particular, concepts that perform badly against criteria with a high RIR should be examined carefully to see if the problem can be designed out. Frequently, this leads to a hybridisation of the concepts with the best features of one concept being used to improve poor performance in another.

Because design is an iterative process, the construction of evaluation matrices is likely to be a repetitive activity throughout the PDP whenever choices have to be made between increasingly detailed design alternatives.

	RIR	AEG Santo 2230-1 DT	Weight	Atlant KSMD-215-0	Weight	Beko NF741	Weight	Bosch KSV 2622/04	Weight	Candy CCFF 29/13FF	Weight	Candy Eco CCM 28/12	Weight
Price (£)		400		180		200		370		370		300	
Country of origin		Germany		Belarus		Turkey		Germany		UK		UK	
Annual running cost (£)		26		42		40		33		50		35	
Height x width x depth (cm)		126/55/58		149/58/61		156/60/62		148/60/60		176/55/64		162/55/61	
Fridge storage volume (litres)		148		192		177		172		148		147	
Freezer storage volume (litres)		44		47		66		66		96		75	
Frost free										√			
Adjustable feet		4		2		2		2		2		2	
Bottles fit upright in main comp.						√		√					
Hidden evaporator		√				√		√		√		√	
Fridge shelves (incl half shelves)		4		5		4		4		4		4	
Freezer compartment drawers		1		1		1		1		4		3	
Freezer on top		√		√		√		√					
Fridge on top										√		√	
Thermostat setting		✱		★		✱		✱		★		✱	
Fridge temperature range		✱		✱		✱		✱		✱		✱	
Fridge temperature stability		✱		✱		★		✱		★		★	
Freezer temperature stability		✱		⊥		✱		✱		★		★	
Defrosting		+		⊥		+		+		✱		★	
Electrical efficiency		✱		★		★		✱		★		✱	
Noise		✱		★		+		★		+		+	
Freezing capacity (kg/24hr)		6		Failed test		3		6		9		5	

Legend (left of table):
✱ best
★
★ ↕
+
⊥ worst

Figure 8.17 Product attribute and evaluation matrix for a selection of fridge-freezers

ASSIGNMENT

Assignment 8.1

This assignment provides some practice at identifying requirements, drawing up an evaluation matrix, and evaluating the requirements against a set of given product attributes. It is similar to the example on choosing an answering machine, except this time we are going to choose a fridge-freezer. Again, the product attributes are courtesy of a *Which?* magazine survey, but only a small sample of the devices surveyed by *Which?* are included here to make your task more manageable. Figure 8.17 shows the product attribute chart, but before you are influenced by it write down a list of what attributes would be important to you. Then, rank the attributes by distributing a predetermined number of points between them. Enter the RIRs that this produces into the chart and analyse the extent to which each product meets your requirements before completing the weighting columns. On the basis of your conclusions write a justification of the final choice.

NINE

MARKET AND TECHNOLOGY RISK

OVERVIEW

This chapter explains why the **identification** and **management of risk** is an essential part of the PDP. Risks are to be minimised wherever possible and techniques are available which facilitate an organised approach to their management by the design team. As with other methods, the objective is to provide a common basis by which risks can be identified, measured, and controlled. The section uses examples and case studies to illustrate the methods that are introduced.

OBJECTIVES

When you have finished studying this section, you will be able to:

- identify different types of risk;
- assign values to probability and consequences of failure;
- identify high risk elements and propose appropriate management methods to control these risks;
- understand the implications of poor risk management for project success.

A RISKY BUSINESS

The risk involved in jumping over a ditch depends upon the width of the ditch and its depth. If the ditch is 4 m wide and 200 cm deep, no problem. The high probability of not being able to reach the other side will be inconsequential in risk terms because the consequences of failure are negligible. On the other hand, leaping over a 1 m wide ditch which is 10 m deep is much easier, but the risk is considerably greater. Thus, risk depends upon two factors: the **probability** of failure, and the **consequences** of failure. An internationally accepted definition of project risk management does not exist, but the following reflects the spirit of most national standards where they exist: 'A process whereby decisions are made to accept a known or assessed risk and/or the implementation of actions to reduce the consequences of occurrence'.

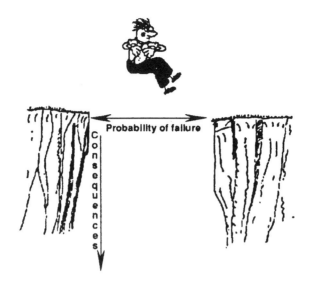

Figure 9.1 The size of the risk depends on the probability of failure and its consequences

Assessing risk and making decisions about appropriate action as a result of the assessment are things that we frequently do throughout our lives. The assessment of risks in a product design environment uses pretty much the same techniques that we use elsewhere, but the need for teamwork and consensus demands that we formalise our approach.

You can read about many different kinds of risk associated with industrial activity. Perhaps the kind most frequently reported by the media is the environmental risk that arises from oil exploration and transport, nuclear power, the generation of greenhouse gases, and environmental pollution of other types. Another type of risk is associated with the possible danger to personal well-being of using certain products or services. Hence, the use of lawn mowers, waste disposal units, electric drills, escalators etc., all carry a risk, although reputable providers will have minimised this risk within the constraints placed by the market requirements and technology.

Although environmental and personal risk are important issues for the product designer, this section is concerned with another type of risk; i.e. that which is associated with the choice of the 'best' project or design idea for development. The following list summarises the areas where risk assessment is important:

- environmental;
- health and safety;
- software systems data handling;
- investment;
- technological;
- marketing;
- commerce (banking, insurance etc.).

One of the key objectives of a company is to maximise its return on investment (ROI). In other words, the company will wish to provide finance for the project or projects that will provide it with the largest possible ratio of income over expenditure. Although there will be constraints applied to this objective that are features of the product type, market environment, short and long term expediencies, and the company's own organisational and technological limitations, the overall objective remains a sound basis on which to make project decisions. Unfortunately, because many factors are involved in arriving at a reliable figure for ROI or income over expenditure ratio, the subsequent decision-making process has a level of risk associated with it. This risk is present regardless of whether the choice being made is between totally different projects (e.g. which of two or more different products to develop), or whether it is between different variants or sub-systems of the same product.

Several models have been developed to help companies choose between different projects. Typical of these is one by Ansoff & Stewart (1967) which is outlined below.

$$\text{Figure of merit } (M_p) = \frac{(M_t + M_b) \times E \times P_s \times P_p \times S}{C_d \times J}$$

where

M_t = Technological merit

M_b = Business merit

E = Estimated total earnings over lifetime

P_s = Probability of success

P_p = Probability of successful market penetration

S = Strategic fit

C_d = Total development time

J = Savings factor from shared resources

If all of the factors on the top line of this equation are large in comparison to those on the bottom line, the figure of merit will be high, and the project that they are associated with will be a good investment in comparison to projects where M_p is lower. Consequently, the risk of a particular project can be represented by a figure of risk (M_r) where:

$$M_r = \frac{C_{ar}}{M_p}$$

and

C_{ar} = The total cost of applied research

Although such models seem to offer a way forward in assessing the merits and risks of alternative projects, in reality they are very difficult to use because of the subjective nature of the process of attributing values to the variables. Some models, like the one described by Kuwahara & Takeda (1990), which provide a figure for the annual profit contribution of various projects do find industrial application, but are of limited use to product designers who need methods that are robust throughout the PDP phases.

From the product designer's point of view it is convenient to identify two types of risk. These are **market risk** and **technological risk**. A definition of the scope of these two types of risk will be useful at this point.

Market risk is concerned with the possibilities that:

- the market requirements have not been correctly defined in the first place;
- the market requirements have been correctly determined but they have not been correctly or adequately recorded in the PDS;
- the market requirements were correctly specified originally, but have changed during the time taken to prepare the product for launch.

Technological risk is concerned with the possibilities that:

- an adequate technical solution cannot be identified for one or more of the product's sub-systems.
- an identified technical solution turns out to be inadequate on functional, cost, time for development, or other grounds;
- a supplier of a key sub-system or component fails to provide a suitable solution.

Market and technological risk meet at the PDS, although a well managed PDP will bridge the two types of risk by having marketing and technical staff working together throughout the PDP development process from market investigation to product launch. Under these conditions, technical staff will be updated at appropriate intervals with new market information, and will have access to comments from marketing personnel regarding the

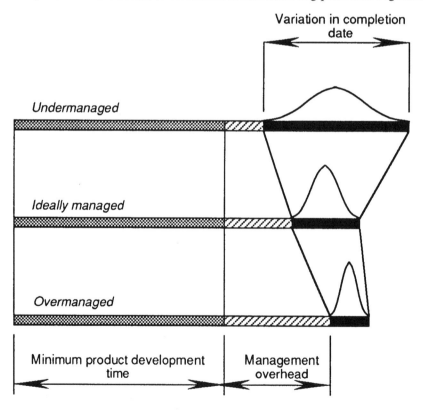

Figure 9.2 Undermanaging risk leads to increased uncertainty about project completion dates, while, over-managing risk can introduce unacceptable management overheads

implications of technical decisions for the product's market potential. Similarly, marketing staff benefit from early contact with technical staff to identify technology related objectives and issues that may carry high cost overheads. As with the remainder of the PDP, the most effective relationship between the marketing and technical functions is one where risks are minimised through communication and iteration.

As we will see later in this section, it is important to identify risks as soon as possible, and make sure that the probability of failure and its consequences are minimised or removed. This requires active management of the design activity, although this can give rise to problems if a satisfactory balance is not achieved. Figure 9.2 shows the possible consequences of under-and over-management of project risk.

At the extremes, the trade-off between high risk and excessive management is about development lead times. 'Going for broke' and risking everything on the design team's ability to overcome problems as and when they arise can result in a very short lead time between making the decision to go ahead and getting the product to market. The risk is that when problems **do** arise they will be more intractable than envisaged, no fall-back solutions will have been established, and the consequences will be excessive cost, a substantial increase in the hoped for lead time, or a total project failure. On the other hand, overmanagement of risk can lead to lost market opportunities because the longer than necessary lead time means that market conditions have changed, and an opportunity has been lost.

Product lead time frequently determines whether it is market or technological risk that is the most important. Product types that traditionally have short lead times (e.g. computers, calculators, computer games) are less likely to attract high market risk because the market requirements have a relatively small chance of changing during product development. For these products, the rush to get them to market means that technological risks are predominant. Whilst the converse is not entirely completely true, there is an increased chance that changing market conditions will be a major risk factor in long lead time projects.

All risks have an active phase. Some will be active during the early stages of the PDP, whilst others will be relevant during later stages. Typical PDP stages that carry their own types of identifiable risks are pre-development, project budgeting and approval, start-up, management, product delivery, and disposal.

IDENTIFYING AND EVALUATING RISK

Technological Risk

For the product design team, the first requirement is to identify the elements of the project that carry a risk. Once identified, the probability of each risk occurring and the severity of its consequences must be investigated, agreed, and recorded. Each element of risk is then assigned an overall weighting, with the most severe risks attracting the highest weightings. Each risk is then assigned to a person who is responsible for its management with, if possible, the most competent people being assigned the highest weighted risks.

During the early stages of the PDP, the best strategy is to identify all of the sub-systems in a design, and treat them as risk elements. However, it is also important to remember

Technology difficulty	Risk factor Rd
We are using existing technology with which we have personal experience, in an application identical to the one proposed.	1
We are using existing technology with which: (1) We do not have personal experience or, (2) In an application different to the one proposed.	2
We are making a new development from a proven technology with which we have personal experience in an application close to the one proposed.	3
We making a new development from a proven technology with which we have no personal experience or in an application different to the one proposed.	4
We are developing new technology in an area where we have little or no previous experience.	5

Figure 9.3   Risk factors attached to varying degrees of technical difficulty on a 5-point scale

that some of the most difficult problems arise from incompatibilities at the interfaces between sub-systems, and each of these interfaces should also be included as a risk element. Having identified all of the elements, each one must be assessed; first to determine the probability of not being able to make the element work in the manner required by the overall system, and second to determine the consequences of such a failure for the project.

In most cases, decisions about the probability of failure and the consequences will be subjective, and are best reached by informed discussion and consensus. Because of this, 3-or 5-point scales are frequently used to ease the task. The scales shown in Figure 9.3 are typical of those used to quantify technical difficulty. We will look at how these factors can be used later, but for the time being it is sufficient to note that the greater the level of uncertainty that is attached to the use or development of a particular technology, the larger the risk factor attached to it will be. It is never easy to assign the appropriate risk factor with a high level of confidence, but the rule is always to assign the highest risk factor within the range of uncertainty. Hence, if you could not decide what the technological difficulty was for a sub-system it should automatically be assigned the value 5, if you were using the scale in Figure 9.3.

Consequence of failure	Risk factor Rc
If the technology fails to provide the required performance, it will either: (1) Have no consequences for the success of the project, or it (2) Can be replaced by existing fully proven technology without adversely affecting performance, lead time or cost.	1
Failure of the technology will mean that an already tried and tested backup can be incorporated but with downgrading of the product specification.	2
If the technology fails, it is possible that a backup could be developed from existing technology	3
If the technology fails, new unfamiliar technology would have to be developed.	4
If the technology fails, there is no backup available, and the entire project would fail.	5

Figure 9.4 Consequence factors attributable to the results of technological failure

The assessment of technological difficulty must include an appraisal of all aspects of technology that influence each sub-system under consideration. In addition to the technology incorporated into electrical, electronic and mechanical elements, this would include the difficulty of providing the production systems, materials, etc. If incorporating all of these aspects of technology into a single sub-system means that it becomes too cumbersome for evaluation, then it will need to be spilt down into smaller sub-systems that are more meaningful in terms of risk.

Figure 9.4 shows factors that can be assigned when evaluating the consequences of failure to achieve the desired performance from a technological system. An overall factor (R) that incorporates Rd and Rc can be obtained from:

$$R = Rd \times Rc$$

The overall risk factor (R) will range from 1 (low technical difficulty with no consequences) to 25 (high degree of technical difficulty with no backup and severe consequences).

CASE STUDY 9.1

There are no golden rules for how a design should be divided into sub-system and interface elements at the start of the risk evaluation exercise. The number and size of the elements will depend upon the stage of product development, the number of identifiable sub-systems in the design, and the nature of the interfaces between them. Indeed, the process of identifying sub-systems and assessing them to see if they are sensible elements for risk evaluation is a vital part of locating technological risk. The best approach is to start with a broad-brush division of the design on functional lines. The following example, based on risk evaluation during the scheme stage of the intestinal stapler introduced in case study 6.1, illustrates some of the issues that need to be considered. Figure 9.5 shows the stapler. The overall size of the device is indicated by the 33 mm dimension which is applied to the body. All other dimensions are in proportion to this.

    The device essentially consists of a stepper motor (2) which rotates the reel (9). A cord which is not shown in the diagram is collected by the rotating reel and pulls the anvil (20) towards it. As the anvil moves towards the motor, the telescopic tube (14) 'collapses' and compresses the spring (18) so that, if required, the motor can be reversed causing the anvil to move away again. In the last few millimetres of movement of the anvil towards the motor, the internal thread (26) in the anvil engages on the threaded extension (10) of the reel, thereby providing a rigid mechanical location for the anvil when it compresses the tissue. When the anvil has reached a position where the intestinal tissue is held tightly in the gap between itself and the staple cartridge (7), the spring (5) is released thus driving the staples (8) through the tissue and into indentations in the anvil where the ends are crimped. At the same time that the staples are pushed through the tissue, a cylindrical knife

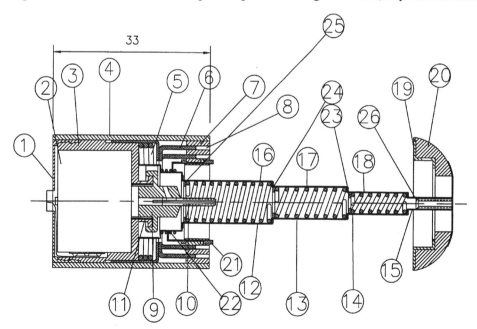

Figure 9.5 Scheme layout of a proposed intestinal stapler

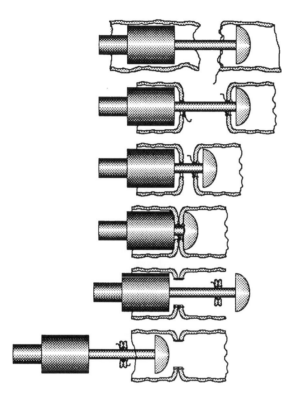

The two cut ends of intestine are pulled over the stapler body and anvil. The diagram shows the position when a `purse-string' suture has been put around one cut end.

With both ends purse-stringed, the suture is tightened to draw the tissue inward towards the stapler shaft.

The anvil is moved closer to the stapler body, bringing the inverted intestines closer together.

Taking care not to damage the tissue from overtightening, the tissue is compressed to ensure a `leak-proof joint after stapling.

The staples are driven through the tissue, and the knife trims the inner edge close to the staple line. The anvil is moved away from the stapler body to remove the force on the tissue and ease removal of the device.

The device is drawn back with the anvil passing through the stapled inverted tissue. The trimmed tissue ring is later examined to ensure that stapling was successful.

Figure 9.6   The stages of the stapling process

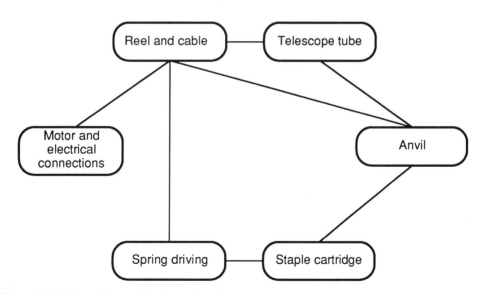

Figure 9.7   Relational diagram for the stapler sub-systems

trims off the inner edge close to the staples to minimise the amount of reduction to the inside diameter of the intestine. Figure 9.6 shows the stages of the stapling process.

To assess risk with this largely untried concept, the design was divided into six interconnecting assemblies as shown in Figure 9.7. These were:

1. Electric motor assembly including electrical and mechanical connections.
2. Reel and cable assembly.
3. Telescopic tube assembly including associated springs.
4. Anvil assembly.
5. Staple driving sub-assembly including spring and spring release.
6. Staple cartridge assembly including driver and knife.

The assemblies represent both individual components and small groups of components that provide a particular function. Care has been taken to include interfaces such as drive connections between motor and reel, and the threaded connection between the reel and the anvil. One way of exploring the presence of interfaces between the various assemblies is to draw a relational diagram that seeks to establish which assemblies influence or control others. Figure 9.7 shows such a diagram for the stapler concept.

Each of the lines in Figure 9.7 show that an interface is required between the two connected assemblies. Hence, a shaft drive is required between the motor and the reel, cable connections are required to the anvil, and a spring driving release mechanism is required for when the reel has taken in all of the cable. The provision of these interfaces must be considered in the risk evaluation chart either by stating them explicitly, or by incorporating them within the other sub-systems.

Figure 9.8 shows the risk assessment chart for the stapler concept. With the assemblies, sub-systems and interfaces incorporated into Figure 9.8, the next task is to decide upon the values to assign to the technical difficulty associated with each sub-system. The scale given in Figure 9.3 has been used for this purpose, and the numbers entered into the 'Difficulty' column reflect the team's assessment. When the team had finished identifying the difficulty factors, they used the consequences scale shown in Figure 9.4 to complete the next column. When making decisions about consequences, it is important not to be influenced by the associated difficulty. Consequence and difficulty are independent, and even when the difficulty of meeting the technical requirements is very low, the consequences of failure might be very high. This is illustrated in the case of the staples and staple cartridge. Failure to make this part of the concept work would have fatal consequences for the project, but the technology is a direct copy of that already existing on other products.

The 'Risk' column contains the product of the previous two, and provides a measure of the relative technical risks for the various parts of the concept. The values in this column could range from 1 to 25, although here they range from 3 to 15. In general, the risk factor will be higher during the early concept development stages than later, when more is known about problems that are being faced. The decision about what constitutes a significant risk is arbitrary because of the subjective nature of assigning difficulty and consequence ratings. However, the risk ranking that emerges from the chart provides the team with an understanding of danger points, and should lead to a close and ongoing management of the most obvious threats to project success. In this case, sub-systems where the risk factor

Assembly	Sub-system	Difficulty	Consequence	Risk	Notes	Staff
Electric motor	Motor	3	5	**15**	Can torque be provided?	A.J.K.
	Cabling	1	3	3	Requirements for sterilisation require watching.	A.J.K.
	Connections	2	3	6		G.P.W.
	Shaft fittings	2	2	4	OK but torque requirements need confirming.	G.P.W.
	Housing locations	2	3	6		G.P.W.
Reel and cable	Reel	4	3	**12**	Best materials still needs determining.	A.J.K.
	Cable	2	3	6		T.D.
	Cable attachments	2	3	6	Solution required to rapid release problem.	N.R
Telescopic tube	Tube segments	2	4	8		T.D.
	Tube location to body	2	3	6		T.D.
	Tube location to anvil	2	3	6	How to make robust?	T.D.
	Springs	2	4	8	Very tight space envelope. Pneumatic backup	T.D.
Anvil	Anvil	1	5	5	Standard technology.	T.D.
	Anvil case	2	4	8	Standard technology. Small space envelope.	A.J.K.
	Collection thread for reel extension	2	5	**10**	Strength calculations required	A.J.K.
Staple drive	Spring	2	4	8	Could use a motor if inadequate space.	N.R
	Spring housing	2	4	8		N.R
	Release mechanism	3	5	**15**	Requires detail design to establish feasibility.	N.R
Staple cartridge	Staples	1	5	5	Standard technology	G.P.W.
	Staple cartridge	1	5	5	Standard technology	G.P.W.
	Staple driver	2	4	8	Modification to standard technology	G.P.W.
	Knife and location	1	5	5	Standard technology	G.P.W.

Figure 9.8 Risk evaluation chart for the surgical stapling concept

has reached double figures were highlighted, and attracted particularly close scrutiny and extensive design effort to reduce the risk as soon as possible.

RISK ASSESSMENT

Having identified the existence of technology and market risk factors, and completed the assignment of probability and consequence factors, there remains the task of deciding what to do about them. The risk map shown in Figure 9.9 provides a useful way of plotting overall risk factors in order to justify actions that need to be taken. The figure represents a 'Boston' matrix where the probability of failure is the vertical axis, and consequences or severity of failure is the horizontal axis. The bottom left hand corner represents a factor of 1 for both probability and severity, while the top right hand corner represents the maximum rating available from both of these criteria. Particular risks can then be marked onto the matrix with a symbol to indicate its position in regard to both criteria. Clearly, the nearer a particular risk is to the top right hand corner, the more closely it needs to be managed. Three zones are marked upon the matrix with different shading. Although these zones are arbitrary in the sense that they do not comply with any national or international standard, they indicate that the probability and severity associated with some risks will make it essential that they are eliminated, either by reducing their probability or severity, or both. In general, the objective will be to move risks towards the bottom left hand corner of the matrix whenever possible. The matrix provides a useful design review tool to enable the project team to keep an eye on outstanding risk issues, and to monitor whether unacceptable risks are being mitigated.

One of the areas of risk management which causes major problems is that of the transfer of risk ownership. As a product passes through the PDP certain risks will be passed from one owner to another. This progression of ownership is inevitable, as personnel with different skills become lead players at different stages of the project. Transfer of ownership is fraught with danger because of the likelihood of the misunderstanding of problems and the mitigation objectives. Careful management of the process of ownership change is essential if these potential problems are to be avoided.

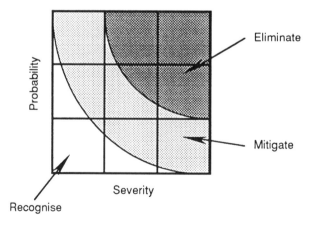

Figure 9.9   Risk mapping

CONTROLLING RISK

Assessing and controlling risks is a management issue. From the manager's point of view, the basic objectives should be as follows:

- involve the key players early;
- commence at project conception;
- identify the risks (difficulties and consequences);
- ensure that each risk has an 'owner';
- classify and assess the risks;
- use cost/benefit analysis to justify risk mitigation decisions.

Although the identification and quantification of risk through the construction of risk assessment charts is a good step towards the removal of unpleasant surprises downstream, it does not by itself make the problem go away. In general, the outcome of research and development programmes is particularly difficult to predict, and that means that they are a source of risk within the PDP process. Whenever possible, product design should build on research programmes that have already been completed. This in turn means that research should be an ongoing strategic activity, not something that is seen as a short-term tactic to solve an immediate problem. Of course, this tactical role of research will always be present to some extent, but it should be avoided wherever possible. The corollary of this is that designers should use existing technology and standard parts unless this proves impossible. This, as can be understood from the risk assessment chart is particularly important where the consequences of failure are significant. On this basis, a useful maxim is to limit new untried technology to sub-systems where there is a proven readily available alternative solution. Having a backup is essential when the consequences of failure are anything other than a 1 or 2 on the Figure 9.4 scale and the difficulty rating is anything other than a 1. This becomes crucial when the project has a tight schedule because there may be insufficient time to set about searching for an escape route.

The higher the risk factor, the more important it is to model and test the proposed solution. Although layouts, detail schemes and even simulations may look convincing on the CAD system, they can rarely be tested sufficiently to examine all of the possible problems that they might carry. The only way to be sure is to provide and test physical models to evaluate for all aspects of performance. Of course, in large expensive systems, the provision of complete prototypes may be excessively expensive, but sub-systems with high risk factors should always be physically modelled as soon as possible. A second benefit of physical modelling can be the opportunities that it provides for customer feedback. Therefore, the model not only clarifies the technical risk, but also tests whether the customer or market like it, thereby helping to establish if there is any element of market risk in the solution that is being proposed.

RECAP

Continuously throughout the PDP, decisions have to be made about which of several choices should be adopted for development. In part, this decision will be made by comparing the attributes of the alternatives with the requirements stated in the PDS, and such decisions may be made easier by the application of techniques like the evaluation matrices described in Chapter 8. An additional factor that must be considered during the selection process is the risk attached to each of the alternative development projects. This project risk assessment should consider both market and technology risk, and each of these involves estimating the probability and consequences of failure.

The method described in this chapter encourages design team members to reach an understanding of the difficulty and consequence factors for each option at their disposal. This understanding enables them to rank the risks and focus their efforts on reducing the most severe. In general, project risks will be high during the early stages of the PDP, but will decrease as effort is applied to developing solutions to problems.

ASSIGNMENT

Assignment 9.1

No two groups of designers will evaluate technical difficulty and the associated consequences in the same way. This is because each group will bring their own knowledge and experience to the problem. Whilst one group may have extensive experience in solving the type of problems being considered, another group might have little or no experience. Because of their experience, the first group may be able to see a clear way through the problems, and be able to identify good back-up technologies in case things go wrong. The second group may not be able (at least initially) to see the way forward so clearly. For the second group, the project will carry a greater risk than for the first. The way that you assess the elements of risk for a particular set of design problems will depend on the experience that you are able to bring to the project. Because of this, your answer to the following assignment will be completely personal. If you are able to attempt the assignment with one or more others, each will also bring his or her own experiences and ideas, with the strong possibility that the risks will be identified more clearly.

Your company is a medium-sized engineering concern, with a good reputation for providing high quality joy-stick controls for military and civil aircraft. The company is a member of a larger group with diverse engineering interests. For some time, the board of directors of your company have been holding discussions with one of the major international suppliers of computer games equipment with a view to supplying them with joy-sticks to assemble into their products. Although a contract has not yet been signed, your board have been informed that a letter of intent will be forthcoming.

The customer will require in the region of 200,000 joy-sticks each year for an initial period of three years. These are quantities that are way above anything that your company has had to deal with in the past, and a new project manager was employed two months ago to oversee the product design, pre-development, project definition, planning, and budgeting phases.

To cope with the production of the new product, your board have decided to convert an on-site warehouse that is currently standing idle, and to install production facilities and an automated assembly line. Three project teams have been formed under the control of the new project manager. These are: (1) building refurbishment and services, (2) manufacturing systems design and installation, (3) product design. An overall budget of £3 million has been sanctioned by the group board.

List the technological and market risks for this project, stating any assumptions that you feel are necessary. Select and apply probability and consequence factors to the risks and complete a risk evaluation chart. Draw a risk map of the type shown in Figure 9.9, and say how you might eliminate or mitigate some of the risks that you have identified.

This assignment has been designed to give you some experience of thinking about the choice of difficulty and consequence factors. In addition, it makes you think about how the risk evaluation method can be applied to issues other than the solution of detail design problems. You will need to produce a slightly modified version of the risk evaluation chart to take account of this fact. Instead of having the 'assembly' and 'sub-system' columns, you will need to have one identified as 'risk description'.

TEN
VALUE ANALYSIS AND ENGINEERING

OVERVIEW

This chapter introduces a systematic method by which changes can be incorporated in the product that will attract more sales and/or greater profits. This is done by seeking to improve the value of the product and, in particular, ensuring that the product offers the potential customer better value than competitor products. After giving the theoretical basis for **value analysis**, a systematic approach is introduced to the tasks of defining function and other value attributes, breaking down material and manufacturing costs between components, and producing value analysis matrices as a precursor to taking appropriate design decisions.

OBJECTIVES

After studying this chapter you should be able to:

- determine the features of a product that make it attractive to a potential buyer;
- take a list of product components and sub-assemblies, and assign manufacturing costs to these elements;
- decide how each component/sub-assembly contributes to the desirable features of the product;
- allocate a manufacturing/material cost to each desirable feature;
- evaluate the feature/cost information to assess value for money;
- propose means by which value can be improved;
- conduct a value study on existing and proposed products.

VALUE AND THE CUSTOMER

The principal objective of manufacturing companies is to produce and sell products in order to make profit. The ability to attract a sufficient number of product purchases is basic to this aim, and to this end it is essential that the customers are offered a product that they consider to be 'good value'.

174

In everyday speech, 'good value' has a number of different meanings. If you are shopping for oranges on the market, the stall that offers the oranges at the lowest price is sometimes said to be offering good value or value for money. What is implied here is that the oranges are cheap in comparison with the offer price at other stalls. However, you might decide not to buy from the stall offering the lowest price if the oranges were obviously of low quality. If the price was low but the oranges were rotten, you might decide that the stall was not offering good value at all, and take your business somewhere else.

For the purpose of the value engineering method, the word 'value' implies that a judgement is being made on the balance between product cost and the desirable features that are being offered to the customer. The concept of value relates the useful features of a product to the cost of producing these features. Let us take a closer look at what this means, and what the implications are.

The only important factors influencing the sale or potential sales of a product are those that the customer can observe and evaluate. These include the functions that the product offers at purchase, long term features like reliability, and the cost of purchase. The product's functions are usually observable at the point of sale, but other features only become evident when the product is used. From the example of the oranges which was introduced earlier, the customer might be persuaded to buy because of the colour, size, and feel of the orange. However repeat purchases might be affected by the taste, texture, amount of juice, etc. These features will be influenced by things like time of harvesting, the type and timing of the fertiliser given to the tree, use of herbicides and insecticides etc. However, the customer is not directly concerned by these issues, only by their effect upon the features that are valued in the product. Hence the stall holder's sign advertises 'sweet juicy oranges', not 'well fertilised oranges'. The same observations are equally true for products that have been produced by engineering processes.

Someone who is thinking about buying a portable cassette player is likely to be much more interested in such features as the on/off switch, automatic reverse, forward/reverse tape drive, normal/CrO_2 switching, belt clip, battery charge indication etc., than they are about the engineering details and processes that provide the features. The engineering team might be justifiably proud of a new tape transport mechanism that controls tape tension, but the customer will only be concerned with sound quality and the expectation that the product does not damage tapes.

In a value analysis study it is only those features that the customer defines as important that we need to be concerned about. Indeed it is most important that **only** the customer (perhaps via the marketing department) provides this list of requirements, and not the engineering team that has been involved with designing the product. Let us get the idea of customer requirements firmly established by using a case study.

CASE STUDY 10.1

In this case study I am using a familiar consumer product as the subject. The reason for this is that I want you to concentrate on the desirable features from the user's point of view. I **could** have chosen an industrial product, but it would have been much more difficult to choose something that everyone was familiar with. My example is the metal hand held torch shown disassembled in Figure 10.1.

Identifying the Functions

Ask yourself what functions you want and expect when you buy a torch like the one shown. Of course, the primary requirement is to produce a beam of light, but there are other important requirements as well. For example, you might list the following:

- ability to turn on and off
- ability to replace batteries
- ability to replace bulb.

If the designer of the torch had forgotten to provide the means of providing these functions, you might be forgiven for thinking that the torch was a poor design and that you would not buy it. Actually, there are many more functions that this torch provides for the user in addition to the ones already identified. Frequently, you can identify additional functions by asking what particular components or sub-assemblies on the product do. For example, what is the glass disc in front of the bulb for. It is certainly not necessary for any of the four functions that have already been identified; the bulb could be extracted and replaced more easily if the glass disc was not there. Of course, the disc is there to **protect** the bulb, and this is yet another 'function' that we might value and expect. Carrying on our search for functions, we might add 'hang the torch on a hook', because this function is provided by the loop on the end cap. If you look closely, you might also see a small button on the switch assembly. Like many torches, this one has been given a facility for flashing the light on and off—yet another function that someone might like.

In examining a product to identify its user-valued functions you should be careful. It is easy (particularly for engineers) to identify vital elements as functions in their own right. As an example, you could look at the component that the bulb fits in and identify 'hold bulb' as an important function. However, this would be a mistake; a potential customer would expect the bulb to be held as a matter of course, and would not choose to buy a particular brand of torch on the basis of this consideration. Let us make a final list of the desirable functions that this torch seems to provide for the user.

Figure 10.1 An electric torch has many functions in addition to 'provide light beam'

- provide light beam
- switch on and off
- replace batteries
- replace bulb
- flash the beam
- protect the bulb
- hang on hook.

Can you think of some additional functions that might influence someone to buy the product. On the other hand, if you disagree with some of the functions that I have identified, this is OK. After all, like practically all design methodologies, value engineering is about thinking through important issues yourself and being able to argue your corner.

ASSIGNMENT 10.1

Most of the following list of products can be found in the home. See if you can get your hands on several of them (the more the better), and write down what you think is the most important function that a potential purchaser would value. Next, list as many other user-valued functions as you can. I will not call functions in this additional list 'secondary functions' because some of them might be just as important as the first function that you identified. Having made the list as exhaustive as you can, make a study of the component parts of the product and try to decide which function or functions each component contributes to. If you find a component that does not seem to contribute to the provision of any of the identified functions, it probably means that you have failed to identify a user-valued function. Here is the list:

- fountain pen
- stapling machine
- opener for food cans (any one of the various types available)

THE COMPONENT/FUNCTION RELATIONSHIP

The next stage of the value analysis process is to decide which user-valued function or functions each component contributes to. In a majority of cases, a component will be found to contribute to more than one function. If, as I hope, you have attempted assignment 10.1, try to decide to how many of the user-valued functions the cap of the pen contributes. My reckoning is that it is involved with at least three. What do you think?

Determining the contribution of individual components to function is not always easy, but asking the following questions usually help:

- 'Would removal of the component be detrimental to the provision of the function?': This needs asking for every possible component/function pairing.
- 'Has manufacturing or material cost been incurred in the production of a component so that it may contribute to the provision of the function?' Again this needs to be asked for all component/function pairings.

If, for any component/function pair, the answer to one or both of these questions is 'yes', then it almost certainly means that the component does contribute to the provision of the function. To ensure that every possible component/function pair is evaluated, a useful technique is to produce a chart which lists the combinations, and explains the interaction between them. You will see an example of a component/function interaction chart in case study 10.2.

ATTRIBUTING COST

With the component/function interactions settled, the next stage of the value analysis process is to divide the cost of producing a component between the functions that it contributes to. In some cases, it will be so difficult to attribute costs in this way that the only way forward will be to divide the component cost equally between the associated functions. However, wherever possible an attempt should be made to differentiate the manufacturing processes and material costs in proportions that reflect their contributions to functionality.

Let us take the pen cap example. The one that I am looking at has a steel tube with a small ridge on the inner diameter to help it snap onto the pen body, a spring clip for securing it into a pocket, and an internal plastic sleeve that fits around the end of the pen to minimise ink drying and leakage. The steel tube also has a small extension at the closed end which is used for securing the clip. The company that manufactures the cap will have access to information on the overall cost of manufacturing it, and a detailed breakdown that can be used to determine the cost of manufacturing each individual feature (like the ridge, sleeve, extension etc.). Since each feature is there to serve a function, it is possible to estimate the total cost of providing the feature necessary for each function on this component. Again, case study 10.2 shows how this can be done through a cost attribution chart.

At this point, you may have some questions to ask about my definition of 'component'. Your pen cap, like mine, may be made up from several parts. Surely, it must be incorrect to call the cap a component when there are several constituent parts? The answer to this question is that value analysis can be carried out at any hierarchical level within the product, depending upon what the objectives are. If the spring clip, plastic sleeve, and steel tube are defined as components, and the study is carried out at that level, then the results are likely to be concerned with improvements to the value of these components. If the objective is to improve the value of the cap as a whole, then the cap requires defining as a component as has been done here. In this case, it is quite possible that the result will be to remove or modify some or all of the constituent parts from which the cap is assembled.

THE VALUE ANALYSIS MATRIX

The next stage of the value analysis process is to prepare the matrix. This matrix is the main tool used to present information on the cost of providing each of the user-valued functions. Figure 10.2 shows a typical value analysis matrix before any data is added.

PRODUCT .... DATE ....
DRAWING NUMBER .... ORIGINATOR ....
HIERARCHICAL LEVEL .... APPROVED ....

Components \ Functions									Component cost (£)	Component cost (%)
Function cost (£)										
Function cost (%)										100

Figure 10.2 The value analysis matrix

The names of the components in the product will be entered in the column on the extreme left of the matrix, whilst the user-valued functions will be entered in the top row. The two columns at the extreme right receive the individual component cost data in the form of monetary units of cost to produce, and as a percentage of the total cost for the product. After completion of the component/function interaction and cost allocation charts, the contribution of appropriate proportions of each component's cost to the functions can be entered into the value analysis matrix. The total cost of providing each function and the percentage of the total cost that this represents can then be entered into the two bottom rows. Finally, the information provided in the completed matrix can be used to guide the design team in their attempts to improve product value.

CASE STUDY 10.2

Figure 10.3 shows a photograph of a beam compass being used to produce large radii curves on a drawing board. Attached to the beam are two mounting pieces, one to hold the point, the other to hold the pencil lead. It is these attachments that are the focus of this case study. The attachments have the following easily defined functions: (a) To hold the point or pencil, (b) to slide along the beam when required, (c) to lock onto the beam securely when required, (d) to guarantee good alignment between the point and pencil. All of these functions are necessary for the functioning of the beam compass, but (a), (b), and (c) are fundamental and may hence be defined as primary functions. Figure 10.4 shows a close up of the attachments, and two views (one sectional) of the attachment mounted on the beam.

Figure 10.3 A beam compass being used to draw large circles

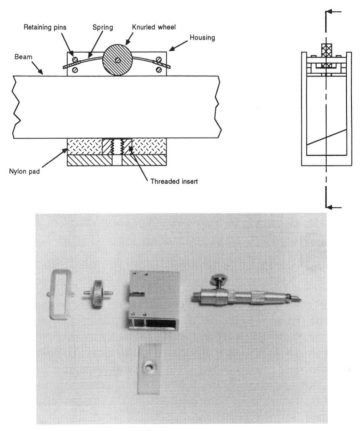

Figure 10.4 Details of the beam compass attachments

In total there are nine components:

Description	Quantity	Cost (£)
Knurled wheel	1	0.20
Knurled wheel shaft	1	0.10
Spring	1	0.30
Retaining pin	4	0.10
Housing	1	1.15
Nylon pad with threaded insert	1	0.18
	Total cost:	2.03

In addition, there is an assembly cost of £0.30 per attachment.

The company that designs and sells the beam compass makes 6000 pairs of attachments per year for sale around the world.

The flat spring that fits over the top of the knurled wheel shaft ensures that the wheel is pressed down firmly against the beam. In this state, the beam, which is a close fit within the housing, is forced into contact with the nylon pad. The pad is tapered from side to side so that the force from the spring pushes the beam into one of the inner side walls of the housing. The attachment is therefore located closely on the beam so that alignment is assured. The position of the attachment on the beam can be changed by using the thumb to rotate the knurled wheel. Although there is no positive locking mechanism, the force that is required to pull it along without the use of the knurled wheel is sufficiently high to make accidental movement possible but unlikely. When the attachment is pulled off the beam for storage, the spring is held in position by the retaining pins. The point or pencil lead are gripped in small holders which screw into the threaded insert in the nylon pad. A hole in the bottom of the housing provides access to the thread. Assembly consists of the following stages:

1. Press the two lower retaining pins into the pre-drilled holes in the housing.
2. Press the knurled wheel onto its shaft.
3. Drop the shaft and wheel into position in the housing.
4. Place the spring over the top of the wheel and shaft.
5. Press the two upper retaining pins into position.
6. Place the nylon pad into the bottom of the housing and screw the holder into position.

Figure 10.5 shows the value analysis matrix with the prime information entered.

The next value analysis stage is to decide the functions that each component contributes to. This task must be undertaken carefully. A useful approach is to ask whether a particular function would be impaired if a component was removed. Figure 10.6 presents a component/function chart which records the interactions.

Based upon the component/function chart, ticks are entered into the value analysis matrix as shown in Figure 10.7.

The next stage of the process is frequently the most difficult. This requires the total manufacturing cost of each component to be divided between the functions that depend upon it. This cost assignment depends on the cost of manufacturing required to achieve each function, together with some measure of the proportional material cost. It is essential

	Hold pencil or point	Slide along beam	Lock onto beam	Provide good alignment	Hold parts together	Cost (£)	Cost (%)
Knurled wheel						0.15	7
Knurled wheel shaft						0.02	1
Spring						0.20	10
Retaining pin						0.06	3
Housing						1.15	55
Nylon pad with insert						0.22	10
Assembly						0.30	14
Total cost (£)						2.10	
Cost (%)							

Figure 10.5 Component cost data entered onto the value analysis matrix

to approach this task in an organised and methodological way if confusion is to be avoided. The technique required involves considering the manufacturing steps through which a component has been put, and deciding which function or functions each step contributes to. The cost of each step may then be divided between the related functions. If the product or some of its component parts are manufactured in-house then it is probable that the costs for each manufacturing step will be available and reliable. In cases where components are bought out, or where an analysis is being carried out on a competitor's product, estimates based upon experience will have to be made.

Only that portion of the component cost that is concerned with manufacturing can be dealt with in the way described. Material, which is the other element of prime cost requires a different treatment. Here, the two issues are **material bulk** and **characteristics requirement**.

Material Bulk

If a single component supports two or more functions, and part of its bulk can be identified with individual functions, then the material cost should be divided between those functions in the same proportions as the amount of material in each associated volume of the component. An example of a component where this sort of discrimination works is the hypodermic syringe for insulin injection shown in Figure 10.8. The body of the syringe is made from a one piece thermoplastic moulding. Two major functions that this component contributes to are: (a) provide temporary drug storage and, (b) facilitate injection. The first of these is provided for by the material in the straight cylindrical portion, whilst the second is provided for by the finger pads. The ratio of material volumes for these two elements is 5:1, so the total material cost for the component of £0.04 is divided in the same

Component	Function	Interaction
Knurled wheel	Hold pencil/point	None. Removal would not affect this function.
Knurled wheel shaft		None. Removal would not affect this function.
Spring		None. Removal would not affect this function.
Retaining pin		None. Removal would not affect this function.
Housing		Pencil/point holder depends upon this for location.
Nylon pad with insert		Pencil/point holder depends upon this for securing.
Assembly		Housing and nylon pad require assembly.
Knurled wheel	Slide along beam	Used to propel the attachment along the beam.
Knurled wheel shaft		Locates the wheel and provide bearing surfaces.
Spring		Provides traction between wheel and beam.
Retaining pin		The upper pins provide reaction for the spring.
Housing		Location for wheel shaft, retaining pins, and nylon pad.
Nylon pad with insert		Low friction for beam, and sideways reaction force.
Assembly		All components involved require assembly.
Knurled wheel	Lock onto beam	Transmits force from spring to beam.
Knurled wheel shaft		Transmits force from spring to wheel
Spring		Force to resist accidental movement of attachment.
Retaining pin		The upper pins provide reaction for the spring.
Housing		Location for wheel shaft, retaining pins, and nylon pad.
Nylon pad with insert		Sideways reaction force.
Assembly		All components involved require assembly.
Knurled wheel	Provide alignment	Transmits force from spring to beam.
Knurled wheel shaft		Transmits force from spring to wheel.
Spring		Force for positive location of beam in attachment.
Retaining pin		The upper pins provide reaction for the spring.
Housing		Location for wheel shaft, retaining pins, and nylon pad.
Nylon pad with insert		Sideways reaction force.
Assembly		All components involved require assembly.
Knurled wheel	Secures parts	None. Removal would not affect this function.
Knurled wheel shaft		None. Removal would not affect this function.
Spring		Holds wheel and wheel shaft in position.
Retaining pin		Hold spring in position.
Housing		Maintains components in position.
Nylon pad with insert		None. Removal would not affect this function.
Assembly		All components involved require assembly.

Figure 10.6 Component/function interaction chart for the beam compass attachment

	Hold pencil or point	Slide along beam	Lock onto beam	Provide good alignment	Hold parts together	Cost (£)	Cost (%)
Knurled wheel		√	√	√		0.15	7
Knurled wheel shaft		√	√	√		0.02	1
Spring		√	√	√	√	0.20	10
Retaining pin		√	√	√	√	0.06	3
Housing	√	√	√	√	√	1.15	55
Nylon pad with insert	√	√	√	√	√	0.22	10
Assembly	√	√	√	√	√	0.30	14
Total cost (£)						2.10	
Cost (%)							

Figure 10.7 The value analysis matrix with interactions identified

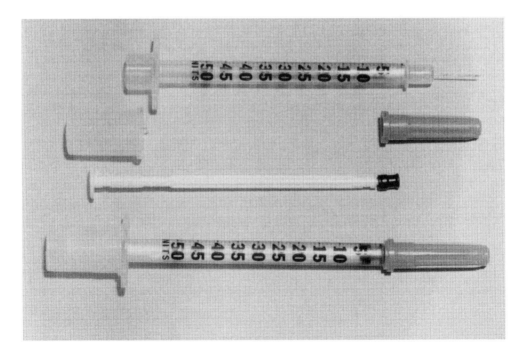

Figure 10.8 Material bulk analysis applied to a hypodermic syringe

ratio between the two functions. i.e. £0.008 to facilitate injection, and £0.032 to provide temporary drug storage. In cases where this sort of functional discrimination cannot be made, the material bulk costs are divided equally between all of the functions involved with the component.

Material Characteristics

In the case of some multi-functional components, it is only one of the functions that drives the specification of the material. The handle of an electrical screwdriver has to: (a) provide a good grip and, (b) provide electrical insulation as its principal functions. Whilst a wide range of cheap materials could be used if function (a) was the only requirement, the addition of function (b) requires the specification of a slightly more expensive material. In this case, if (a) was the only function, the material cost per handle would be £0.12, but to satisfy function (b) a material cost of £0.15 must be incurred. This additional cost of £0.03 must be assigned entirely to function (b). Hence, the material characteristic costs of the two functions are:

(a)   Cost to provide a good grip = £0.12 ÷ 2 = £0.06

(b)   Cost of provide electrical insulation = £0.06 + £0.03 = £0.09

Once again, if the material characteristics requirements are the same for each function, the cost is divided equally between them.

   The chart in Figure 10.9 shows a way of organising the process of breaking down component costs between functions, taking into consideration the manufacturing and material issues introduced. Two of the components from the beam compass are considered.

			Hold pencil or point	Slide along beam	Lock onto beam	Provide good alignment	Hold parts together
Housing	1.15	Manufacturing	0.75	0.05	0.20	0.20	0.20	0.10
		Material	0.40	0.08	0.08	0.08	0.08	0.08
		Cost per function		0.13	0.28	0.28	0.28	0.18
Nylon pad with insert	0.22	Manufacturing	0.08	0.04	0.01	0.01	0.01	0.01
		Material	0.14	0.02	0.06	0.02	0.02	0.02
		Cost per function		0.06	0.07	0.03	0.03	0.03

Figure 10.9   A breakdown of function/cost on the basis of manufacturing and materials

Housing

The overall cost of £1.15 for the housing splits £0.75 to manufacturing, and £0.40 to material. None of the functions are more demanding of material specification than the others so, in this case, the material cost is divided equally between them. Manufacturing cost is divided between the functions on the basis of the cost of the steps involved.

Hold pencil or point

The only manufacturing step required to meet this function is the drilling and finishing of a hole in the base of the housing. Out of a total manufacturing cost of £0.75, this operation is estimated to cost £0.05 by the production engineering department.

Slide along beam

Several machining steps on the housing are involved in the provision of this function. These steps include the provision of: two slots in which the knurled wheel shaft rests; small chamfers on the edges of the slots; two through-holes for the upper retaining pins; and the provision of a highly polished surface on the inside faces. Although these steps are also required to support other functions, a distribution of the operation costs totals £0.02 for this function.

Lock onto beam and provide good alignment

Same as for 'slide along beam'.

Hold parts together

The apportioned cost of drilling the holes for the retaining pins provides a total cost for this function of £0.10

Nylon Pad With Insert

The overall cost of £0.22 is divided £0.08 to manufacturing, and £0.14 to material. Of the manufacturing cost, it is estimated that 50% is associated with the provision of the threaded insert. The remaining cost of manufacturing operations is divided equally between the remaining functions. Only the requirement for the attachment to slide easily along the beam sets the need for anything other than the most basic material specification. The additional material cost to provide this functionality is £0.04 per component, with the remaining £0.10 being divided equally between all five functions.

Division of the manufacturing and material costs between the functions permits a cost per function to be calculated as shown in Figure 10.9. Repeating this procedure for each component in the attachment provides cost per function data that can be entered into the value analysis matrix as shown in Figure 10.10.

In addition to the entry of the cost per function data, the total cost per function has been calculated by summing the individual costs in each column. Finally, the cost of each function as a percentage of the total attachment cost is presented in the bottom row. As a check on the arithmetic, the sum of the total costs per function should give the total attachment cost of £2.10.

The information presented in the value analysis matrix enables the design team to evaluate the effectiveness with which the manufacturing and material costs are being used to provide the product's functionality. Although, in part, this evaluation is always intuitive, there are a number of questions that the team can ask in an attempt to identify problems and possibilities. Although different companies develop their own questioning strategies, the following are useful and quite typical:

- Do the percentage costs assigned to each function seem reasonable in terms of their worth to the customer?
- Do any of the components contribute an excessively large proportion of any function's total cost?
- Can any function be eliminated?
- Can any component be eliminated?
- Can any components be combined?
- Can a cheaper specification of the same material be used?
- Can a different material be used?
- Can waste material be reduced?
- Can any tolerances be relaxed?
- Can any cheaper finishes be used?
- Can any special part be replaced by a standard?
- Can another process make it at a lower cost?
- Can someone else supply the components at a lower cost?

	Hold pencil or point	Slide along beam	Lock onto beam	Provide good alignment	Hold parts together	Cost (£)	Cost (%)
Knurled wheel		0.09	0.03	0.03		0.15	7
Knurled wheel shaft		0.01	0.005	0.005		0.02	1
Spring		0.05	0.05	0.05	0.05	0.20	10
Retaining pin		0.01	0.02	0.01	0.02	0.06	3
Housing	0.13	0.28	0.28	0.28	0.18	1.15	55
Nylon pad with insert	0.06	0.07	0.03	0.03	0.03	0.22	10
Assembly	0.06	0.06	0.06	0.06	0.06	0.30	14
Total cost (£)	0.25	0.57	0.475	0.465	0.34	2.10	
Cost (%)	12	27	23	22	16		100

Figure 10.10 The completed value analysis matrix for the beam compass attachment

Bearing these questions in mind, but not forgetting to use an intuitive approach, let us see what we can make of the beam compass attachment matrix. The first thing that you might notice is that 'slide along beam' and 'lock onto beam' together account for 50% of the cost of the attachment. All of the components in the assembly are used to provide what are essentially simple functions, and the question 'are all these parts and their associated cost essential' must be asked. For example, the knurled wheel contributes £0.09 (16%) to the cost of the 'slide along beam' function. Could this cost be reduced by removing or redesigning this component? In the case of the two functions already identified, plus 'provide good alignment', the housing cost contributes almost 50% or over. Reduction in the cost of this component would have a major influence on reducing the cost of providing the three functions. In addition, the function 'hold parts together' accounts for 16% of the total. It might be worthwhile asking if this function needs to be provided at all. Only the marketing people could determine the correct answer to this question, but it might turn out that the company would do better to sell a cheaper attachment without this function, or invest the £0.34 into providing better functionality elsewhere.

The attachment comprises nine components, and it may be beneficial to investigate whether some of these could be combined to provide acceptable functionality at a lower cost. In addition to having the potential to reduce the cost of manufacturing components, such a step would almost certainly lead to a reduction in assembly cost which, at present, accounts for 14% of the total. Because the parts are assembled into the housing, it might be worth considering if they can be combined with the housing, or with each other prior to assembly.

Clearly, some of the design decisions that have to be taken will depend on the quantities that are required. In the design shown in Figure 10.4 the use of metal cutting predominates, with the addition of pressing for the spring, and injection moulding for the nylon pad and its insert. If a way could be found of producing a one-piece housing incorporating some of the other components, cost might be reduced. Thermoplastic, possibly a grade of nylon, could be attractive because of its strength and low friction properties. Indeed, a simple moulded or extruded box section might be used to replace the housing, nylon pad, and retaining pins, if a way could be found to control sliding and locking. Of course, there are other important issues to consider other than the pure functionality of the attachment. One of these is whether the 'solid' well engineered appearance of the current design provides esteem value to the people who use it, and if so, how important this is to sales. Clearly, there would be no point in making a cheaper product with the same functionality, if its appearance and 'implied quality' made potential customers go elsewhere. The correct course of action might be any one of the following:

- Modify the existing design.
- Produce a completely new design for the current and additional market segments. Drop the old design.
- Produce a completely new design for new market segments. Maintain the old design in its current or modified form for the existing market segment.

What is the right answer? It all depends on how the market would respond, and which option would produce more profits for the company. Figure 10.11 shows an alternative attachment design that might come out of the value analysis study that we have just completed.

Figure 10.11   A different approach to the beam compass design

VALUE ENGINEERING OR VALUE ANALYSIS?

While value analysis is concerned with the application of value improvement techniques to existing products, value engineering applies the principles during the product concept phase. Essentially, the objectives, the information that is required, the charting procedures, and the questions that need to be asked are the same in both cases. The most obvious difference is the availability of the information, and the **form** in which it will be available.

Design teams can undertake value analysis studies on their own products and those of their competitors. Indeed, value analysis is a very useful tool for benchmarking competitor products. The main problem with this is that precise figures on the cost of producing individual components will not be available, and it will be necessary for the design team to use their experience in assigning overall costs, and costs to component features. In some cases, the problems associated with assigning costs can be reduced by deciding to express costs as percentages rather than in units of currency. However, despite and even because of the difficulties involved, the need to conduct an in-depth study of the competitor's product can be highly beneficial to understanding its strengths and weaknesses.

It should be the objective of all design teams to be well informed about the requirements of the customer. The process of building functional, quality, and price-related requirements into a new design must commence from the earliest stage of the PDP if costly redesign and project delays are to be avoided. Getting the balance of functionality and cost correct is vital for product success, and is an issue that the value approach can assist with.

During the early stages of the PDP there are likely to be many design options to be considered and evaluated. By relating the functionality of each design option to what is known of its constituent parts, a value approach can be used to assess strengths and weaknesses. This activity will require preliminary costings to be carried out on sub-systems of the overall design. This necessity to study cost implications during the concept development phase forces the design team to think clearly about the function/cost relationships in their design proposals so that nasty surprises are less likely to occur later. Uncertainty about costs and the means of achieving certain functions should not be used as an excuse for not attempting a value engineering approach during the earliest stages of the PDP. Giving the study your best shot helps to focus the mind on exactly what is known and what is still uncertain or unknown. Addressing these uncertainties, and running a value engineering study alongside a project risk analysis can prove invaluable when making concept related decisions.

LIMITATIONS TO THE VALUE METHOD

In many products the customer puts great value on product attributes that are difficult to cost in the way described. For example, implied quality might, for some people, be the paramount attribute that a particular product carries with it. Car manufacturers like BMW, Rolls Royce, and Mercedes have built their companies image on high Quality over the years. In the field of domestic products, AEG also sell their products on the Quality ticket. In the case of products from companies like these, the implied Quality issue may be more important than the availability of usage functions. However, the cost of Quality for each product, or the cost of Quality in each component is very difficult to determine, and is not easily dealt with in the value method described.

Other user-valued attributes like aesthetics are also difficult to deal with. In consumer products like hi-fi systems, automobiles, and kitchen appliances, aesthetics are at least as important as functionality in attracting people to buy. In some cases, aesthetic appeal can be listed as a function in the value analysis matrix, and the cost of providing the aesthetic attributes of (say) the hi-fi housing and controls apportioned. The problem is to separate the purely aesthetic cost from the cost of producing the basic housing, which would be required anyway to support other functions. Regardless of these problems, the principal objective of the value study would be to determine if the company was putting a reasonable proportion of the product's prime cost into providing an acceptable level of aesthetic appeal, either in absolute terms or in comparison with major competitors.

RECAP

The way that the customer perceives the value of a product is a major contributory factor in making the decision of whether to purchase it or not. Hence, it is vital that the design team actively considers value throughout the PDP. The principles of value study are equally applicable at the early or late stages of the PDP, and may be used both prior to (value engineering), and after (value analysis) a prototype or production version of the product is available. Value principles may also be applied in the benchmarking of competitor products to help establish reasons for market success or failure.

The method involves the assignment of manufacturing and material costs to each of the functions that the customer values. This enables the cost of producing each function to be calculated. The function/cost data enables the design team to see if the cost of producing the product is being shared between the functions in a way that makes sense in terms of their relative importance. The value analysis matrix also helps the team to answer questions about the means by which cost could be reduced without decreasing value, or whether value could be enhanced.

ASSIGNMENT 10.2

Figure 10.12 provides details of a treasury tag punch. The punch is used to place a single hole near the corner of sheets of paper so that they can be secured together by the treasury tag. Other than for the fact of punching only one hole, this product is similar in functionality and construction to a normal two-hole punch. When disassembled, the product is found to be made up of 10 separate components although, as a part of the manufacturing process, the base and support bracket are riveted together.

Assume that this product is manufactured by a competitor company, and that you have been given the task of benchmarking it. Your marketing department have provided you with a list of functions that customers value, together with an assessment of the importance of each function to the buyer. This information is given in Figure 10.13.

Your production engineering department have made a list of each component and using their experience have estimated the manufacturing cost of each. They have also assigned elements of component cost to each of the user-valued functions on the list provided by the marketing department. This information is provided in Figures 10.14 and 10.15.

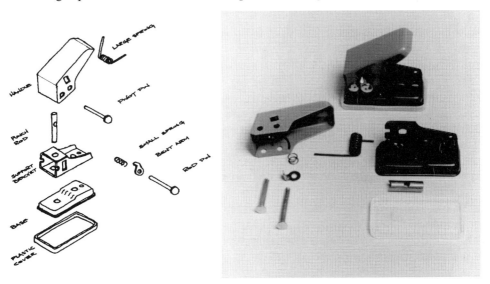

Figure 10.12   An exploded view of the treasury tag punch

Function	Customer rating
Punch hole	High
Hold punchings	Medium
Allow punchings to be removed	Medium
Automatic resetting of handle	Medium
Handle locks down to reduce size	Low

Figure 10.13   Customer ratings of the punch functions

Component	Manufacturing plus material cost (£)
Plastic cover	0.05
Base	0.08
Support bracket	0.12
Pivot pin	0.03
Punch rod	0.02
Spring (large)	0.04
Spring (small)	0.01
Bent arm	0.02
Handle	0.08
Rod pin	0.03

Figure 10.14   Manufacturing and material costs for the punch components

Function \ Component	Plastic cover	Base	Support bracket	Pivot pin	Punch rod	Spring (large)	Spring (small)	Bent arm	Handle	Rod pin
Punch hole		0.04	0.12	0.03	0.02				0.08	0.02
Hold punchings	0.02	0.03								
Allow punchings to be removed	0.03	0.01								
Automatic resetting of handle						0.04				
Handle locks down to reduce size							0.01	0.02		0.01

Figure 10.15   Cost/function information for the treasury tag punch

Using a photocopy of the value analysis matrix in Appendix 1, complete an analysis for the punch. State what changes you might consider making to the punch to improve its value to the customer. Also state any assumptions that you are making about the market or manufacturing processes.

ELEVEN

FAILURE MODES AND FAULT TREES

OVERVIEW

This Chapter deals with **fault trees** and **failure mode and effects analysis**. Both methods are concerned with explaining the relationships between product failures and their causes. The methods are not an alternative to prototype testing and development, but they do provide a structured way of gaining an understanding of the events that can lead to failure, and thereby focus attention on potential problems in the design. A variation on failure mode and effects analysis which uses the concepts of failure probability and detectability is also introduced. This method is called **failure mode, effects and criticality analysis**. All the methods introduced in this chapter can be used qualitatively or quantitatively although, for reasons given below, this introduction is limited to the qualitative approach. A brief explanation of the use of Boolean algebra for the interpretation of fault tree truth tables is also provided.

OBJECTIVES

When you have finished studying this chapter, you will be able to:

- understand the meaning of the symbols used for fault tree construction;
- identify top level events and analyse the faults that can give rise to them;
- construct a fault tree to portray the various ways in which the top level event can occur;
- apply truth tables and Boolean algebra to identify key combinations of faults that might lead to the top level event;
- construct and complete a failure mode and effects analysis worksheet;
- choose severity, probability and detectability ratings and apply these to calculating criticality ratings in failure mode, effects and criticality analysis worksheets.

CONSEQUENCES OF FAILURE

In time, all products develop faults that render them unsuitable for the purposes that they were designed to fulfil. These failures may be dealt with by repairing the product, or by replacing it with a new one. There are many good reasons why the designer of a product needs to understand the ways that it can fail. Sometimes, the safety of the user might be put at risk by particular types of failure. Designers of medical appliances like anaesthetic delivery systems; braking systems, airbags, and seat belts on motor cars; and even home appliances like liquidisers and hedge trimmers, all need to understand how various components or sub-assembly failures can affect the user of the product. Product failures that have safety consequences are not the only type of failures that it is important to understand. If product failures occur after a shorter time or with a higher frequency than customers decide is reasonable, the good name of the product may be damaged. The result of this might be that repeat sales are reduced due to adverse customer experience, and new sales jeopardised because of adverse publicity. Even the sales volume of other products produced by the company may be reduced due to customers' perceptions that there is an overall quality problem with its products. On top of this and the inevitable consequences for sales volume and profits, the company can also find itself facing problems from an unforeseen and expensively high level of warranty claims.

During the process of product design, many companies produce prototypes that they test before putting the final version on the market. In addition to helping the company to verify if the product meets performance requirements, prototypes are also used to examine the ways in which failure occurs. Although prototype testing is a widely used and valuable approach to gaining an understanding of product reliability, it does have the limitations listed below:

- By the time that it is possible to build prototypes, a large commitment in staff time and money will have been committed to the design. Major changes at the prototype stage are likely to be costly and introduce delay into the product launch process.
- Although prototype testing is likely to simulate a broad range of working conditions and environments, it may not be possible to subject the prototype to all of the conditions under which failures can occur.
- With the normal range of statistical variation that is present in assemblies of many components, it may be necessary to test a large number of prototypes before all possible types of failure have been observed and analysed.
- With some types of product it is difficult or virtually impossible to build prototypes. Frequently, this is the case for products that are expensive, and only one or a small number are to be manufactured. Examples include one-off process lines, and special purpose machine tools.

This chapter introduces two methods that can help the designer to think about failures during the early stages of the PDP. By using these methods, the designers attempt to minimise the risk of unforeseen failures occurring at the prototype test or product launch stages, and hence reduce cost and time to market. The methods that are introduced are Fault Trees and failure mode and effects analysis (FMEA). Each of the methods use a different logical approach to understanding faults and their consequences in the proposed design.

Both fault trees and FMEA can be used at various stages of the PDP. In cases where there is detailed information available about the probability of certain components failing under a particular set of circumstances, the methods can provide a basis for a quantitative analysis of the probability of failure. However, such analysis is beyond the scope of this chapter, which limits the introduction to qualitative applications. For those wanting to read further, there are many specialised texts available.

FAULT TREES

Fault Trees use a deductive, top-down method of analysis to identify which component failures might be responsible for particular system failures.

definition

failure   *n.*   **1** lack of success; failing. **2** an unsuccessful person, thing, or attempt. **3** non-performance, non-occurrence. **4** breaking down or ceasing to function.

fault   *n.*   **1** a defect or imperfection of character or of structure, appearance etc. **2** a break or other defect in an electrical circuit.

There is a clear, if subtle distinction between a failure and a fault, and an example will help to clarify this. If a headlamp of a car does not emit light when the driver throws the switch, and when all the associated electrical circuitry and power supplies are fully operational, then there is a headlamp failure. However, if the headlamp does not function because of loose wiring somewhere in the circuit, this is not classified as a headlamp failure but a headlamp fault. Logically, all failures are faults, but not all faults are failures.

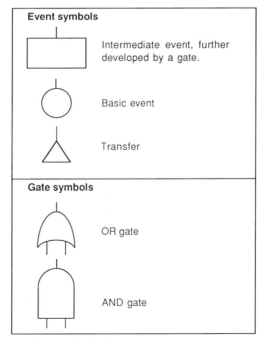

Figure 11.1   Event and gate symbols used in fault trees

Because fault trees use a top-down approach, the first step is to define the top level 'system failure-modes' that are to be examined. These system failure-modes are the end results of the lower order failures that can give rise to them, and it is these that the method attempts to discover by repeatedly asking the question 'what can cause this?' The initial statement of the system failure-mode under investigation and the repeated interrogation of cause leads to the construction of a tree-like structure that shows the logical relationships between lower order failures. The process stops when component level failure events, termed **basic events** are encountered. In the majority of cases, several fault trees will be constructed for a particular product, each one addressing a different system failure-mode.

In seeking causes for failures, various logical relationships between the causes can be identified. Before some failures can occur, two or more causes must be present simultaneously, as in the case of some aircraft control systems where backup arrangements are provided. In other cases, failures will occur if any of two or more causes are present. These, and other types of relationship between failures are identified on the fault tree by logical **gate** symbols, whilst the occurrences are represented by **event** symbols. Because of the introductory nature of this chapter, not all of the gate and event symbols will be used or described. Those that are used in the examples are shown in Figure 11.1.

Figure 11.2 shows how the gate and event symbols might be used in a simple fault tree dealing with an explosion in a domestic gas central heating boiler. The tree has been developed by first determining the system level failure that is to be investigated. In this case, the system level failure has been defined as 'gaseous explosion', and the remainder of the tree examines the lower order failures that may result in this.

Note how the logical AND gate has been used to show that the presence of an explosive gas mixture and a source of ignition are both required at the second level to bring about the system level failure. This gate is used again to show that both a gas escape and inadequate ventilation are required to cause the presence of the gas mixture. The gas escape may be

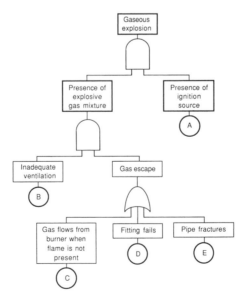

Figure 11.2 Fault tree showing possible causes of a boiler explosion

caused by one of several possible causes, and this is described by the use of the logical OR gate at level three. Although, for this tree, it has been decided that the presence of an ignition source, inadequate ventilation, and the various possible causes of a gas leak are basic events, they could have been investigated further, thus leading to additional lower levels.

Deciding upon the top-level system failure mode, and the boundaries of the analysis is important if the study is not to be too wide or too narrow for the desired purpose. If the tree shown in Figure 11.2 had 'dangerous system failure' at the top level, the tree would have had to deal with modes of failure additional to 'gaseous explosion'. These might include the emission of excess levels of toxic gases into the home environment, and explosion of the heat exchanger. Like other design methods, fault trees are at their most useful when they are used by teams to encourage dialogue and communication. Consequently, the best strategy is usually to commence work with a broad system level failure to make sure that nothing has been overlooked, and then to focus attention on each of a number of second level failures with separate trees.

At the early stages of the PDP, the prime reason for constructing fault trees is to make sure that everyone has a clear view of what system failures can occur, and what the root causes of these failures might be. Even without quantifying the probability of these failures, the knowledge enables designers to take subjective decisions relating to the importance of component reliability. From a project management point of view, it enables resources to be allocated to areas of the design that appear to have important consequences for product failure modes.

As stated earlier, not all failures have consequences for health or safety. Indeed, the majority of system failure modes merely cause inconvenience to the customer. Nevertheless, from the point of view of customer perceptions and their effect upon sales, all system failures need to be logged and understood as early as possible in the PDP. Let us take a simple example to show how a Tree is constructed.

Suppose that you had just invented the three pin 13 amp electric plug that is now common in the United Kingdom (Figure 11.3). You have decided that you want to construct a fault tree for the plug to identify the ways in which failure could occur.

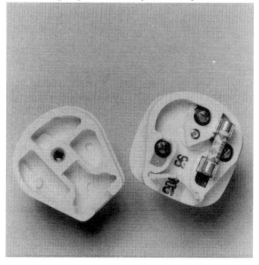

Figure 11.3 Three pin electric plug

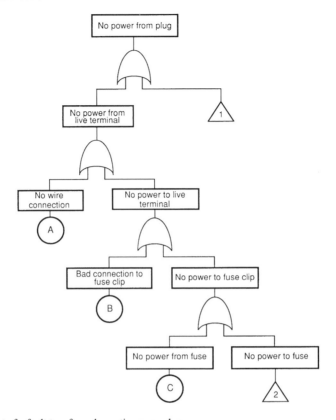

Figure 11.4 Part of a fault tree for a domestic power plug

As a top-level system failure, you have decided upon 'no power available from plug'. Asking the 'what can cause this?' question should lead you to two possible causes: (a) there is no power from the live terminal, or (b) there is no power from the neutral terminal. Asking the question of cause (a), would lead to either (a1) there is no power **to** the live terminal, or (a2) there is no wire connection at the live terminal. You might decide that there is no point in interrogating (a2) further, although you may want to explore the possible causes like the stripping of the terminal thread. However, (a1) clearly needs developing further with the result that either of the following might be identified as causes: (a1.1) no power to fuse clip, or (a1.2) no connection between live terminal block and fuse clip. Interrogation of (a1.1) produces either (a1.1.1) no power to fuse, or (a1.1.2) no power from fuse. If power is available going into the fuse, but not on the output side, the implication is that the fuse has blown, which is a basic event, but (a1.1.1) could be developed further. Figure 11.4 shows the logical layout of all these failures. From the design point of view, it is the basic events that indicate where action may be required to improve reliability. In this case we might ask if it is possible to design better terminal blocks to prevent wires becoming loose, or fuses with less variation in their 'blow' voltage. In recent years, designers have tried to improve both of these aspects with varying degrees of success.

ASSIGNMENTS

Assignment 11.1

Complete the fault tree shown in Figure 11.4 by developing it from the points indicated by the transfer symbols 1 and 2. When continuing a tree like this on a new sheet, it should start by referencing the transfer symbol from which it is being developed. The correct way of doing this is shown in Figure 11.5.

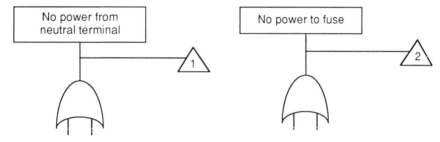

Figure 11.5   The use of transfer symbol on continuation trees

Assignment 11.2

Complete a fault tree for a battery powered torch, using 'bulb does not light when the torch is switched on' as the top-level system failure. Because torches vary in their construction, it is best to get hold of one and take it to bits before starting the tree. Some torches have sealed bodies, and are difficult to disassemble, so choose one that comes apart easily. The metal type shown in Figure 10.1 is ideal for this purpose.

This assignment is sufficiently close to the last example not to give you too many problems in its completion. Nevertheless, you need to progress through the tree carefully, always seeking replies to the 'what can cause this?' question. Try to proceed in a series of small steps, making sure that you do not make 'logical leaps' that will cause you to miss something important.

Starting the first and second levels of a tree is frequently the most difficult part, so Figure 11.6 shows one possible way of doing this.

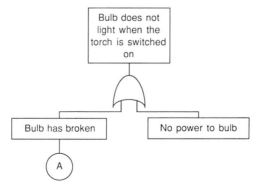

Figure 11.6   One way of commencing work on the torch fault tree

CASE STUDY 11.1

Here are two case studies to illustrate the use of some further symbols used in fault tree construction. The tree shown in Figure 11.7 is related to a water supply system for an automatic fire extinguisher in a factory. In the case of this emergency system, there are two sources of water supply, both of which are automatically pumped into a common delivery pipe when a fire is detected. The top-level failure is specified as 'partial loss of water supply on demand'. Figure 11.7 shows the way of dealing with this problem.

Note the difference between the exclusive OR gate used in Figure 11.7 and the normal OR gate used earlier. The normal OR gate allows one or more of the inputs to be present before the output event occurs. The exclusive OR gate only allows one of the input events to occur. If more than one input to an exclusive OR gate occurs, the output event would not occur.

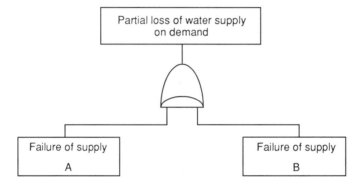

Figure 11.7   Use of the exclusive OR gate when one but not both of the two input events occur

CASE STUDY 11.2

The second example shown in Figure 11.8 indicates the use of a 'house event' symbol to indicate an event that is normally under the control of personnel, and hence can be deemed

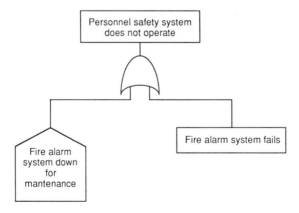

Figure 11.8   House event symbols are used to identify two-state events

to either occur or not occur. Figure 11.8 provides a simple example of the use of this symbol by using it to indicate the effect of a maintenance procedure on the availability of a system.

During the PDP, house events can be used to model user actions, such as incorrect assembly or usage. Hence, the tree can be used to indicate the consequences of pressing a wrong button, or failing to ensure that two components are correctly joined together.

QUALITATIVE FAULT TREE ANALYSIS

The purpose of constructing a fault tree is to determine the effect of the occurrence of basic events on the system. Although large and complex fault trees require the help of computers to carry out this analysis, many can be dealt with 'longhand', particularly at the concept

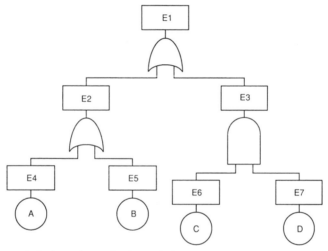

Figure 11.9 An example fault tree for qualitative analysis

Case	A	B	C	D	System
1	W	W	W	W	W
2	W	W	W	F	W
3	W	W	F	W	W
4	W	F	W	W	F
5	F	W	W	W	F
6	W	W	F	F	F
7	F	F	W	W	F
8	W	F	W	F	F
9	F	W	F	W	F
10	F	W	W	F	F
11	W	F	F	W	F
12	F	F	F	W	F
13	F	F	W	F	F
14	F	W	F	F	F
15	W	F	F	F	F
16	F	F	F	F	F

W = Works; F = Fails

Figure 11.10 Truth table for the fault tree shown in Figure 11.9

development stage. To see how this analysis is carried out, here is an example. Figure 11.9 shows a fault tree with two OR and one AND gate, and four basic events, A, B, C, and D.

Figure 11.10 shows a truth table for the fault tree. The table lists every possible state of the system based upon whether none, all, or some of the basic events have occurred.

A **system failure mode** is a unique way in which the system can fail due to various combinations of basic events. The collection of basic events that cause the top event is called a 'cut set', and the list of basic events that are necessary and sufficient to cause system failure are called the 'minimum cut set'. For example, if A, B, and C are the basic events that will guarantee failure, but A and B are necessary and sufficient to cause failure, then the state of C is immaterial. By inspection of the truth table in Figure 11.10, it can be seen that if basic events A or B occur the system fails. This is not the case for basic events C and D, which are only involved if both C and D fail. If a third state is introduced to the truth table, using the symbol – for 'don't care' then in all the rows in which A has failed, B, C, and D can be replaced by don't care as shown in Figure 11.11.

Similarly, it can also be seen that the system fails when either B, or C and D fail. Figure 11.12 shows the minimum combination of events that are necessary and sufficient to cause system failure.

Here, the minimum cut sets are {A}, {B}, and {CD}. The number of failures in each cut set is called the 'order' of the set. Hence, {A} and {B}, are first order sets, whilst {CD} is a second order set. In general the design team might feel it worthwhile to pay particular attention to first order minimum cut sets, because they only require the failure of one component or sub-system to bring down the entire system. However, the general rule of low order sets being the ones to study first does not always apply. If the probability of {A} or {B} occurring is very low, whilst the probability of {CD} occurring is very high then the general rule may not hold true.

A	B	C	D	System
W	W	W	W	W
W	W	W	F	W
W	W	F	W	W
W	F	W	W	F
F	–	–	–	F
W	W	F	F	F
W	F	W	F	F
W	F	F	W	F
W	F	F	F	F

Figure 11.11 Reduced truth table rationalised for basic event A failure

A	B	C	D	System
–	F	–	–	F
F	–	–	–	F
–	–	F	F	F

Figure 11.12 Combinations of basic events giving rise to system failure

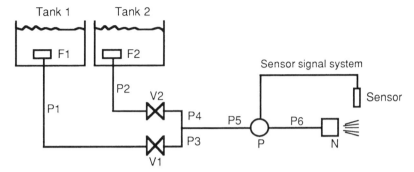

Figure 11.13 Diagrammatic representation of the emergency system

Although this intuitive method of identifying the combination of basic events resulting in system failure is possible with small truth tables, most problems are too large to be dealt with in this way. The number of cases in any truth table is equal to 2^n where n is the number of basic events. Hence, in Figure 11.10 there are four basic events and the number of cases is equal to $2^4 = 16$. By the same calculation, in the following case study the system shown in Figure 11.13, and represented in the fault tree shown in Figure 11.14 has 14 basic events and a staggering 16,384 cases in its truth table. Needless to say, it is not reproduced here.

CASE STUDY 11.3

Figure 11.13 provides a diagrammatic representation of a fire protection system. When the sensor is activated by heat from the fire, a signal is sent to the motor driving pump P. When the pump starts working, water is drawn through valves V1 and V2 from tanks T1 and T2. The water outlet pipe in each tank is fitted with a filter F1 and F2, to prevent sediment and other debris being drawn into the system. The valves are always kept open, except when maintenance to the pump is required. They are then closed to prevent water running from the tanks when the pump is disconnected. Water from the pump is pushed along pipe P6 to the nozzle N, where it emerges as a spray.

The pump can draw sufficient water for the system from either tank T1 or tank T2. For simplification, the sensor and sensor signal system are not included in the tree shown in Figure 11.14.

IDENTIFYING MINIMUM CUT SETS USING BOOLEAN ALGEBRA

Fortunately, computer aids are available to work out the solutions to large problems. These computer-based systems use Boolean algebra to calculate the minimum cut sets using a top-down method which starts at the top event and repeatedly substitutes the Boolean events represented by the gates. This continues until the bottom of the tree is reached. As an example, look at the tree shown in Figure 11.15, and then satisfy yourself that the truth table shown in Figure 11.16 describes how the top event is influenced by the basic events. If you agree with this, you will also be able to see that Figure 11.17 identifies that the minimum cut sets are {A} and {B}.

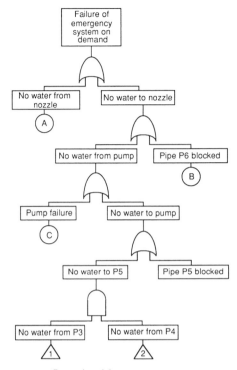

Figure 11.14(a) Part of the emergency fire extinguisher system

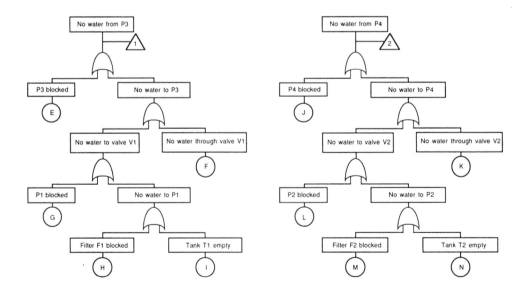

Figure 11.14(b) Final part of emergency fire extinguisher system

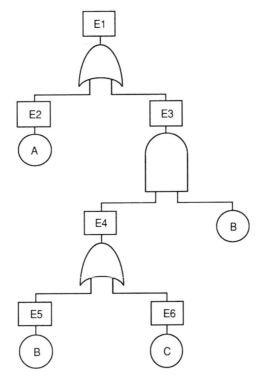

Figure 11.15 Example fault tree for Boolean analysis

Case	A	B	C	System
1	W	W	W	W
2	W	W	F	W
3	W	F	W	F
4	F	W	W	F
5	W	F	F	F
6	F	W	F	F
7	F	F	W	F
8	F	F	F	F

Figure 11.16 Truth table from Figure 11.15

A	B	C	System
F	–	–	F
–	F	–	F

Figure 11.17 Minimum cut sets by inspection

Now let us see if we can identify the same minimum cut sets by using Boolean algebra directly on Figure 11.15.

Remembering that in Boolean notation $X \cap Y \equiv X$ AND Y, and $X \cup Y \equiv X$ OR Y, then:

$$E1 = E2 \cup E3$$
$$= A \cup B \cap E4$$
$$= A \cup B \cap (B \cup C)$$
$$= A \cup B \cap B \cup B \cap C$$

but $B \cap B = B$, and by the absorption law $B \cup B \cap C = B$

Therefore, $E1 = A \cup B$

In other words, E1 fails when A or B fails; and this agrees with the minimum cut sets identified in Figure 11.17. The failure of C is immaterial to the occurrence of top-level failure in this system.

ASSIGNMENT 11.3

Figure 11.18 shows a diagrammatic representation of part of the cooling system on a motor car. The positions of the engine and radiator with respect to other components are not indicated.

Only the following four components are shown:

- a pump which forces the cooling water through the system;
- a thermostat which is closed until the coolant reaches the best temperature for high engine efficiency, but which opens to allow coolant to flow as soon as this temperature is reached;
- a transducer which senses the temperature of the cooling water and sends an appropriate signal to the display inside the car;
- a temperature display on the car fascia which informs the driver if the coolant temperature is normal or abnormal.

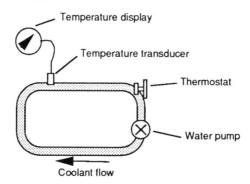

Figure 11.18 A diagrammatic representation of part of a motor car cooling system

An excessively high coolant temperature can cause damage to the engine, and it is important that the driver is informed when such a condition arises so that remedial action can be taken. A situation where the temperature is excessively high and where the driver is unaware of the situation is therefore to be avoided. Using 'engine coolant overheats without the driver's knowledge' as the top-level system failure, draw a fault tree which contains the failure of the four identified components as basic events. Complete the truth table and find the minimum cut sets from it by inspection. Finally, use Boolean algebra to corroborate your answer.

FAILURE MODE AND EFFECT ANALYSIS

The application of fault trees provides a way of thinking about the causes of system failures using a 'top-down' approach. This requires the designers to define one or more types of system failure. These, in turn, are investigated to find out how such failures could occur, and what the combination of sub-system or component failures are that might give rise to them. Another method of thinking about failures is to start with the components or sub-systems, decide how each of these could fail, and then determine what the effects would be on the overall system. This 'bottom-up' approach is called failure mode and effect analysis (FMEA), and is introduced in this section. Although FMEA can be used to provide numerical failure rates, only qualitative applications are examined here. Like fault trees, there are many specialised books dealing with FMEA. Interested readers might like to read *Reliability, Safety & Risk Management* by Cox & Tait (1991), together with other texts in the reference section.

The steps necessary to undertake a FMEA are shown below.

- Define the system that is to be analysed.
- Construct a functional block diagram to show how the components or sub-systems interact.
- List the components or sub-systems and identify their failure modes.
- Complete an FMEA worksheet, assessing the effect of each failure on the overall system performance.
- Assign severity ratings and evaluate the criticality of each failure mode on system performance.
- Use the worksheet to identify critical components and make recommendations for design improvement.

System Definition

At the start of the analysis, it is essential to decide upon the boundary of the system to be studied. In the case of large complex systems, it will be necessary to draw this boundary around sub-systems that are small enough to be dealt with effectively. Products like aircraft will be broken down into sub-systems like landing gear hydraulics, air conditioning, cabin pressurisation etc., and large sub-systems like avionics will in turn be divided into smaller sub-systems for analysis. Even in much smaller and considerably less complex products such as a washing machine, the product will be divided into sub-systems like water pumping and control, and electrical power and interlocks. In cases where sub-systems cross the FMEA system boundary, this must be carefully documented to ensure that the effect of system failures on other systems are not overlooked.

If the system has more than one operational mode, each of these must be recorded, and the expected effects of environmental and operational stress noted. Finally, a decision must be made about the hierarchical level at which the study is to be carried out. To a large extent, this will depend upon the level at which the effect of failures can be determined. If you are dealing with a system constructed from bought out items like pumps, valves, motors, and electronic controllers, the effect of failures of components within these items may be difficult to ascertain. In this case, the correct hierarchical level for the study is unlikely to be at the individual component level.

Functional Block Diagram

These are required to record how sub-systems and/or components at the chosen hierarchical level are interconnected. Block diagrams are the most useful in products or systems associated with flow processes, e.g., where the flow of electrical power, fluid, or components on a processing line can be represented. Figure 11.19 shows a functional block diagram for a process line for the preparation of carrots for supermarkets.

The diagram in Figure 11.19 is prepared at a high hierarchical level. Lower levels would successively reveal sub-assemblies within each of the functional areas, and components within the sub-assemblies. This hierarchical structure can be represented as shown in Figure 11.20, where each sub-system and component is identified by a unique number.

Listing the Components or Sub-systems

When the level at which the study is to be carried out has been determined, all of the known components and sub-systems at that level are identified and listed. During the early stages of the concept development process, and until the scheme stage is complete, many of the elements within the study will be sub-systems with incomplete component definitions. Even at this stage, a FMEA study can be useful in drawing the design team's attention to consequences of sub-system failure. This can provide knowledge about potential problem

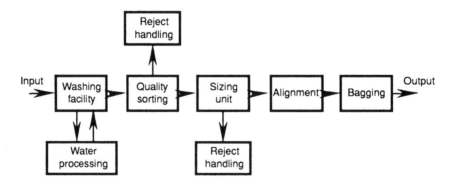

Figure 11.19 A block diagram for a carrot processing line

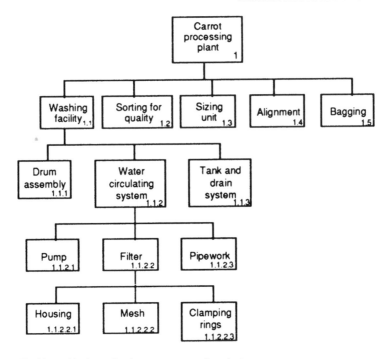

Figure 11.20 The hierarchical tree for the carrot processing plant

areas that will require the assignment of additional resources, and closer monitoring and management control. As the details of the design solution become more completely defined, the study is modified to include components at a lower level in the hierarchy. The exception to this is when bought out sub-systems such as amplifiers, pumps, solenoids etc. are to be incorporated. In most cases, sub-systems like these are treated as components in their own right, because the design team choosing them may not have control over their internal components or layout.

In cases where the failure rate data are available for the components or sub-systems, the information is collected and collated at this stage of the FMEA study. Failure rate data are usually expressed in failures per hours of use; for example 50 failures per 10^6 hours. For the purpose of this introduction to FMEA, I am only going to show you how to take a qualitative approach to assessing the likely frequencies of failure.

The FMEA Worksheet and Severity Ratings

There are almost endless variations on the structure and column headings of FMEA worksheets. Many companies develop sheets to best suit their own and their customers' requirements. The sheet shown in Figure 11.21 contains the most common features to be found.

The first two columns provide a means of identifying the components or sub-systems being considered in the FMEA study. The 'item' column may be used to provide a sequence of numbers 1,2,3 . . . etc., which can be referenced elsewhere, or could carry additional

SYSTEM: ....
HIERARCHICAL LEVEL: ....
DRAWING: ....
MODE OF USE: ....

DATE: ....
SHEET: .... OF ....
ORIGINATOR: ....
APPROVED: ....

Item	Description and Function	Failure Mode	Failure Effect		Detection Method	Severity	Remarks
			Local	System			
1	2	3	4	5	6	7	8

Figure 11.21 An FMEA chart showing the most commonly encountered features

information about part numbers from drawings or other schedules. The second column provides space for a brief description of the component in terms of its name and function. For each component or sub-system entered in columns 1 and 2, a list of the possible failure modes are provided in column 3. Each component or sub-system may have one or more failure modes, and all of these should be listed so that their severity may be evaluated as a basis for taking appropriate design decisions. So that these decisions can be made effectively, the influence of each failure mode on the system must be determined. This is done by first considering the effect of the failure on the same hierarchical level of the system structure as the failure itself. When these 'local' effects have been determined, identifying the 'knock-on' effects at system level will be much easier. Columns 4 and 5 provide space for recording the design team's opinions on the local and system effects of each failure mode.

Frequently, an important aspect of FMEA is the ease with which a particular failure mode can be detected. In the motor car cooling example shown in Figure 11.18, the failure of the thermostat or water pump would be far less likely to have severe consequences for the health of the engine if the failure could be detected by the temperature warning light. If the presence of failures with severe consequences cannot be detected easily, then the design team need to consider if this is satisfactory. If not, then perhaps the solution might involve decreasing the severity or increasing the detectability or both. Whatever the case, the team need to be aware of failure detectability, and column 6 makes those involved think about the issue.

Effect of failure on the system	Severity rating
No effect upon system performance environment, or safety.	1
Minor degradation of system performance. All important functions still available. No environmental or safety implications.	2
Loss of non essential function(s) and/or impairment of essential function(s). No safety implications. Minor environmental consequences.	3
Loss of major function(s), and/ or minor safety and/or environmental implications.	4
Complete loss of system, and/or major safety and/or environmental implications	5

Figure 11.22 Qualitative severity scale for use in FMEA worksheets

Column 7 is for the assignment of a severity index. For the type of qualitative FMEA study that we are considering here, the usual approach is to assign a severity rating from a scale of values. In the process industry, the scale most frequently used is from 1 to 4, with 1 being the most severe and 4 the least. However, for product designers, this arrangement does not seem to fit comfortably with the feeling that increasing severity should be reflected by higher numbers. The 'inverse' 1 to 4 scale also has some drawbacks when considering criticality, but I will deal with this later. Unless you are working in an industry where codes of practice require you to adopt a particular approach, you are free to discuss and agree your own scale. In the meantime, I suggest the scale shown in Figure 11.22 as reasonable for most early PDP problems, and this scale is used in the examples that follow.

The reasons for entering particular severity ratings against failure modes are rarely clear other than to those who have entered the numbers. The 'remarks' column gives the opportunity to explain what the factors were that persuaded the team that particular values applied to each mode. Because these decisions are subjective, it is inevitable that disagreements will occur, and the bases for these disagreements need stating. In most cases, the disagreements will stem from different assumptions about the mode and its consequences held by different people, and it is important that these assumptions are stated in column 8.

Identifying Critical Components and Sub-systems

The completed FMEA worksheet provides the design team with a means of identifying the components and sub-systems which, if they fail by one of the modes identified, will have the most significant detrimental effects upon system performance, the environment, or safety. Although the severity ratings are applied to the failure modes, and not the components, the implications for the design and choice of the system, sub-systems, and components are clear. A useful technique is to present the failure modes in a Pareto chart which will readily identify the important failure modes and the associated components. Starting with the mode with the highest severity rating, the design team need to examine the causes and effects in detail before deciding if, and what, design improvements are called for.

CASE STUDY 11.4

Figure 11.23(a) shows a low pressure sensing unit that is used to determine if pressure is present or absent in a pneumatic circuit. Loss of pressure in this pneumatic circuit is potentially dangerous, and the presence of such a condition must be made evident to personnel. The large tension spring pulls the left hand end of the swinging arm against the pivot, thereby lowering the right hand end until it contacts the support. This is the condition when there is no pressure in the pneumatic circuit and the bellows are not extended. The switch contacts are open, and the absence of a current passing across them is used to signal loss of pressure. There is a small compression spring inside the switch which forces it open whenever the position of the arm allows this. With the circuit pressurised, the bellows are extended as shown at (b). The extension spring is extended as the arm rotates anti-clockwise about the fulcrum, and the switch is closed by the arm pushing the lower contact upwards. Positions (c) and (d) show two conditions under which the switch would give an incorrect signal. In (c) the pivot is misplaced and, even though

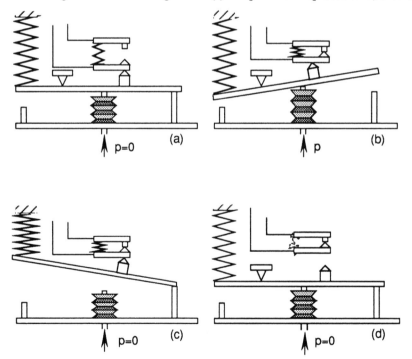

Figure 11.23 Two normal and two failed states for a pressure switch

SYSTEM: ......Low.pressure.sensing.unit......................
HIERARCHICAL LEVEL: ...3.....................................
DRAWING: ....LPS-1.3...................................
MODE OF USE: ...Normal..................................

DATE: ....15.June.1996..................
SHEET: ....1..... OF .2.................
ORIGINATOR: ...J.R.F......................
APPROVED: ...T.W..............................

Item	Description and function	Failure mode	Failure effect		Detection method	Severity	Remarks
			Local	System			
1	Compression spring. Opens contacts when arm returns to horizontal.	Fracture or disconnection	Contacts stay closed	Notification not provided when pressure is low.	None	4	Would be better if switch could fail safe in this failure mode.
2	Pivot. Provides fulcrum for arm.	Displaced	Arm is pulled upwards by extension spring and closes contacts.	Notification not provided when pressure is low.	None	4	Would be better if switch could fail safe in this failure mode.

Figure 11.24 FMEA worksheet showing two failure modes for the low pressure sensing unit

there is no pressure in the circuit, the extension spring has pulled the arm upwards so that the switch is closed, thereby indicating that there is pressure. In (d) the compression spring in the switch has broken so that the contacts remain closed when there is a loss of pressure.

Figure 11.24 shows a FMEA worksheet for the low pressure sensing unit. The worksheet shows that there is no system for detecting the presence of either failure mode other than the occurrence of the system failure. The severity rating assigned to each mode will depend upon the outcome. In this case it has been evaluated at 4, but in other applications and under other circumstances may have been higher or lower. In the remarks column, the observation is made that the design might be improved if the unit was to fail safe on the occurrence of these failure modes. This means that the design team might look for a modification where failure of the small spring or pivot would automatically cause the contacts to open.

ASSIGNMENTS

Assignment 11.4

Using the example given in Figure 11.23, what would be the outcome of the following failure modes: (1) a leak in the bellows, (2) the extension spring breaks? Construct a FMEA worksheet, entering the two failure modes. State any assumptions that you need regarding the operation of the unit.

Assignment 11.5

Re-design the unit so that the contacts are open when pressure is present, and closed when it is absent. Construct a new FMEA worksheet, entering details of the four failure modes mentioned so far. Is the new switch better, worse, or the same in terms of failing safe?

SYSTEM: ....
HIERARCHICAL LEVEL: ....
DRAWING: ....
MODE OF USE: ....

DATE: ....
SHEET: .... OF ....
ORIGINATOR: ....
APPROVED: ....

Item	Description and function	Failure mode	Failure effect		Severity	Probability	Detection method	Detectability	Criticality
			Local	System					

Figure 11.25 A typical layout for a FMECA worksheet

FAILURE MODES, EFFECTS AND CRITICALITY ANALYSIS

Although FMEA is an extremely useful and widely used tool, it can be observed to have some limitations. These limitations are centred around the absence of any consideration of the combined effect of failure severity, the probability or likelihood of failure, and the ease with which the failure can be detected before its consequences can take effect. **Failure mode, effects and criticality analysis** (FMECA) attempts to take all of these factors into account. The FMECA worksheet is similar to that used for FMEA but usually contains three additional columns; probability, detectability, and criticality. Figure 11.25 shows a typical layout.

In addition to the ratings for the severity column, which are provided in the same way as for FMEA, similar consideration needs to be given for the probability and detectability columns. Because we are limiting our study to a qualitative assessment, we need a set of criteria against which to make evaluations. Figure 11.26 provides a basis for such evaluations.

In cases where numerical failure rate data is not available for components of sub-systems, the selection of qualitative assessments for the probability of failure, and failure detectability is similar to the methods used in project risk analysis. Usually, it is the severity of failure that is examined first, and an appropriate severity rating chosen. If the severity rating is low, there is a tendency to pick low values for the probability rating, simply because the consequences are slight. However, the probability and detectability ratings must be chosen purely on the information that is available in regard to them. Automatic

Probability of failure	Rating P or D	Detectability of failure
Will not occur during the predicted life of the system regardless of any forseen abuse or lack of maintenance. The design team have experience of the reliability of this component or sub-system in an identical application. All aspects of the design are under the control of the design team.	1	The existence of the failure mode will be brought to the attention of those monitoring or using the system.
The design team are familiar with the application of this component or sub-system in a similar situation and are confident that there is a low chance of failure irrespective of any foreseen abuse or lack of maintenance. All aspects of the design are under the control of the design team.	2	The existence of the failure mode will be immediately apparent to those monitoring or using the system.
The design team are unfamiliar with the reliability of this component or sub-system in regard to the failure modes being considered. However, third party suppliers or coroborated information from elsewhere suggests that reliability is acceptable.	3	Existence of the failure mode can be identified during normal inspection or usage procedures.
Uncorroborated evidence suggests that this component or sub-system will provide acceptable reliability in regard to the failure modes being considered.	4	Examination beyond that required during normal inspection or usage procedures is required to identify the existence of the failure mode.
There are doubts about the reliability of this component or sub-assembly in regard to the failure modes being considered.	5	The existence of the failure mode is not detectable and, on its occurence, nothing can be done to prevent the system failure.

Figure 11.26 Probability and detectability ratings for FMECA

cross-linking between the three ratings must be avoided at all cost. Uncertainty in regard to which rating is the most appropriate for a particular situation must be reflected in the choice. In other words, if you really do not have any idea about the probability of failure, the severity of failure, or the detectability, they must all be set at 5. In cases of doubt, always choose the highest rating that may be appropriate until more information is available to justify or revise the decision.

CASE STUDY 11.5

Figure 11.27 shows an example of a FMECA worksheet for an inverter on an underground train system. Here the design engineers were working on a power regeneration system which would generate DC power whenever the train was braking. The DC current required converting to AC before being put back into the electrical grid, and the inverter is the device that accomplished this conversion. The design required an inverter to be fitted to each train, and the FMECA worksheet was produced as a part of a much larger study early in the PDP. Within the hierarchical structure defined by the team, this study was carried out at level two, level one being the entire inverter system, level two the sub-system, and level three the component level. Three sub-systems are defined on the worksheet, with only one failure mode identified for each sub-system. Local and system consequences are recorded, and severity ratings selected. Finally, the criticality of each failure mode is assessed as the product of the three ratings. Each failure mode was then revisited by the design team to check if its criticality rating fairly reflected the risks associated with it. Consideration was given to the acceptability of each criticality factor, and any design options that were available by which it might be reduced.

SYSTEM: ....DC.: AC. Inverters....................... DATE: ....9 April 1996......................
HIERARCHICAL LEVEL: ..2... SHEET: .....1.........OF ....1.......
DRAWING: ....TD/387780-3............................. ORIGINATOR: ...P.D..Richards....................
MODE OF USE: ....Normal................................... APPROVED: .....F..Disley..........................

| Item | Description and function | Failure mode | Failure effect | | Severity | Probability | Detection method | Detectability | Criticality |
			Local	System					
1	Inverter commutation cicuits. Inversion of DC supply to AC	Short circuit of DC supply through inverter arms	Generation of 125Hz AC supply	Interference with signalling system	4	2	Inverter output monitoring system	1	8
2	Inverter voltage/current sensors. Detects voltage level on DC system	Voltage/current sensors not operative on both inverter and train	Excessive voltage rise on DC system	Localised fire risk	3	2	Test during maintenance procedures	3	18
3	Inverter casing. Protects equipment and safeguards staff	Breakdown of insulation	Casing is live during maintenance	Electrocution of staff	5	1	Regular maintenance checks of insulation condition	2	10

Figure 11.27 A FMECA worksheet for an underground train inverter

CASE STUDY 11.6

Figure 11.28 shows a diagrammatic representation of a yarn accumulator for a spinning machine. When cotton yarn is produced and wound onto tapered bobbins or 'packages', the rate of yarn production is constant. However, the demand by the package onto which it is being wound varies, because the peripheral speed of the package at the large diameter

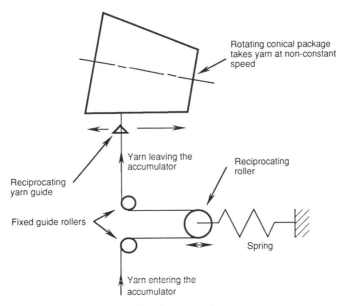

Figure 11.28 Diagrammatic representation of a spring accumulator

end is greater than that at the small end. This means that an accumulator is required to store and release yarn as the yarn guide traverses backwards and forwards along the package. Without the accumulator, there would be a higher yarn tension at the large end than the small end, and this would be unacceptable for subsequent processes.

There are several problems with this type of accumulator, but the most important is the limitation in the maximum speed at which it can operate. The frequency of motion of the reciprocating roller is the same as that of the yarn guide and, on increasing the speed of the machine, a speed is reached beyond which the spring/roller system cannot keep up because of the mass and inertia of the roller.

A design team working on an improved accumulator that would not be affected by such speed limitations proposed the design represented in Figure 11.29. Here, the yarn passes around a groove on the periphery of a disc. The disc is placed inside a housing through which a stream of air is passed. As yarn demand rises and falls, the disc floats to the left or right in order to decrease or increase the size of the loop. Gross variations in yarn tension are thereby avoided. The volume of air flowing into the housing is slightly larger than that being removed. This results in a small amount of air being forced out of the housing at the slots where the yarn enters and exits. This ensures that cotton fibres and dust floating in the air outside the housing are not sucked in to cause blockage and build-up within the system. This pressure balancing arrangement also ensures that excessive 'whistle' caused by air entering or leaving the slots is avoided. The low inertia of this new system means that it can be operated at three times the speed of the spring-mass system.

At the concept stage of the PDP, the design team working on the new accumulator completed a FMECA worksheet as a part of the process of attempting to identify potential problems before making a final commitment to the idea. The team decided that the following failure modes were the ones that they wanted to address: (a) absence of input air at the inlet port due to disconnection of piping or airline puncture, (b) absence of suction

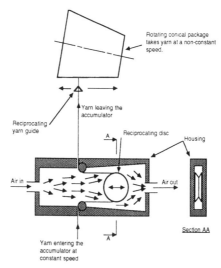

Figure 11.29 The new pneumatic accumulator

SYSTEM: Yarn accumulator
HIERARCHICAL LEVEL: 3
DRAWING: BRg/A223
MODE OF USE: Normal

DATE: 3 June 1995
SHEET: 1 OF 1
ORIGINATOR: P. Skillet
APPROVED: J. Thomson

Item	Description and function	Failure mode	Failure effect		Severity	Probability	Detection method	Detectability	Criticality
			Local	System					
1	Air inlet pipe. Brings compressed air to the housing	Pipe punctured or becomes detached from fitting on housing	Loss of forced air supply to housing	Air is drawn in through yarn slots causing excessive noise	3	1	Audible increase in noise level	2	6
				Air causes ingestion of debris	5	1	Visual observation of yarn quality. Eventual breakage triggers alarm	4	20
2	Air outlet pipe. Extracts air from housing	Pipe fractured or becomes detached from fitting on housing	Loss of suction to housing	Air loss with gross increase in noise level	3	1	Audible increase in noise level	2	6
				Pressure drop affects yarn tension and yarn quality	4	1	Post processing quality checks	5	20
3	Disc. Collects a loop of yarn and maintains it against varying demand	Yarn abrasion causes wear in 'v'-notch	Yarn snags in the notch	Yarn breakage causing machine down-time	5	3	Maintenance check. Otherwise yarn breakage	4	60
		Excessive wear on sides of disc through contact with housing	Decrease in pressure drop across disc	Decreased disc force affects yarn quality	4	3	Maintenance check. Otherwise yarn quality check	4	48
			Disc flutter due to larger clearance	Increased wear at disc edges	2	3	Routine maintenance	3	18

Figure 11.30 FMECA worksheet for a pneumatic yarn accumulator

at the outlet port due to the same causes, (c) wear on the periphery of the disc, and (d) wear on the side surfaces of the disc. Figure 11.30 shows the FMECA worksheet for these failure modes.

Three items or components are shown: The air inlet pipe, the air outlet pipe, and the disc. In the case of the air inlet pipe, only one failure mode is identified. This failure mode (pipe puncture/detachment) has one local effect, but two system effects. The first of these is concerned with the increase in noise level, whilst the second is concerned with debris collection. Although the probability of these system effects are the same because they arise from the same failure mode, their severity ratings are different. The failure mode detection is in both cases through the effects themselves; and because one of the effects is easier to detect than the other, the detectability ratings also differ. Although the failure mode with the higher severity rating is also the most difficult to detect, its presence could be recognised by the higher noise level associated with the other effect. In this case then, it would be sensible to assign severity level 5 rating with a detectability 2 rating, thereby giving a criticality of 10. For item 3, the disc, two failure modes have been identified. The first of these is excessive wear at the base of the notch, whilst the second is wear to the flanks. While the first of these has one local and one system effect, the second has two local effects, each giving rise to a different system effect.

The issues raised in the FMECA illustrated in Figure 11.30 strongly influenced the embodiment design of the accumulator prototype. In particular, it resulted in the introduction of profiled grooves in the side walls of the housing to generate an air flow pattern that kept the disc away, thereby reducing the risk of direct disc to housing contact. In addition, it was decided to use a ceramic coating in the peripheral disc notch to minimise wear due to yarn abrasion. Although product development through trial and error was still a part of the PDP, there is no doubt that careful consideration of failure modes at the concept stage reduced lead times and costs. Figure 11.31 shows the first prototype mounted on a spinning machine under test.

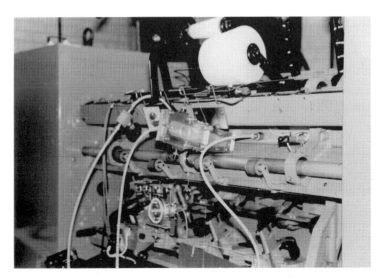

Figure 11.31 The prototype accumulator under test

RECAP

Fault trees provide a top-down approach to establishing the component and sub-system failures that might give rise to a pre-defined system failure. The tree shows the logical linking between the failure occurrences by means of gates and event boxes, and the logic encapsulated in the tree can be represented in a truth table listing all of the possible system states. From the truth table, minimum cut sets can be defined using either an intuitive approach or Boolean algebra. The minimum cut sets describe the combination of component and/or sub-system failures that are necessary and sufficient to cause system failure. Lower order cut sets are often the ones that should be examined when designers are seeking to improve system reliability.

FMEA and FMECA worksheets are used by designers to present the relationships between sub-system failures and system failures. Both methods use a bottom-up approach, starting at the component or sub-system level and expressing the consequences of these failures at local and system levels. In FMEA, the severity of each failure mode is expressed as a rating. In FMECA, the severity rating is combined with probability and detectability ratings to yield a criticality rating for the system.

Although this chapter has been limited to qualitative use of the methods, they are frequently used with quantitative data in industry, particularly in the latter stages of the PDP when such data are more likely to be available.

ASSIGNMENTS

Assignment 11.6

Using the switch problem introduced in Assignment 11.4, draw a FMECA chart and provide criticality ratings for each of the identified failure modes. Assume that the switch is a vital element in the control of a chemical plant that processes toxic waste. State any assumptions that are necessary for the completion of the chart.

Assignment 11.7

On the same basis as above, produce a FMECA chart for the redesigned switch developed for Assignment 11.5.

TWELVE

QUALITY FUNCTION DEPLOYMENT

OVERVIEW

This chapter introduces the **Quality function deployment** (QFD) method. QFD provides a structured approach to ensuring that the needs of the customer are considered whenever decisions that affect those needs are taken. The method relies upon a system of interlinked charts. The first chart relates the customer needs to the 'engineering characteristics' that are under the control of the design team. The second chart relates engineering characteristics to parts characteristics, and so on until the charts are dealing with issues like machine settings, staff training etc. Decisions relating to these 'bottom-level' issues can be linked back through the charts to customer needs, thereby ensuring that the customer is considered whenever decisions are made.

In reality, many companies that use QFD only use the first, or the first and second charts because of the time overheads involved in their construction. Indeed, during the early stages of the PDP there is frequently either insufficient information available to construct more than the first two charts or a feeling that the time required would tend to 'freeze' the design rather than keep it fluid and 'dynamic'. While introducing the concept of the multiple charting approach to QFD, this chapter concentrates on the first two charts because of their relevance to the early stages of the PDP.

OBJECTIVES

When you have finished studying this section, you will be able to:

- understand the potential benefits of using the QFD method;
- construct QFD charts using customer need and product information;
- use a QFD chart to ascertain the consequences of making changes to a product's characteristics;
- Understand the role of QFD charts in Total Quality Management.

LINKING CUSTOMER NEEDS TO PRODUCT CHARACTERISTICS

Like other design methods described in this book QFD is concerned with building customer valued attributes into products. In previous chapters, this activity has involved: (a) the methodological determination of customer requirements and/or, (b) the analysis of attributes under various conditions to determine if the requirements are being satisfied. In general, customers are only concerned with 'if', and not 'how' their requirements are satisfied. In cases where 'how' is specified by a customer it immediately becomes yet another requirement, and the 'how' question is then concerned with engineering matters with which the customer is not concerned. For example, the purchaser of a lawn mower might insist on a petrol engine rather than an electric motor, hence specifying as a requirement how the power should be provided. However, this buyer is much less likely to specify engineering characteristics like compression ratio or swept volume as requirements, and will be content to leave these 'hows' to the design team.

Although customers will appraise, compare, and select products on the basis of the extent to which the attributes meet their requirements, and not on the basis of how the attributes have been achieved, there is usually a strong link between these two aspects. Although the average lawn mower purchaser will not have requirements relating to engineering characteristics, these will have a strong influence on attributes like power, fuel consumption etc. Unfortunately, the effect that engineering characteristics have on customer-valued attributes can easily be overlooked by design team members due to the continuous pressure of solving technical problems, and meeting internal company requirements.

QFD provides a formalised method of linking customer-valued attributes to the engineering, manufacturing, and process decisions that companies need to make. Because the Quality of a product is defined by the extent to which these attributes are present, the term 'Quality function deployment' is used to identify the method by which they are linked to, or deployed throughout, the various product related characteristics.

According to Hauser and Clausing (1988), QFD originated in Mitsubishi's Kobi shipyard in Japan in 1972. The method was adopted and developed by Toyota, who eventually made all of their suppliers use it to control product Quality. In Japan, the method has been used by manufacturers of consumer electronics, home appliances, clothing, integrated circuits, synthetic rubber, construction equipment, and agricultural equipment. Even the providers of services find that QFD can be beneficial in making them think about Quality issues. Utilisation of the method is thought to be much higher in Japan and the USA than in the United Kingdom and the remainder of Europe. Many companies in the United Kingdom now use QFD to some extent, although many of these are large companies with fairly complex data (Wright *et al.*, 1996).

The QFD method uses multi-disciplinary project teams to prepare the data required for the completion of a series of charts or matrices. The first chart links customer requirements to the engineering characteristics over which the design team has control. Figure 12.1 shows an example of a requirement-characteristic chart produced for the hairdryer introduced in Chapter 4.

Down the left hand side of the chart are listed the attributes that the customer has defined as being important. In this case, to keep the chart simple, only a few of the customer-valued attributes have been entered. It is important that the attributes are stated

Engineering characteristics

Customer voiced quality attributes	RIR	Wire resistance (Ω)	Current (A)	Voltage (V)	Heat output (I²R)	Length of wire in matrix (mm)	Thermal resistance of housing (W/m°C)	Thickness of housing (mm)	Heater matrix to housing air gap (mm)	Exit air velocity (m/sec)	Volume flow rate of air (m³/sec)	Minimum section of air duct (m²)	Air outlet temperature (°C)	Fan speed (rev/min)	Fan efficiency (%)	Fan power (W)	Force to move heat setting switch (N)	Free switch movement (mm)	Distance of CG to forefinger (mm)
Dries hair quickly	3	√	√	√	√	√				√	√	√	√	√	√	√			
Casing does not get hot	1	√	√	√	√	√	√	√	√	√	√	√	√	√	√	√			
Switches feel positive	3																√	√	
Comfortable to hold	2																		√

(Convenience of use)

Figure 12.1 A QFD chart for some of the segment M hairdryer requirements

in the way that the customer originally expressed them. If the customer says that the hairdryer must 'dry the hair quickly', then this must not be converted into 'powerful heater' by the design team. The whole point about this chart is that it expresses the customer's desires in the words that the customer uses. Inevitably, when views have been collected from hundreds of customers or potential customers, it will be necessary to find a form of words that expresses their combined view about a particular issue. However, care must be taken to avoid stating the attribute in a way that reflects the in-built preferences and experiences of the design team. Hence, although 'powerful heater' might be a way to dry the hair quickly, there are other factors that influence this particular attribute such as air velocity. Any tendency for requirements to be expressed in 'technical' terms can often be countered by asking the question 'why'. For example, if 'powerful heater' appeared in the customer requirements list, asking the question 'why' several times should eventually bring it back to something that the customer would accept. Why do we need a powerful heater? So that we can have high temperature air. Why do we want high temperature air? So that the hair can be dried quickly!

Along the top of the chart lie the 'engineering characteristics' that influence the attributes that the customer values. These are the characteristics that the design team may have some control over, and hence be able to change in an attempt to influence the attributes that the customer values. Frequently, the process of identifying these engineering characteristics is surprisingly difficult, and not as obvious as it might first appear. In the case of an existing product, the reason for this difficulty is frequently over-familiarity with the product. In the case of the 'dry hair quickly' attribute, there might be a tendency to list 'heater matrix power output' as the important engineering characteristic that influences it. On more careful consideration, there are several more basic characteristics such as heater matrix wire length, and the wire resistance that the heater matrix power output depends upon. These are the characteristics that we need along the top of the chart.

The central area of the chart identifies the relationships between the customer-valued attributes and the engineering characteristics that influence them. In this case, the existence of a relationship has been identified by the placing of a √ in the appropriate box. This can also be difficult, because we need to identify negative as well as positive influence. For the example given, it is obvious that many of the engineering characteristics like current, wire length, fan speed etc., influence the speed with which the user can dry their hair. However, these characteristics also influence the 'casing does not get hot' attribute because higher air temperatures will have a knock-on effect in terms of the increased rate of heat transfer to the surrounding parts.

The purpose of QFD is two-fold. First, it helps the design team to identify the engineering characteristics under its control that might enable it to change customer valued attributes for the better. Secondly, it informs the design team about the possible detrimental effects on some customer-valued attributes of making improvements to others. Figure 12.1 shows that decreasing the time taken to dry the hair by increasing the length of the heater matrix wire, might well have a detrimental affect on the surface temperature of the hairdryer and hence the comfort of holding it. QFD charts frequently show this positive and negative influence of engineering characteristics on customer-valued attributes by using different symbols. Various symbols can also be used to show whether a particular characteristic has a strong, medium, or weak influence on attributes. The following case study shows how different types of symbol can be used to show different relationships.

CUSTOMER ATTRIBUTES FOR A CAR DOOR

Primary	Secondary	Tertiary
Good operation and use	Easy to open and close	From outside Stays open on hill From inside No kick-back
	Isolation	Does not leak No road noise No wind noise No drips when open No rattle
	Arm rest	Soft Comfortable In right position
Good appearance	Interior trim	Non-fade Attractive (non-plastic)
	Clean	Easy to clean No grease from door
	Fit	Uniform gaps

Figure 12.2 A selection of customer valued attributes for an automobile

CASE STUDY 12.1

QFD has found widespread application in the automobile industry, with companies like Ford, Nissan, and Toyota enthusiastically supporting its use.

A survey of automobile buyers identified attributes that were considered important when making decisions about which product to buy. Figure 12.2 shows the tabularised results of a small part of the survey relating to the door. The table contains a list of the desirable attributes associated with the operation and appearance of the door, and breaks both of these 'top-level' attributes down into two further levels of detail. This process of developing primary attributes into secondary and tertiary levels is an important prerequisite for the production of the first QFD chart, and is often accomplished by using a requirement tree or similar method.

The second stage of preparing the attributes for the QFD chart is to assign RIR (re-read Chapters 5 and 8 if you need to recap on relative importance ratings). Once again, these RIR must be set as a result of the customers evaluation of importance. Figure 12.3 shows how RIR might be added to some of the attributes from Figure 12.2.

An additional use for the first QFD chart is to express the success of competitor products in meeting the needs of the customers. Usually, this is done by asking customers to rate products attributes by assigning success values to them. If the company seeking this information already has a competitive product in the market, this can also be included in the study. Hence, Figure 12.4 shows how customers rate one manufacturer's automobile door in comparison to those of two competitors. Charting methods like the one shown in Figure 4.7 can be useful in the preparation of this type of information. Customer evaluations, combined with RIRs help the design team to see where their product stands in regard to the attributes that customers consider to be the most important. Clearly, a poor performance on an important attribute is a cause for concern, and the team need to look at the engineering characteristics that can be used to improve performance.

The QFD chart produced from the investigation into customer-valued attributes for the automobile door is shown in Figure 12.5. The chart also includes some additional features not shown in the chart for the segment M hairdryer.

Basically, the chart is the same as that shown in Figure 12.1 in that its central part consists of a matrix that relates customer-valued attributes to engineering characteristics.

Bundles	Customer attributes	RIR
Easy to open	Easy to close from outside	7
	Stays open on a hill	5
Isolation	Does not leak in the rain	3
	No road noise	2
	.	.
	.	.
	.	100%

Figure 12.3 RIR are assigned to customer valued attributes

CUSTOMER EVALUATION OF COMPETITOR PRODUCTS

Bundles	Customer Attributes	RIR
Easy to open and close	Easy to close from outside	7
	Stays open on hill	5
Isolation	Does not leak rain	3
	No road noise	2

Worst 1 — Best 5

◳ Our door

■ Competitor A

▨ Competitor B

Figure 12.4 Product evaluation

In Figure 12.5 attributes are divided into three level of detail, and RIRs are provided for each one. The major difference is in the way that the attributes and engineering characteristics are linked in the central matrix area. In this chart, symbols have been used to show whether a particular engineering characteristic has a strong, medium, or weak influence on an attribute. This information can be useful when the design team are looking for the most influential characteristics under their control when changes need to be made to some of the product's attributes. To the extreme right hand side of the central matrix is comparative information based on customer perceptions about the company's product and its two principal competitors. This information can be used in conjunction with the RIRs to see how the product is perceived to perform on the most important attributes. It also provides a basis for the benchmarking of competitor products to find out the reasons why they are perceived to be better in some areas. Finally, a poor perceived performance in regard to some attributes can be linked to the engineering characteristics that might be used to improve the situation.

In some cases, making a change to the magnitude of one engineering characteristic has 'knock-on' consequences for others. In this case, the positioning of the handle that the customer uses to close the door from the inside will have obvious repercussions on the force required. A handle situated near the door hinge will require a higher force applied to it than a handle further away from the hinge. These relationships can be very important, particularly when changes to one characteristic aimed at improving an attribute results in detrimental changes to another. The triangular matrix sitting on top of the chart in Figure 12.5 carries information on which engineering characteristics are linked with others. Again, symbols have been used to show whether the relationship is a strong, medium, or weak one. The existence of a relationship between the 'door closing effort' and the 'door pull handle location' is recorded by a ○ at the intersection of the diagonals flowing from the characteristics. Other characteristics that affect the door closing effort are shown to be the door's performance in the leak test (a door seal that provides a high contact force would also tend to make the door more difficult to close), and the static and dynamic force

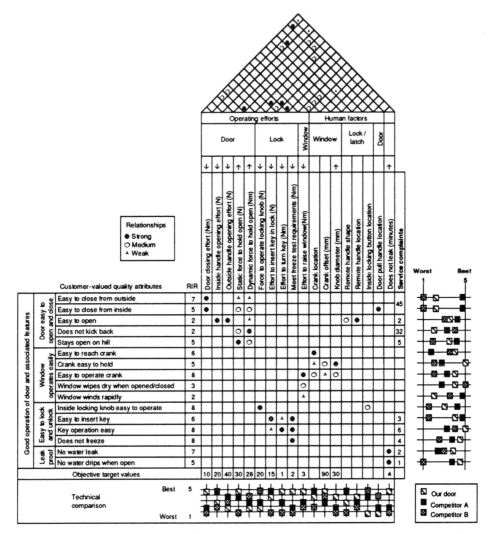

Figure 12.5 A QFD chart for an automobile door

required to overcome the mechanism that prevents the door swinging shut when the vehicle is parked facing up a hill. The leak test, and static and dynamic hold forces are good examples of characteristics that influence others in a negative sense. Clearly, customers value the attributes associated with non-leaking doors and doors that do not swing shut on a hill. However, by changing the characteristics that improve these attributes, the door will be made more difficult to close. QFD charts are particularly useful at recording relationships between attributes and characteristics as a way of making design team members think about the consequences of their decisions, and encouraging them to consider alternative courses of action.

At the bottom of the Figure 12.5 chart is a technical evaluation of the characteristics. The evaluation has been undertaken by design team members, and relates to the engineering characteristics under their control. Like the customer perception information, it contains an evaluation based upon the company's own product, and its two main competitors. The technical comparison can be combined with information from the customer perception data and the main body of the matrix to suggest courses of action to improve the product. In the QFD chart for the automobile door, there is a general agreement between the customer's perceptions of the success in meeting various attributes, and the technical comparisons of the engineering characteristics. For example, companies A and B are seen as being inferior in terms of the non-leak and non-drip attributes; and this view is confirmed by the company's engineers who have found that their door performs best in the leak test. This tends to confirm that the characteristics that they are trying to control are indeed the most important. However, although the design team have discovered that their door requires the lowest closing effort, the customers are not happy, and rate it a poor second behind the door of competitor A. This could be due to the high dynamic hold force, but may equally be due to some other factor that may not have been considered, such as poor ergonomic design of the handle or the positioning of the seat back making it difficult to apply the force in the optimum direction. Neither of these characteristics actually change the magnitude of the closing effort characteristic but they might well alter the customer's perception of the force that is required. The result is that the design team are forced to think about the characteristics that affect the customer's perception of product Quality.

Finally, the chart shows the number of claims that have been made in regard to certain attributes, and the values that the design team would like to achieve to optimise the various characteristics. There are no standards on the contents or layout of QFD charts, and companies tend to design them to suit their own purposes. Whilst some are as basic as the one shown in Figure 12.1, some contain even more detail than in Figure 12.5. For example, some charts contain the characteristic magnitudes for all of the competitor products, a rating for the technical difficulty in achieving target values, and the estimated costs associated with achieving them.

MULTIPLE QFD CHARTS

If you thought that you had seen all that there was to see in the automobile door QFD chart, you will be surprised. The attribute-characteristic chart is merely the first in a sequence of four or more charts that can be used to link customer-valued attributes to manufacturing processes and production requirements. Figure 12.6 shows the links that are presented in each of the four charts.

The first chart, as we have seen, links customer valued attributes to the engineering characteristics (ECs) that are under the control of the design team. The second chart, maps the relationships between these engineering characteristics and 'parts characteristics'. These parts characteristics (PCs) are the descriptors that describe features of the product's components that influence or determine the ECs. In the majority of cases, the PCs can be determined by asking the question 'what are the component characteristics that influence or determine each engineering characteristic in the first chart?'. For example, if this question was asked of the EC 'door closing effort', PCs such as: weight of door assembly, stiffness of 'hold-open' spring, and door seal stiffness might rapidly come to mind. By

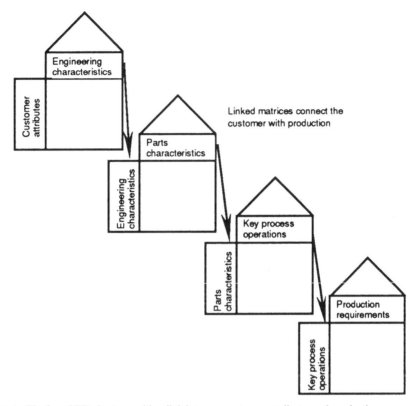

Figure 12.6 The four QFD charts provide a link between customer attributes and production

placing these and other PCs along the top edge of the second chart, we can look for relationships between them and the engineering characteristics that would be placed along the left hand edge. Once again, we can evaluate what the relationships are, and whether they are strong or weak. We can also investigate whether there are links between different PCs, and map these relationships into the triangular area at the top of the chart. By preparing the second chart, we link the parts characteristics, through the engineering characteristics, to the customer-valued attributes, and this enables us to assess the impact of part modifications on customer perceptions. Because each EC is frequently influenced by several PCs, the number of columns in chart 2 can be large. For this reason, the parts characteristics chart shown in Figure 12.7 only includes some of the parts characteristics that could be developed. As in the first chart, comparisons are shown between the company's own product and those of two competitors. This comparison includes the ECs which were part of chart 1, but now also covers a comparison of PCs. The chart provides space for the design team to enter the specific values that can be attributed to the various measures applied to the PCs. Note that not all ECs are related to a controlling PC. This is frequently the case when the EC relates to a 'spatial relationship' like 'door handle location', although this could be related to the position of the holes. Again, the aim is to identify which PCs influence customer-valued attributes, and what the consequences of change will be.

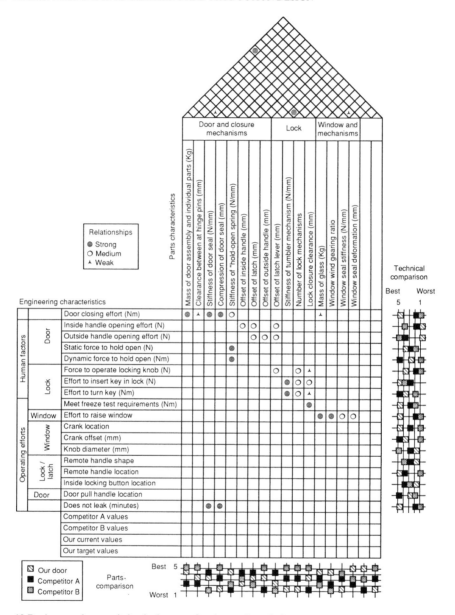

Figure 12.7 A parts characteristics deployment for the car door design

The third QFD chart seeks to establish the relationships between the PCs identified in chart 2, and key process characteristics. Figure 12.8 gives an example of how part characteristics from the door seal attributes could be developed and linked to the process characteristics that control them. This chart also shows that the relative importance of process characteristics can be expressed by adding together the RIR of the customer-valued attributes that they positively influence. This technique is particularly important in involving process and production engineers with customer requirements (Ferguson (1990)).

	Extruder cross die	Extruder speed	Back pressure	Bulb material	Base material	Reinforcement	
Relationships ■ Strong 9 / ◎ Medium 3 / X Weak 1							
Compression load				■	◎		
Bulb height	■	◎	◎	X	X		
Bulb O/D	■	◎	◎	X			
Bulb I/D	■	◎	◎	X			
Base dimensions	■	◎	◎		X	■	
Importance rating	36	13	13	21	8	9	

Figure 12.8 A process deployment chart for a part of the door seal design

Finally, the fourth QFD chart provides the links between process characteristics and production requirements. These production requirements might include the settings on particular machine tools or manufacturing processes, on-line quality control requirements, inspection of bought out components, and even the training requirements of process operators. Customer-valued attributes can thereby be linked through to the actions of individual operators, quality control staff, and the purchasing and staff training functions.

BENEFITS AND PROBLEMS OF USING QFD

Companies that use QFD as a part of a formal TQM strategy frequently claim that the method can bring substantial benefit to the customer orientation of the organisation. A principal reason for this effect is the necessity for multi-functional teams including personnel from all aspects of the company's operations to be involved in the QFD charting process. These activities are basic requirements for effectively facilitating a TQM strategy. An advantage that is often claimed for the application of QFD is the reduction of a product's time to market or lead time. If the production of the QFD charts go hand-in-hand with the product design process, the design team is made aware of the consequences of their decisions by increased liaison with other company staff. Although this increased pre-production activity may increase the pre-launch costs, this can be more than compensated for by reduced problem solving (start-up) costs after launch. Figure 12.9 typifies the claims made for QFD in terms of product development cost reduction, and also indicates how the time to product launch is decreased. A study of two automobile companies in the 1980s showed marked differences in the number of design changes that the companies had to make during the design process, and in the period following product launch. The Japanese company Toyota showed substantially fewer pre-launch changes, and relatively few after launch changes. The USA company Ford, showed somewhat higher pre-launch changes but, significantly, a large number of after launch changes. The differences were attributed at least in part to the use of QFD by the Japanese company. Figure 12.10 represents the finding of the study.

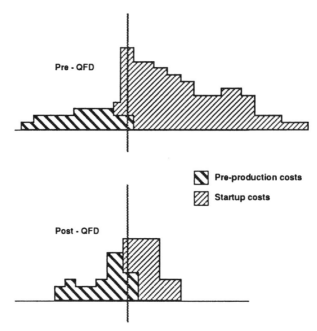

Figure 12.9 The effect of QFD on design costs

COMMUNICATION AND DOCUMENTATION

QFD charts can provide valuable documentation for design review, TQM, or ISO 9000 purposes. Because they link customer-valued attributes with engineering and manufacturing characteristics, they have strong relationships with many of the other methods described in this book, as shown diagrammatically in Figure 12.11.

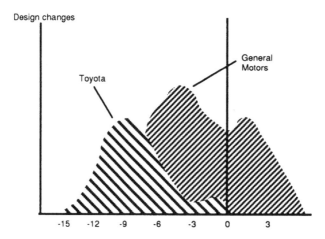

Figure 12.10 It is claimed that QFD reduces the number of forced design changes both pre- and post-product launch

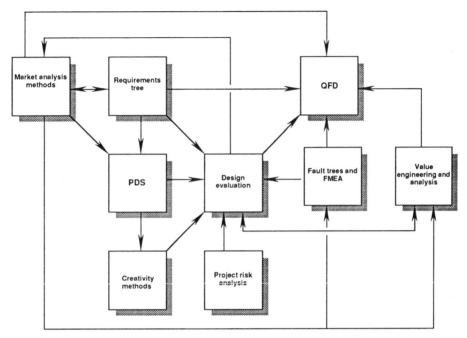

Figure 12.11   Information flow between QFD and other design methods

The gathering of customer perceptions through market research, generation of requirement trees, and the assignment of RIRs all provide information for the first QFD chart. Establishing engineering and parts characteristics, process operations and production requirements, and the links between them and customer requirements, is made easier by the use of value engineering and analysis techniques because of the attention that they give to these issues. The use of fault trees and FMEA also link customer requirements to technological aspects of the design.

RECAP

Quality function deployment is a method by which the requirements of the customer can be linked to the decision-making processes within the company. The linkage between the requirements and engineering characteristics, parts characteristics, process operations, and production requirements is established through a series of charts. The charts can also be used to record current and target values of the characteristics that they include, and the performance of competitors in terms of the requirements and characteristics.

Although QFD carries a large overhead in terms of staff time, substantial benefits are claimed by some companies, particularly if use of the method commences during the early stages of the PDP. If this is done, there is evidence that QFD can help to reduce the number of post product-launch design changes, and thereby reduce development costs and time to market.

ASSIGNMENTS

Assignment 12.1

Figure 12.1 shows an engineering characteristics deployment for some of the customer-valued attributes for the segment M hairdryer. Using this as a base, complete a more detailed engineering characteristics deployment chart including as many customer-valued attributes and engineering characteristics as you can identify. Use the customer perception data in Chapter 4 to help provide an evaluation on the chart, and assign RIRs to each customer-valued attribute. Instead of merely identifying the existence of relationships between customer-valued attributes and engineering characteristics with a tick, decide whether they are strong, medium, or weak and identify them with suitable symbols. Use the relationships that you have identified and the RIRs to assign an importance rating to each engineering characteristic. Also incorporate a 'roof structure' as shown in Figure 12.5, and record relationships between different engineering characteristics. In some cases, you will need to make some assumptions about the nature of the design solution. You could use an enlarged photocopy of the QFD chart provided in Appendix 1 instead of making up your own chart.

Assignment 12.2

Using the engineering characteristics that you developed in Assignment 12.1, produce a parts development chart along the lines of the one shown in Figure 12.7. Make any assumptions that you wish about the nature of the parts that are manufactured 'in-house' or purchased from outside suppliers. Identify relationships between part characteristics and assign importance ratings by looking at their influence on the previously weighted engineering characteristics.

STANDARD FORMS

Appendix 1 contains standard forms for some of the more complicated charts that have been introduced. These may be photocopied freely for use when solving the assignments and for other applications of the methods. In some cases, it would be an advantage if the copies were made at A3 size because of the amount of information that need to be entered into each field.

Users of these charts should note that there are no broadly accepted standards, and that different companies tend to use their own design.

Features

	No importance	Little importance	Quite important	Very important
	☐	☐	☐	☐
	☐	☐	☐	☐
	☐	☐	☐	☐
	☐	☐	☐	☐
	☐	☐	☐	☐
	☐	☐	☐	☐
	☐	☐	☐	☐
	☐	☐	☐	☐
	☐	☐	☐	☐
	☐	☐	☐	☐
	☐	☐	☐	☐
	☐	☐	☐	☐
	☐	☐	☐	☐
	☐	☐	☐	☐
	☐	☐	☐	☐
	☐	☐	☐	☐
	☐	☐	☐	☐
	☐	☐	☐	☐
	☐	☐	☐	☐
	☐	☐	☐	☐
	☐	☐	☐	☐
	☐	☐	☐	☐
	☐	☐	☐	☐

Figure A1.1   User preference chart

PRODUCT FEATURES	PRODUCTS																							
	Very poor	Poor	Good	Excellent	Very poor	Poor	Good	Excellent	Very poor	Poor	Good	Excellent	Very poor	Poor	Good	Excellent	Very poor	Poor	Good	Excellent	Very poor	Poor	Good	Excellent
	☐	☐	☐	☐	☐	☐	☐	☐	☐	☐	☐	☐	☐	☐	☐	☐	☐	☐	☐	☐	☐	☐	☐	☐
	☐	☐	☐	☐	☐	☐	☐	☐	☐	☐	☐	☐	☐	☐	☐	☐	☐	☐	☐	☐	☐	☐	☐	☐
	☐	☐	☐	☐	☐	☐	☐	☐	☐	☐	☐	☐	☐	☐	☐	☐	☐	☐	☐	☐	☐	☐	☐	☐
	☐	☐	☐	☐	☐	☐	☐	☐	☐	☐	☐	☐	☐	☐	☐	☐	☐	☐	☐	☐	☐	☐	☐	☐
	☐	☐	☐	☐	☐	☐	☐	☐	☐	☐	☐	☐	☐	☐	☐	☐	☐	☐	☐	☐	☐	☐	☐	☐
	☐	☐	☐	☐	☐	☐	☐	☐	☐	☐	☐	☐	☐	☐	☐	☐	☐	☐	☐	☐	☐	☐	☐	☐
	☐	☐	☐	☐	☐	☐	☐	☐	☐	☐	☐	☐	☐	☐	☐	☐	☐	☐	☐	☐	☐	☐	☐	☐
	☐	☐	☐	☐	☐	☐	☐	☐	☐	☐	☐	☐	☐	☐	☐	☐	☐	☐	☐	☐	☐	☐	☐	☐
	☐	☐	☐	☐	☐	☐	☐	☐	☐	☐	☐	☐	☐	☐	☐	☐	☐	☐	☐	☐	☐	☐	☐	☐
	☐	☐	☐	☐	☐	☐	☐	☐	☐	☐	☐	☐	☐	☐	☐	☐	☐	☐	☐	☐	☐	☐	☐	☐
	☐	☐	☐	☐	☐	☐	☐	☐	☐	☐	☐	☐	☐	☐	☐	☐	☐	☐	☐	☐	☐	☐	☐	☐
	☐	☐	☐	☐	☐	☐	☐	☐	☐	☐	☐	☐	☐	☐	☐	☐	☐	☐	☐	☐	☐	☐	☐	☐
	☐	☐	☐	☐	☐	☐	☐	☐	☐	☐	☐	☐	☐	☐	☐	☐	☐	☐	☐	☐	☐	☐	☐	☐
	☐	☐	☐	☐	☐	☐	☐	☐	☐	☐	☐	☐	☐	☐	☐	☐	☐	☐	☐	☐	☐	☐	☐	☐
	☐	☐	☐	☐	☐	☐	☐	☐	☐	☐	☐	☐	☐	☐	☐	☐	☐	☐	☐	☐	☐	☐	☐	☐

Figure A1.2 Customer perception chart

	Comments				
FEATURE					
PRODUCT					

Figure A1.3 Product feature chart

Specification				
Sub-assembly and/or product title:			**Prepared by:**	
Date of preparation:		**Sheet** .... **of**	**Approved by:**	
Reference number	**Requirements - compliance criteria must be provided**		**Revision number**	**Responsible**

Figure A1.4 Product design specification

	IDEA 1	IDEA 2	IDEA 3
Team member 1			
Team member 2			
Team member 3			
Team member 4			
Team member 5			
Team member 6			

Figure A1.5   6–3–5 chart

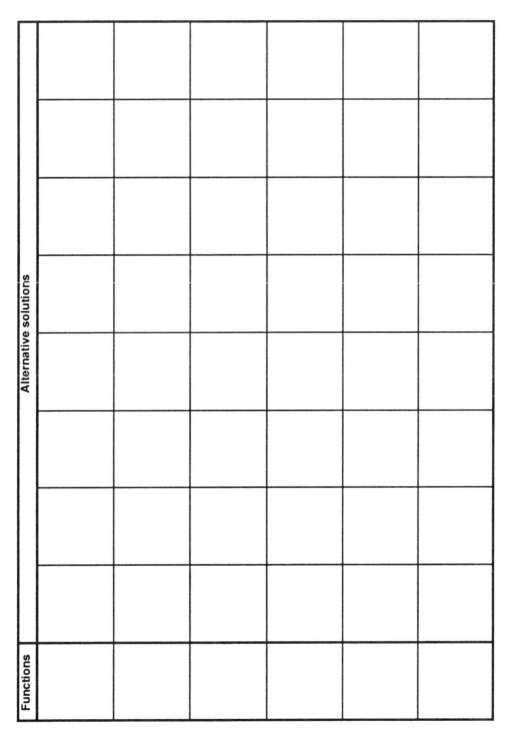

Figure A1.6 Morphology chart

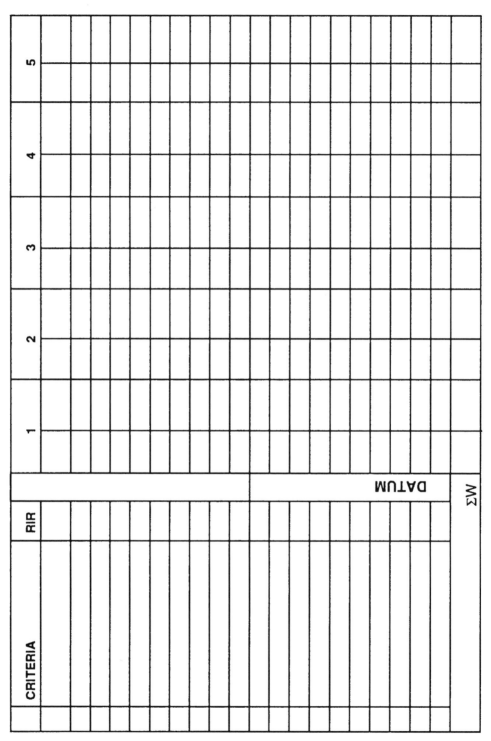

Figure A1.7 Evaluation matrix

Assembly	Sub-system	Difficulty	Consequence	Risk	Notes	Responsibility

Figure A1.8 Risk analysis chart

PRODUCT ....
DRAWING NUMBER ....
HIERARCHICAL LEVEL ....

DATE ....
ORIGINATOR ....
APPROVED ....

Components	Functions								Component cost (£)	Component cost (%)
Function cost (£)										
Function cost (%)										100

Figure A1.9 Value engineering chart

Component	Function	Interaction

Figure A1.10 Component/function interaction chart

Customer valued attributes

Components	Component cost	Cost elements					
		Manufacturing					
		Material					
		Cost per function					
		Manufacturing					
		Material					
		Cost per function					
		Manufacturing					
		Material					
		Cost per function					
		Manufacturing					
		Material					
		Cost per function					
		Manufacturing					
		Material					
		Cost per function					
		Manufacturing					
		Material					
		Cost per function					
		Manufacturing					
		Material					
		Cost per function					
		Manufacturing					
		Material					
		Cost per function					
		Manufacturing					
		Material					
		Cost per function					
		Manufacturing					
		Material					
		Cost per function					

Figure A1.11 Function/component cost chart

SYSTEM: ....
HIERARCHICAL LEVEL: ....
DRAWING: ....
MODE OF USE: ....

DATE: ....
SHEET: .... OF ....
ORIGINATOR: ....
APPROVED: ....

Item	Description and Function	Failure Mode	Failure Effect		Detection Method	Severity	Remarks
			Local	System			
1	2	3	4	5	6	7	8

Figure A1.12 FMEA worksheet

Item	Description and function	Failure mode	Failure effect		Severity	Probability	Detection method	Detectability	Criticality
			Local	System					

SYSTEM: ....
HIERARCHICAL LEVEL: ....
DRAWING: ....
MODE OF USE: ....

DATE: ....
SHEET: .... OF ....
ORIGINATOR: ....
APPROVED: ....

Figure A1.13 FMECA worksheet

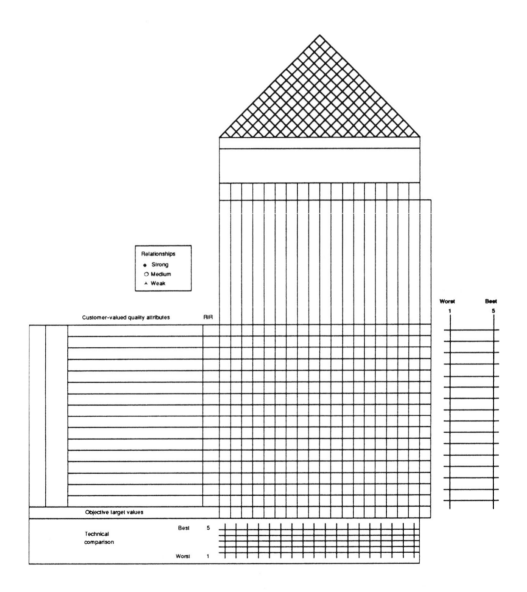

Figure A1.14 QFD matrix

MODEL ANSWERS

Some assignments in this book are concerned with the evaluation of products and marketing techniques. Where the outcome of such a study depends upon factors that are likely to change over a short period of time, the answers provided in this appendix have been given in general terms rather than in reference to a product or advertising strategy current at the time of writing.

ASSIGNMENT 4.1

Automobile manufacturers identify many segments for their products. Three segments that are often identifiable in their advertisements are the following:

1. *Young, single, first time buyers of new vehicles. These customers are often identified as adventurous, open-minded, and risk-taking, with a considerable amount of disposable income.*
2. *Married with a young family. This segment demonstrates interest in safety, economy, and space for the accoutrements of family travel.*
3. *Middle- or late middle-aged. This segment can be seen to include people at the peak of their earning power, and with diminishing demands imposed by their children. Disposable income tends to be higher in this segment than in segment 2.*

Which publications might an automobile manufacturer use to reach each of the above segments? Although some publications will overlap two or all three of the segments, most will only be suitable for reaching one. Obtain one or more issues of different publications that are targeted at the segments and look at the automobile advertisements. In most cases, the company will use a form of words and images that will attempt to make the product attractive to the relevant segment. In each case, make a list of the attributes and usage occasions that are introduced in the advertisement that address the needs of the segment.

Can you find examples of the same model being sold on the basis of different attributes and usage occasions to two segments? Even companies that sell painkillers do this when selling their product to young or old, and men or women.

Although each advertisement on TV or in publications tends to target a well defined and relatively narrow segmentation, the company will want to pick up sales from as many segments as possible. For this reason, the literature available from the distributors tends to be much wider in its coverage of attributes and usage occasions.

There is a lot of overlap in these segments in terms of disposable income. Clearly, not all people in segment 3 are more affluent than everyone in segment 2, and many people in segment 1 (e.g. students) have little disposable income. Many older people are just as adventurous as segment 1 buyers because of their reduced family responsibilities, which presents them with the opportunity to go in for more adventurous purchases. Nevertheless, regardless of these reservations, discrimination in the placing of advertisements in magazines is relatively easy to find. Typical of the magazines that target advertisements for these segments are:

Segment 1:

Many womens' magazines can be classified on the basis of the age group to which they are aimed. Those that target the younger age groups carry advertisements for automobiles at the lower end of the price range, but concentrate on freedom and the social benefits that can accrue from ownership. Specialist car magazines tend to be aimed at young and middle-aged males, and hence carry the sort of information that these segments are supposed to be interested in. Advertisements concentrate on technical specification and a sporty or macho styling.

Segment 2:

Magazines aimed at women in their mid-twenties to thirties frequently carry advertisements that stress the family benefits of the automobile. Storage space and safety play a predominant role in these advertisements. There is little difference between the advertising strategy for young single males and married males in a family group. Some men still seem to yearn for macho sporty models (cars that is) independent of their marital status; or at least, that is what the marketing people have decided.

Segment 3:

This group is notoriously difficult to reach through advertising. Although there are a few specialist magazines that are aimed at the senior citizen, their reading matter differs little from that of segment 2. For that reason, advertisements aimed at this group tend to be combined with segment 2 advertising. Some magazines typified by the 'country lifestyle' and 'investment weekly' type of publication carry advertisements depicting older people enjoying the freedom that an automobile can bring. Selling points tend to be based around comfort and economy.

ASSIGNMENT 4.2

Read some computer magazines and look through the window of any popular computer retailer in the high street. On the basis of the products that are available, what can you say about market segmentation for PCs? Make a list of these segments, identifying some of the characteristics of the people that make them up. Complete the study by identifying one or more computers that seem to be targeting each segment. You will almost certainly find that each manufacturer attempts to broaden the appeal of its product by providing attributes that are attractive to more than one segment.

Commercial applications including secretarial and business applications. Advertisements aimed at these segments tend to sell 'bundled' solutions, where the computer comes with word processing, spreadsheet, database software etc. The productivity advantages of using the most up-to-date systems are stressed strongly. However, ease of use and friendly user interfaces are put forward as key issues to persuade non-experienced buyers that the system is easy to use, and that training requirements are minimal. Pricing is important, but the features are 'sold' strongly.

Home use is a rapidly growing market for PC suppliers. Two sub-segments that can be identified are children and adults. While recognising that in many cases adults and children will use the same computer, advertisers tend to separate them quite distinctly in their advertising strategies. Although the majority of children want a computer to play games, parents can often be persuaded to buy a PC for them on the basis of its combined games and educational capabilities. The advertisements aimed at the child segment therefore stresses both aspects, one to persuade the child that a computer is essential to have fun, and the other so that the parents feel that they are doing their duty. In the United Kingdom, public use of the Internet has lagged behind that found in the USA. There is plenty of evidence that the marketing of Internet facilities on PCs is growing rapidly in the home segment.

ASSIGNMENT 4.3

From your experience, and based upon the examples given earlier, identify three consumer products that are targeted using each of the following strategies:

1. *Undifferentiated marketing*
2. *Differentiated marketing*
3. *Concentrated marketing*

In each case, explain why that targeting strategy had been chosen. Repeat this exercise for industrial products.

Products selling into an undifferentiated market can often be identified by the lack of advertising associated with them. Advertising an undifferentiated product may produce an increase in overall sales volume, but this is just as likely to benefit competitor products as it is your own. Unbranded products in supermarkets often fall into this category. Although customers may identify these products on the basis of segmentation advertising from branded competitors, unbranded products are frequently treated as though they are being sold into a largely undifferentiated market by their distributors. Fruit, vegetables, and the output of utility industries (i.e. gas, electricity, and water) also belong to undifferentiated markets.

The majority of products fall into the differentiated market category. Some of the segments are real (e.g. male and female purchasers behaving differently towards particular types of product), or they may be artificial in that the advertising strategy tries to convince potential purchasers that they need something different. Although marketing strategies for automobiles are clearly differentiated on the basis of income, usage occasions etc., there are many more interesting examples. Cosmetics are predominantly aimed at the female segment, but a rapidly growing male segment for skin care products is now being addressed by many manufacturers. The train companies identify a large number of segments including students, young families, and senior citizens, and produce a sometimes bewildering array of promotions aimed at potential customers. Companies like the Microsoft Corporation have several ways of differentiating the market. Factors such as various hardware environments, usage situations (e.g. business/professional, home/hobby, scientific/technical), clarity of software needs, and country and language, are used by Microsoft to differentiate the market and hence help to guide product development and advertising strategy.

A concentrated marketing strategy usually requires a product that is finely honed to meet the requirements of its chosen segment. Specialist cars (frequently very expensive) are good examples of this type of product. Many manufacturers of industrial products build up a high level of expertise in designing and selling their product to a few customers. This design and manufacturing expertise is difficult to attain by potential competitors who would like to break into the market. In other words, it carries all the hallmarks of a concentrated market. Examples include: companies that manufacture transmission elements or electrical equipment for one or two major automobile companies to the almost total exclusion of other products; some suppliers of specialist equipment to the aerospace or military communications industries; companies that concentrate on products for customers with a particular physical disability.

ASSIGNMENT 4.4

Using the product feature chart in Figure 4.5 as a guide, produce a similar chart for one of the product classes in the following list. Limit your chart to eight brands.

1. *Domestic food-mixers.*
2. *Electric shavers for men and women (four of each).*
3. *Compact disc players.*
4. *Electric kettles*
5. *Electric drills*

Remember to include price as an attribute, and identify those attributes that are mentioned on the packaging.

PRODUCT	Keyless chuck	Voltage	Charge time (hours)	Number of forward speeds	Reverse	Number of torqued settings	Hammer action	Cost (£)	Comments
Black & Decker KC8441C	Yes	8.4	3	2	Yes	0	No	58	
Black & Decker KC9651C	Yes	9.6	3	∞	Yes	5	No	80	
Black & Decker KC9682C	Yes	9.6	1	∞	Yes	14	Yes	115	
Elu SBA55K	No	12	1	∞	No	0	No	300	Combination screwdriver. Comes with 2 battery packs.
De Walt DW976K2	Yes	12	1	∞	Yes	0	Yes	300	Electronic brake. Comes with 2 battery packs.
De Walt DW921K2	Yes	9.6	1	1	Yes	0	No	150	Comes with a kit box and 2 battery packs.

Figure A2.1 A product feature chart for a range of electric drills

As an example, Figure A2.1 is a product feature chart for electric drills where six products from three manufacturers are listed. Eight features have been chosen on the basis of the attention given to them by the manufacturers as a part of their product description in advertisements and on packaging.

ASSIGNMENT 4.5

Make a list of the attributes identified in your study from Assignment 4.4 and present it in a similar way to that shown in Figure 4.4. Provide a copy of the form to a small sample of 20 people or more (the more the better) and collate the results into a single sheet summary. It will help in getting some consistency in your results if the members of your sample are of a similar age or background, i.e. all students, parents, male, female etc. In other words, try to identify a segment on which to carry out your customer preference survey.

Rank the preferences in descending order, i.e. the most highly valued attribute at the top. Is it likely that a study of a different segment would show a different ranking? Is this reflected in the product range or advertising? If not, why is there a range of product brands for this class?

Figure A2.2 shows the details from the User Preference Chart with averaged perceptions of importance from a sample of 50 males between the age of 35 and 45 years. Charge time and hammer action were the most important features for this sample. Perhaps a sample consisting of users who were DIY car enthusiasts would have rated 'reverse' and 'torqued settings' more highly.

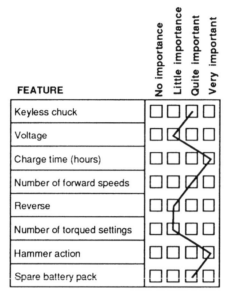

Figure A2.2   An attribute list for a survey of customer preferences for an electric drill

ASSIGNMENT 5.1

Imagine that you are a consulting engineer who has been given a brief to undertake a feasibility study on the design of a machine to take loads of recently lifted carrots and prepare them ready for sale in high class retail outlets. A market survey has revealed that the customer wants the carrots to be prepacked in sealed 1 Kg packs. Draw a requirement tree for the machine. Can you get down as far as fourth level objectives in all branches? At some stage during the preparation of the tree you may have to make some assumptions about the problem.

Figure A2.3 shows part of a requirement tree for the carrot processing problem. Although not completed because of space limitations, the Tree indicates how a second level consisting of five requirements might be developed in some of the branches.

ASSIGNMENT 5.2

You have made such a success of the carrot problem that you have been 'head hunted' by a company that makes electrical domestic products. In your new capacity, you are working with the marketing department to specify the objectives for a new design of hair dryer to meet the needs of the 17 to 25 year old single male market. Making any assumptions that you want about the market, draw a requirement tree. Many of the objectives will be the same as for any other type of hairdryer, but include them in your tree just the same.

Figure A2.4 is my attempt at the hairdryer tree based upon the information to hand. I have set the bottom-level requirements in boxes with a thicker outline to bring them to your

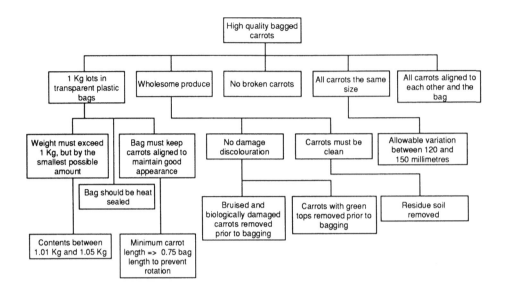

Figure A2.3   A requirement tree for the carrot processing problem

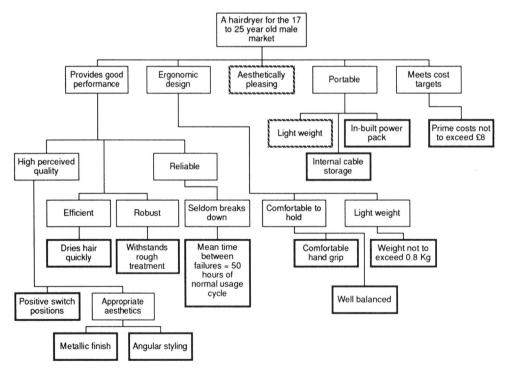

Figure A2.4   A requirement tree for the Segment M hairdryer

attention. In the case of 'aesthetically pleasing' and 'lightweight', the requirements occur at two different places in the tree, so I have not bothered to develop the second occurrences. Some of the requirements like 'seldom breaks down' and 'meets cost targets' have been developed a step further into constraints. With a little bit of work more constraints could be developed. Your tree will certainly be different to mine, but should be dealing with similar sets of requirements.

ASSIGNMENT 5.3

Using either the requirement tree that you produced for Assignment 5.2, or the hairdryer tree in Appendix 2, develop weightings for all of the bottom-level objectives. Use the top-down approach, working alone or (preferably) with two or three colleagues. Remember to make a record of why each decision was taken, paying particular attention to unresolved conflicts where you agreed to disagree.

I removed the constraints and recurring requirements from the basic tree before starting the weighting. Because the 'portable' second level objective carried 40% of the overall weight, and because it only developed into two sub-objectives, the weighting for a built-in power pack was particularly high. This may indeed reflect its importance to potential buyers, or it might mean that there are other third level requirements that the tree shown in Figure A2.5 has not developed.

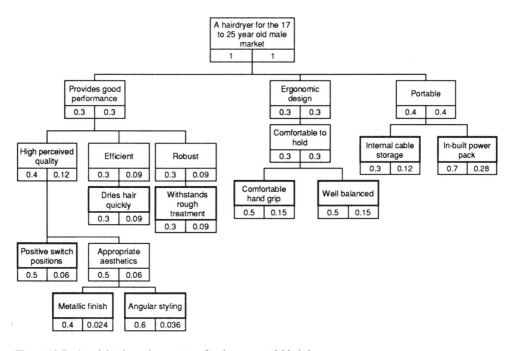

Figure A2.5   A weighted requirement tree for the segment M hairdryer

ASSIGNMENT 5.4

Make a list of the bottom level objectives that you worked on in Assignment 5.2 and assign weightings to them using the bottom-up approach. Ask at least six of your colleagues to rate each objective on a scale from 1 (not important) to 5 (vitally important) as was done earlier in this chapter with the shoe cleaning problem. Are the weightings obtained by the two methods different, and what may be the reason for this?

Using the bottom-up approach, a small sample (80 people) from the target group ranked the objectives as follows:

Objective	Points
Dries hair quickly	340
In-built power pack	315
Withstands rough treatment	298
Well balanced	243
Internal cable storage	224
Comfortable hand grip	220
Positive switch positions	185
Metallic finish	92
Angular styling	55

If you present customers with a list of product attributes and ask how important they are in influencing purchasing decisions, there is often a reluctance to admit that subjective issues like styling are important. Many people feel happy to say that they purchased their car because of its miles per litre, acceleration, or internal space. Far fewer admit that it was the chrome strip, alloy wheels, and imitation wood inlays that persuaded them to part with their hard won money. This tendency is also revealed in the bottom-up ranking of the hairdryer attributes. On the other hand, when people are asked to make direct comparisons between attributes at a high level in a requirements tree, they seem to be more comfortable in acknowledging that things like aesthetics do have a very important part to play. It is only when they get down to the detail of what they mean by aesthetics that they get nervous.

ASSIGNMENT 6.1

In Chapter 5 you did an assignment which entailed the construction of a requirement tree for a hairdryer. I now want you to use this requirement tree to produce a PDS. If you wish, you can use the sample tree that I provide in the Appendix, but it would be much better if you developed your own. Remember to quantify as many items as possible and, in the case of those that you cannot quantify, think of ways that you might be able to resolve differences of opinion when assessing potential design solutions.

Specification			
Sub-assembly and/or product title: Re-chargeable battery powered hairdryer		Prepared:: A.J. Dewhurst	
Date: 25 March 1996	Sheet......1..... of........2.	Approved: H. Budarkewicz	
Reference number	Requirements - compliance criteria must be provided	Revision number	Owner
1	30-minutes operation on 3-hour re-charge time.		A.D.T
2	Output 1500 Watts		A.D.T
3	Plugs into mains re-charger		A.D.T
4	Maximum weight 350 grams		S.S.P
5	Ergonomics to human factors document E90221 and approved by TD227889.		S.S.P .
6	Comb and nozzle attachments for short hair		S.S.P .
7	Positive switch positions. Approved by customer sample under document TD227889		J.G .
8	Styling to industrial design requirements IDR556 and approved by TD227889.		J.G .
9	Withstands rough treatment. 1m drop test.		A.D.T

Figure A2.6 A PDS for the hair dryer

Because you are producing this PDS from the requirement tree, it is inevitable that it will specify basic requirements without any restrictions on the various forms of solution that may be developed from it. Figure A2.6 shows some of the items that your PDS may contain. Each item should describe a requirement in a form in which compliance can be checked at a later date. In some cases this can be done by assigning constraints like maximum weight or power. In other cases, compliance will need to be checked by customer sampling.

ASSIGNMENT 7.1

Rather than have me provide you with some problems to solve, I would like you to generate a list yourself. I call this sort of list a 'bug-list', because the things that generally appear on them are problems that annoy or 'bug' us. Just sit down, and write down a list of things that annoy you, and where you think that it might be possible to find a solution to the problem. I sometimes give this task to my students so that we will have a 'store' of problems to apply the creativity techniques to. Ideally, you would try to find solutions to other peoples' problems rather than the ones that you had generated yourself, but obviously there are no rules about this. The following list is part of one that a small group of students generated in less than 10 minutes. I have omitted those that might have prevented this book being published.

- *Doors that squeak*
- *Doors that stick in damp weather*
- *Glasses that 'mist-up'*
- *Cold toilet seats*
- *Toilets where the paper has run out*
- *Big bunches of keys*

- *Polishing shoes*
- *Lecturers*
- *Loose change*
- *Pens that don't work*
- *etc.,*

After you have generated your own list, select two problems that you would like to work on. Choose problems that you consider can be handled in a reasonable period of time; obviously this would tend to exclude things like 'travel to the moon on a number 2 bus' but, on the other hand it is better if the problem does not have a clear means of solution at the outset. The reason for this being that there is then a tendency to cling on to the obvious rather than generate other novel ideas.

Take the first problem, and apply the 6–3–5 method in an attempt to generate solutions. Re-read the notes on the method carefully before starting. If you are working in a group of n people, try to generate at least 2 × n distinct ideas plus a similar number of hybrids. Of course, the number of ideas that you produce will depend upon the size of the problem, the experience and background of members of the team, and serendipity.

When you have finished, make some reasonably neat sketches of the ideas that came out of the sessions (you may need more than one), and provide a short paragraph for each idea describing its strengths and weaknesses.

The diagram in Figure A2.7 is a part of the 6–3–5 chart produced by a group dealing with the 'glasses that mist-up' problem.

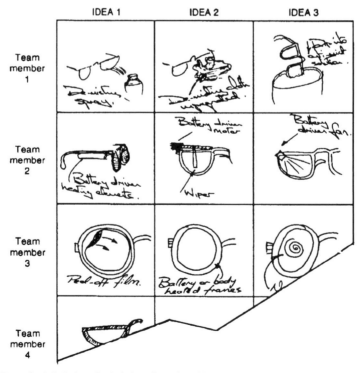

Figure A2.7 Part of a 6–3–5 chart for 'misting glasses' problem

It is important to remember that practice is necessary to make any of the brainstorming techniques work effectively for you. Whichever technique you use, brainstorming is simply the stage during which you combine the efforts and abilities of your group to breakthrough problems. Developing the outcome of the brainstorming process, either by further brainstorming and/or detail design, is the next stage of the PDP.

ASSIGNMENT 7.2

Take the second of the two problems selected from the bug-list of Assignment 7.1, and apply the controlled input method to its solution. Again, read the notes on the method carefully before proceeding, and complete the session with a written summary.

Which of the two methods do you prefer? Is this because of some basic advantage of one method over the other, because one method requires more practice than the other, or simply because one of the problems was more conducive to brainstorming than the other? Whatever your conclusions, remember that all these techniques need a lot of practice before you can get the best out of them.

As I said in Chapter 7, the various methods of brainstorming appeal to different people at different times. Most people prefer the 6–3–5 method initially, because there are fewer intrusive rules to follow. This does not mean that the 6–3–5 method is superior. Experienced users tend to switch between the methods. If one does not give the desired results then try the other.

ASSIGNMENT 7.3

Take one of the ideas generated during Assignments 7.1 or 7.2 and draw a mind map like the one shown in Figure 7.2 to explore the problems that will be involved in bringing it to completion.

Figure A2.8 shows a mind map for problems associated with one of the concepts dealing with preventing spectacles from misting up. The concept involves providing batteries to provide current to elements on or in the lens material. There are many problems associated with this concept, and the diagram lists some of them. Three main problem areas are identified. These are: the batteries, which raise questions relating to the power requirements, battery life, and the battery technology i.e. alkaline, NiCd, rechargeable, the elements, and whether these are mounted on or embedded in the lens material, and switching i.e. whether the user switches the power on, or whether a sensor based on temperature change and/or humidity is used.

ASSIGNMENT 7.4

Using figure 7.7 as an example, draw a problem diagram for an automatic system to change a tyre on a car wheel. Assume that the system is to be installed in one of the high-street retailers that you can go to for replacement tyres or exhausts. Remember that you do not need to think

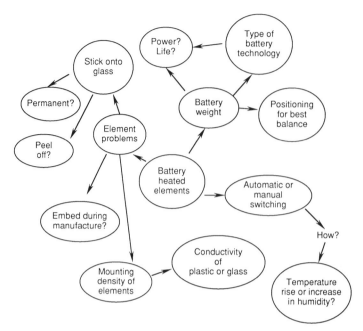

Figure A2.8 A mind map for problems associated with the 'misting glasses' problem

of detailed solutions to any parts of this problem; only what the events are, in what sequence they are required, what materials must be provided and disposed of, and if there are any information 'feed-back' or feed-forward requirements. Get this one right and you may be able to retire earlier than you had thought.

Your problem diagram will depend upon your perception of the problem, where you decide to draw the system boundaries, and the direction that your creativity takes you.

In Figure A2.9 I have assumed that the car will be driven into a work bay so that it is adjacent to the tyre changing system. At this stage, I have made no commitments as to which stages in the process are automatic, and which will need to be accomplished manually. These decisions will depend upon the technical difficulties and the associated costs, and the effect that these costs have on the commercial viability of the system. Therefore, the problem diagram closely represents the manual process of tyre changing. If an automatic system was developed, some of the stages represented here may be removed or re-ordered. For example, the system might suspend the car and drop the floor away thereby requiring the third element in the diagram to be rewritten.

ASSIGNMENT 7.5

Construct a morphology chart, and enter the functions that were identified from the tyre problem that you worked on in Assignment 7.4. Use either the 6–3–5 or controlled input methods of brainstorming to generate several possible solutions for each of the functions, and enter these onto the morphology chart.

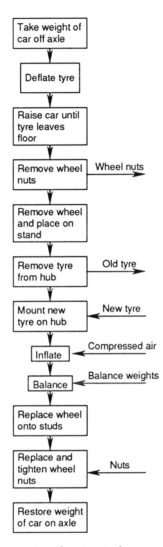

Figure A2.9 A problem diagram for an automatic system to change car tyres

Can you identify any logical linkages between solutions for the various functions; perhaps based on the type of power requirements or services? Identify two or three combinations of solutions that you consider to have potential for development. Which solutions do you feel might be the most difficult to develop fully? Based on the morphology chart, write a one-page report for the company's technical director outlining the options available.

There are several examples of morphological charts in Chapter 7. Use these as a guide in the preparation of the one for the car tyre problem. Place the various elements from the problem diagram down the left hand side, and generate as many solutions as you can for each of these using one of the brainstorming methods. Enter the outcome of the brainstorming sessions into the morphological chart.

Think about the services that the system will require to operate. Clearly, compressed air will be needed to inflate the new tyre. Is it reasonable to use compressed air for any of the other functions that the system will have to provide. If other types of power systems are required, e.g. hydraulics to raise the vehicle, can this also be used to provide the torque necessary for releasing and tightening the wheel nuts? Will materials such as the tyres (new and old) and the balance weight be conveyed and presented manually, or will they be stacked and withdrawn automatically? If you have not already got them, add these material handling functions to the left hand side of the chart, and provide each with some possible solutions. Use the morphological chart to help you evaluate the options, look for promising combinations of solution, and identify areas where further thought is required.

ASSIGNMENT 8.1

This assignment provides some practice at identifying requirements, drawing up an evaluation matrix, and evaluating the requirements against a set of given product attributes. It is similar to the example on choosing an answering machine, except this time we are going to choose a fridge-freezer. Again, the product attributes are courtesy of a Which? *magazine survey, but only a small sample of the devices surveyed by* Which? *are included here to make your task more manageable. In Figure 8.17, I have provided the Product Attribute Chart, but before you are influenced by it write down a list of what attributes would be important to you. Then, rank the attributes by distributing a predetermined number of points between them. Enter the RIRs that this produces into the chart and analyse the extent to which each product meets your requirements before completing the weighting columns. On the basis of your conclusions write a justification of the final choice.*

Remember that the objective is not to pick the 'best', but to identify the product out of those listed that most closely meets **your** requirements. Unless you have an absolute upper limit on what you are prepared to pay, it is difficult to put a RIR value against cost. This is because cost is just one factor in your assessment of the 'value' of the product, and can only be assessed in conjunction with other attributes. Even when you have thought carefully about the attributes that you want or would like from a fridge-freezer, and evaluated each of the ones listed against these attributes, it is unlikely that the final choice will be obvious. Clearly, you would want to see the product that you were considering buying to make sure that the design detail met with your approval. Your views on this may be influenced by aesthetics, internal layout, and ergonomic details. This influence of a very broad range of factors on the marketability of a product occurs in industrial as well as consumer products

ASSIGNMENT 9.1

Your company is a medium-sized engineering concern, with a good reputation for providing high quality joy-stick controls for military and civil aircraft. The company is a member of a larger group with diverse engineering interests. For some time, the board of directors of your company have been holding discussions with one of the major international suppliers of computer games equipment with a view to supplying them with joy-sticks to assemble into their products. Although a contract has not yet been signed, your board have been informed that a letter of intent will be forthcoming.

The customer will require in the region of 200 000 joy-sticks each year for an initial period of 3 years. These are quantities that are way above anything that your company has had to deal with in the past, and a new project manager was employed two months ago to oversee the product design, pre-development, project definition, planning, and budgeting phases.

To cope with the production of the new product, your board have decided to convert an on-site warehouse that is currently standing idle, and to install production facilities and an automated assembly line. Three project teams have been formed under the control of the new project manager. These are: (1) building refurbishment and services, (2) manufacturing systems design and installation, (3) product design. An overall budget of £3 million has been sanctioned by the group board.

List the technological and market risks for this project, stating any assumptions that you feel are necessary. Select and apply probability and consequence factors to the risks and complete a risk evaluation chart. Draw a risk map of the type shown in Figure 9.9, and say how you might eliminate or mitigate some of the risks that you have identified.

You might identify the following project risk factors from the question:

Market
- The company to which the product is being supplied may have underestimated or overestimated the size of market that they can command.
- Your company's market image may be adversely affected by their expansion into a 'lower quality' mass market product.

Technological
- Product design lead time may overrun.
- Technical problems may occur with the product leading to overrun on project time.
- Technical problems may occur with the product leading to a larger than expected product cost.
- Problems in converting the warehouse to house production facilities.
- Problems in designing and commissioning the manufacturing facility leading to larger than expected costs or time overrun.

In addition to these broadly stated areas, there could be other risk factors, including the availability of adequate staff resource to carry out the project successfully.

The details of the risk evaluation chart will depend upon your view of the situation regarding each of the factors that you have listed.

ASSIGNMENT 10.1

Most of the following list of products can be found in the home. See if you can get your hands on several of them (the more the better), and write down what you think is the most important function that a potential purchaser would value. Next, list as many other user value functions as you can. I will not call functions in this additional list 'secondary functions' because some of them might be just as important as the first function that you identified. Having made the list as exhaustive as you can, make a study of the component parts of the product and try to decide which function or functions each component contributes to. If you find a component that does not seem to contribute to the provision of any of the identified functions, it probably means that you have failed to identify a user-valued function. Here is the list:

- *A fountain pen*
- *A stapling machine*
- *An opener for food cans (any one of the various types available)*

Fountain pen

1. Provide a line on paper

2. Store ink

3. Allow ink to be refilled

4. Clip into pocket

5. Prevent ink from drying when not being used

6. Protect carrier from ink stains

7. Provide good grip

Components/sub-assemblies	Functions
Cap	4, 5, 6
Clip	4
Body	3, 6, 7
Nib assembly	1, 2, 3, 6
Ink reservoir assembly	1, 2, 3, 6

A stapling machine

1. Secure sheets of paper together

2. Hold a supply of staples

3. Allow staples to be refilled

4. Allow staple points to be either inward or outward facing

5. Stand on desk without damaging the surface

6. Handle automatically resets

Components/sub-assemblies	Functions
Base sub-assembly	1, 4, 5, 6
Anvil sub-assembly	1, 4
Cartridge release sub-assembly	2, 3
Staple slide	2, 3
Staple delivery sub-assembly	1

An opener for food cans

1. Remove the top from food cans
2. Retain the lid after removal
3. Demand little physical effort

Components/sub-assemblies	*Functions*
Cutter-wheel sub-assembly	1, 2
Serrated-wheel sub-assembly	1
Wheel mounting plate	2
Handle sub-assembly	3

ASSIGNMENT 10.2

Figure 10.12 provides details of a treasury tag punch. The punch is used to place a single hole near the corner of sheets of paper so that they can be secured together by the treasury tag. Other than for the fact of punching only one hole, this product is similar in function and construction to a normal two-hole punch. When disassembled, the product is found to be made up of 10 separate components, although as a part of the manufacturing process, the base and support bracket are riveted together.

Assume that this product is manufactured by a competitor company, and that you have been given the task of benchmarking it. Your marketing department have provided you with a list of functions that customers value, together with an assessment of the importance of each function to the buyer. This information is given in Figure 10.13.

PRODUCT ....Treasury tag punch .... DATE ....23/9/97...............
DRAWING NUMBER .....TP/16A........... ORIGINATOR ........I.E.S...............
HIERARCHICAL LEVEL ....2....................... APPROVED ..........I.C.W...........

Components \ Functions	Punch hole	Hold punchings	Remove punchings	Auto reset	Handle locking				Component cost (£)	Component cost (%)
Plastic cover		0.02	0.03						0.05	11
Base	0.04	0.03	0.01						0.08	17
Support bracket	0.12								0.12	25
Pivot pin	0.03								0.03	6
Punch rod	0.02								0.02	4
Spring (large)				0.04					0.04	8
Spring (small)					0.01				0.01	2
Bent arm					0.02				0.02	4
Handle	0.08								0.08	17
Rod pin	0.02				0.01				0.03	6
Function cost (£)	0.31	0.05	0.04	0.04	0.04				0.48	
Function cost (%)	65	11	8	8	8					100

Figure A2.10 A value engineering matrix for the treasury lag punch

Your production engineering department have made a list of each component and, using their experience have estimated the manufacturing cost of each. They have also assigned elements of component cost to each of the user-valued functions on the list provided by the marketing department. This information is provided in Figures 10.14 and 10.15.

Using a photocopy of the value analysis matrix in Appendix 1, complete an analysis for the punch. State what changes you might consider making to the punch to improve its value to the customer. Also state any assumptions that you are making about the market or manufacturing processes.

Encouragingly, from a design point of view, 65% of the prime cost of the punch is concerned with providing the basic and most important function, 'punch hole'. On the basis of the analysis, the design team might decide to examine the handle lock mechanism. This function, which receives a low importance rating from the customer's accounts for the same percentage of prime cost as two of the medium rated functions. This *may* be necessary, and make good marketing sense, but alternative options need to be evaluated. Would it be better to remove the lock completely, and either reduce the price and hope to increase the volume of sales, or keep the price at the existing level and make an increased profit on each punch? Alternatively, the cost saved by omitting the lock could be used to improve other attributes.

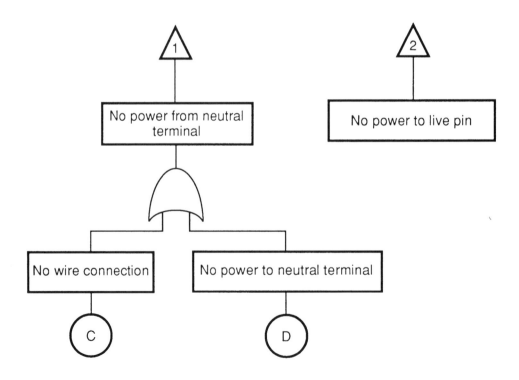

Figure A2.11 The continuation of the plug fault tree from transfer symbols 1 and 2

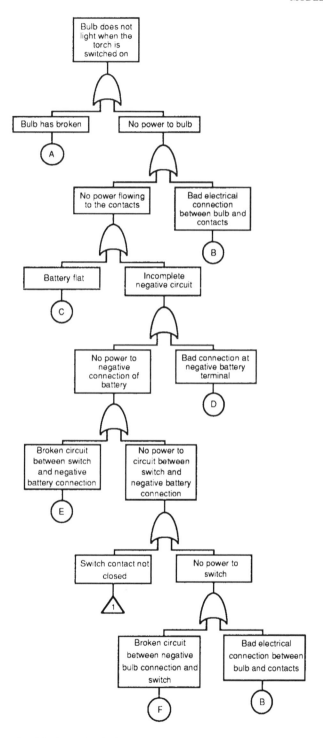

Figure A2.12 A completed fault tree for the battery powered torch

ASSIGNMENT 11.1

Complete the fault tree shown in Figure 11.4 by developing it from the points indicated by the transfer symbols 1 and 2. When continuing a tree like this on a new sheet, it should start by referencing the transfer symbol from which it is being developed. The correct way of doing this is shown in Figure 11.5.

ASSIGNMENT 11.2

Complete a fault tree for a battery powered torch, using 'Bulb does not light when the torch is switched on' as the top-level system failure. Because torches vary in their construction, it is best to get hold of one and take it to bits before starting the tree. Some torches have sealed bodies, and are difficult to disassemble, so choose one that comes apart easily. The type shown in Figure 10.1 is ideal for this purpose.

Figure A2.12 show's how a fault tree might develop from this question.

ASSIGNMENT 11.3

Figure 11.18 shows a diagrammatic representation of part of the cooling system on a motor car. The positions of the engine and radiator with respect to other components are not shown.

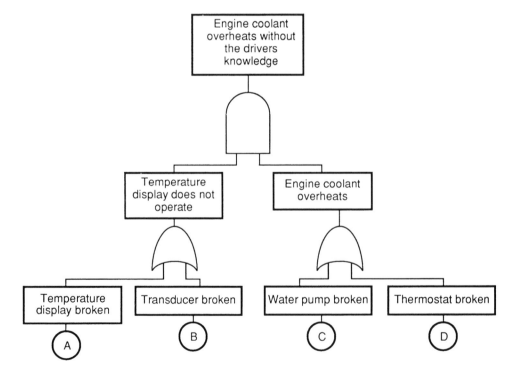

Figure A2.13   Fault tree for the engine cooling system with four basic events

Only the following four components are shown:

- *A pump which forces the cooling water through the system.*
- *A thermostat which is closed until the coolant reaches the best temperature for high engine efficiency, but which opens to allow coolant to flow as soon as this temperature is reached.*
- *A temperature transducer which senses the temperature of the cooling water and sends an appropriate signal to the display inside the car.*
- *A temperature display on the car fascia which informs the driver if the coolant temperature is normal or abnormal.*

An excessively high coolant temperature can cause damage to the engine, and it is important that the driver is informed when such a condition arises so that remedial action can be taken. A situation where the temperature is excessively high and where the driver is unaware of the situation is therefore to be avoided. Using 'Engine coolant overheats without the driver's knowledge' as the top-level system failure, draw a fault tree which contains the failure of the four identified components as basic events. Complete the truth table and find the minimum cut sets from it by inspection. Finally, use Boolean algebra to corroborate your answer.

In this example, the system, level failure has been defined as being: 'Engine coolant overheats without the driver's knowledge'. This is shown at the top level in Figure A2.13. Two faults, 'temperature display does not operate' *and* 'engine coolant overheats' must occur simultaneously for the top-level system failure occur. The AND symbol is used to specify this on the diagram. In the simplified system that we are considering, occurrence of each of the two second level faults only require one of two possible lower level faults to exist. The diagram uses OR symbols to link the basic events to the second level faults.

The following table shows the 16 possible system states, with all combinations of basic events.

Case	A	B	C	D	System
1	W	W	W	W	W
2	W	W	W	F	W
3	W	W	F	W	W
4	W	F	W	W	W
5	F	W	W	W	W
6	W	W	F	F	W
7	W	F	F	W	F
8	F	F	W	W	W
9	W	F	W	F	F
10	F	W	F	W	F
11	F	W	W	F	F
12	W	F	F	F	F
13	F	F	F	W	F
14	F	W	F	F	F
15	F	F	W	F	F
16	F	F	F	F	F

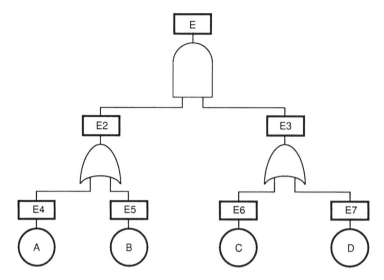

Figure A2.14 The generalised fault tree for the car cooling system

By inspection, the minimum cut sets are:

A	B	C	D	System
–	F	F	–	F
–	F	–	F	F
F	–	F	–	F
F	–	–	F	F

To confirm this using Boolean algebra, I have first drawn a fault tree (Figure A2.14) representing all of the faults symbolically (E1, E2, E3 etc.).

Then, applying Boolean algebra:

$$E1 \ = E2 \cap E3$$
$$= (A \cup B) \cap (C \cup D)$$
$$= (A \cap C) \cup (B \cap C) \cup (A \cap D) \cup (B \cap D)$$

Which is equivalent to: A and C, or B and C, or A and D, or B and D, which agrees with the minimum cut sets derived from the truth table.

ASSIGNMENT 11.4

Using the example given in Figure 11.23, what would be the outcome of the following failure modes: (1) a leak in the bellows, (2) the extension spring breaks? Construct a FMEA worksheet, entering the two failure modes. State any assumptions that you need regarding the operation of the unit.

Item	Description and function	Failure mode	Failure effect		Detection method	Severity	Remarks
			Local	System			
1	Bellows. Responds to air pressure to operate switch	Puncture causing air leak	Contacts open even if air pressure is satisfactory	False alarm of pressure loss	Routine maintenance. Otherwise none except system observation	2	Fail safe
	Extension spring. Rotates arm to collapse bellows on loss of pressure	Spring breaks	Contacts closed even if air pressure is lost	No alarm at loss of air pressure	None other than routine maintenance	5	Fail to danger

Figure A2.15   A FMEA worksheet for two failure modes of the pressure switch problem

The worksheet (Figure A2.15) presents details of the two components, their functions, and the failure modes being considered. In the case of the bellows, failure through leakage results in the contacts being open even when air pressure in the main system is at a satisfactory level. This is a fail safe situation because a warning will be given even though the situation does not demand it. On the information given, and under the assumptions applying, the result would be inconvenience to operators and perhaps some temporary loss of the process if it was shut down pending investigation. Failure of the extension spring is potentially much more dangerous because this could allow the swinging arm to rotate counter clockwise under its own weight, thereby closing the contacts even when air pressure has been lost from the system.

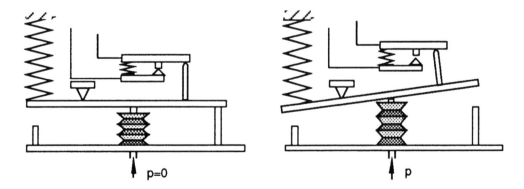

Figure A2.16   A FMEA worksheet for the modified switch

Item	Description and function	Failure mode	Failure effect		Detection method	Severity	Remarks
			Local	System			
1	Bellows. Responds to air pressure to operate switch	Puncture causing air leak	Contacts close even if air pressure is satisfactory	False alarm of pressure loss	Routine maintenance. Otherwise none except system observation	2	Fail safe
2	Extension spring (large). Rotates arm to collapse bellows on loss of pressure	Spring breaks	Contacts open even if air pressure is lost	No alarm at loss of air pressure	None other than routine maintenance	5	Fail to danger
3	Provides fulcrum for arm	Displacement	Arm rotates clockwise. Contacts open	No alarm at loss of air pressure	None other than routine maintenance	5	Fail to danger
4	Extension spring (small). Closes contacts when bellows collapse	Spring breaks	Contacts fail to close on loss of pressure	No alarm at loss of air pressure	None other than routine maintenance	5	Fail to danger

Figure A2.17 A FMEA worksheet for the modified switch

Item	Description and function	Failure mode	Failure effect		Severity	Probability	Detection method	Detectability	Criticality
			Local	System					
1	Bellows. Responds to air pressure to operate switch	Puncture causing air leak	Contacts open even if air pressure is satisfactory	False alarm of pressure loss	2	3	System alarm	1	6
2	Extension spring. Rotates arm to collapse bellows on loss of pressure	Spring breaks	Contacts close even if air pressure is lost	No alarm at loss of air pressure	5	2	None other than routine maintenance	5	50

Figure A2.18 A FMECA worksheet for the original switch

Item	Description and function	Failure mode	Failure effect		Severity	Probability	Detection method	Detectability	Criticality
			Local	System					
1	Bellows. Responds to air pressure to operate switch	Puncture causing air leak	Contacts close even if air pressure is satisfactory	False alarm of pressure loss	2	3	Routine maintenance. Otherwise none except system observation	1	6
2	Extension spring (large). Rotates arm to collapse bellows on loss of pressure	Spring breaks	Contacts open even if air pressure is lost	No alarm at loss of air pressure	5	2	None other than routine maintenance	5	50
3	Provides fulcrum for arm	Displacement	Arm rotates clockwise. Contacts open	No alarm at loss of air pressure	5	1	None other than routine maintenance	5	25
4	Extension spring (small). Closes contacts when bellows collapse	Spring breaks	Contacts fail to close on loss of pressure	No alarm at loss of air pressure	5	2	None other than routine maintenance	5	50

Figure A2.19 A FMECA worksheet for the modified switch

ASSIGNMENT 11.5

Re-design the unit so that the contacts are open when pressure is present, and closed when it is absent. Construct a new FMEA worksheet, entering details of the four failure modes mentioned so far. Is the new switch better, worse, or the same in terms of failing safe?

Figure A2.16 shows one way in which the switch might be re-designed so that the contacts are open when the system is pressurised, and closed when pressure is lost. A leak in the bellows causes the contacts to close and give a warning of system pressure loss regardless of the real situation; this represents a fail safe situation. As was the case with the previous assignment, breakage of the large extension spring could result in the swinging arm rotating clockwise or anti-clockwise depending upon the distribution of mass and the strength of the small extension spring in the switch. Anti-clockwise rotation could give rise to a fail to danger situation where the contacts were kept open regardless of system pressure. Displacement of the pivot could result in the left hand end of the arm being pulled upwards by the large extension spring with the possibility of the contacts being opened. Failure of the small spring in the switch could result in the contacts failing to close when pressure is lost. Figure A2.17 provides details of these four failure modes.

ASSIGNMENT 11.6

Using the switch problem introduced in assignment 11.4, draw a FMECA chart and provide criticality ratings for each of the identified failure modes. Assume that the switch is a vital element in the control of a chemical plant that processes toxic waste. State any assumptions that are necessary for the completion of the chart.

Figure A2.18 provides a sample FMECA chart for this problem.

ASSIGNMENT 11.7

On the same basis as above, produce a FMECA chart for the redesigned switch developed for Assignment 11.2.

Figure A2.19 provides a sample FMECA chart for the modified switch.

ASSIGNMENT 12.1

Figure 12.1 shows an engineering characteristics deployment for some of the customer valued attributes for the segment M hairdryer. Using this as a base, complete a more detailed engineering characteristics deployment chart including as many customer-valued attributes and characteristics as you can identify. Use the customer perception data in Chapter 4 to help provide an evaluation on the chart and assign RIRs to each customer-valued attribute. Instead of merely identifying the existence of relationships between customer-valued attributes and engineering characteristics with a tick, decide whether they are strong, medium, or weak and identify them with suitable symbols. Use the relationships that you have identified and the RIRs to assign an importance rating to each engineering characteristic. Also incorporate a 'roof structure' as shown in Figure 12.5, and record relationships between different engineering characteristics. In some cases, you will need to make some assumptions about the nature of the design solution.

The preparation of a QFD chart makes you think about customer needs and the engineering characteristics that are under your control. For each need, you have to think carefully about the ways that you can provide influence. Ask if there are any needs for which you have not listed controlling characteristics, or if there are any characteristics that you are controlling that do not seem to have a direct link to a customer-defined need. The QFD chart shown in Figure A2.20 is for the segment M hairdryer. This limited chart collects the engineering characteristics under four convenient headings: heater, fan, comfort, and ergonomics. Assignment of strengths to relationships is subjective, so do not be too worried if your decisions are not the same as mine. The important thing is to reach a consensus view among team members. In this case, I have assigned weightings to engineering characteristics by looking at the number of times that each characteristic is identified as having influence on a customer need. I then counted a 3 for strong, 2 for medium, and 1 for weak. The totals are provided in the bottom row of the chart. Information on two potential competitors is given at the right hand side of the chart.

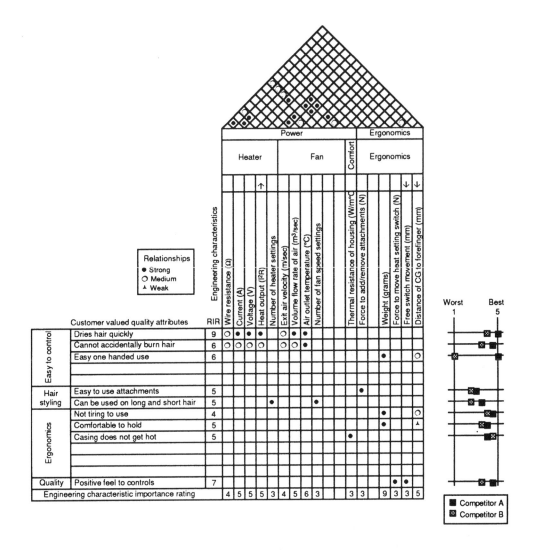

Figure A2.20 Attribute/characteristics QFD chart for the segment M, hairdryer

ASSIGNMENT 12.2

Using the engineering characteristics that you developed in Assignment 12.1, produce a parts development chart along the lines of the one shown in Figure 12.7. Make any assumptions that you wish about the nature of the parts that are manufactured in-house or purchased from outside suppliers. Identify relationships between part characteristics and assign importance ratings by looking at their influence on the previously weighted engineering characteristics.

The engineering characteristics generated from the solution to Assignment 12.1 have been entered down the left hand side of the parts deployment chart shown in Figure A2.21.

Characteristics that describe parts of the hairdryer, e.g. materials, geometry, mass, are entered along the top. As before, relationships between the parts are shown in the 'roof structure'. For example, the position of the centre of gravity is strongly affected by the mass and position of major components like the motor and heater matrix.

The strength of the relationship between individual engineering characteristics and the part characteristics is also recorded in the main body of the chart. Weightings for part characteristics are calculated by multiplying the engineering characteristic weighting with a number representing the strength of the relationship. In this case, 3 for strong, 2 for medium, and 1 for weak. Totals are given in the bottom row of the chart. These provide a subjective measure of the importance of individual part characteristics to customer needs.

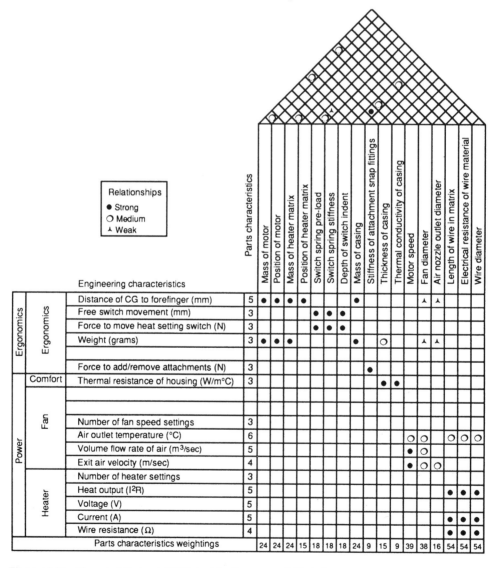

Figure A2.21 Characteristics/parts QFD chart for the segment M hair dryer

REFERENCES AND OTHER SOURCES

Papers, books, and other works provided in this section represent a combined list of material referenced from within the text, and sources of general background reading. Referenced works are identified in the text by the name of the first author listed.

Acar, B.S. (1966) A new model for design processes. *Proceedings of the Institution of Mechanical Engineers*, Series E, **210**. pp. 135–138.

Ansoff, H.I., Stewart, J.M. (1967) Strategies for technology-based business. *Harvard Business Review*, **45**(6). pp. 71–83.

Baynes, K., & Pugh, F. (1981) *The Art of the Engineer*. Lutterworth Press, Guildford, England. ISBN 0 7188 2506 3.

Berk, J., & Berk, S. (1993) *Total Quality Management*. (Sterling Publishing Company Inc., New York, USA. ISBN: 0 8069 7453 2.

BS7000 (1989). *Guide to Managing Product Design*. British Standards Institution.

Clausing, D. (1994) *Total Quality Development: a Step-by-Step Guide to Concurrent Engineering*. ASME Press, New York, USA.

Cooper, R.G., & Kleinschmidt, E.J. (1994) Determinants of timeliness in product development. *Journal of Product Innovation Management*, **8**(4). pp. 381–396.

Cooper, R.G., & Kleinschmidt, E.J. (1995) Benchmarking the firm's critical success factors in new product development. *Journal of Product Innovation Management*, **12**(5). pp. 374–391.

Cooper, R.G., & Kleinschmidt, E.J. (1996) Winning business in product development – the critical success factors. *Journal of Research-Technology Management*, **39**(4). pp. 18–29.

Corey, E.R. (1991) *Industrial Marketing: Cases and concepts*. Prentice Hall International Inc., Englewood Cliffs, USA. ISBN: 0 13 457573 3.

Cox, S.J., & Tait, N.R.S. (1991) *Reliability, Safety and Risk Management: An integrated Approach*. Butterworth-Heinemann, Oxford, England. ISBN: 0 7506 1073 5.

Crimp. M. (1990) *The Marketing Research Process*. Prentice Hall International (UK) Ltd., Hemel Hempstead, England. ISBN: 0 13 556515 4.

Cross, N. (1994) *Engineering Design Methods: Strategies for product design*. John Wiley and Sons Ltd., Chichester, England. ISBN: 0 471 94228 6.

Curtis, C. (1994) *Business and Marketing for Engineers and Scientists.* McGraw-Hill Book Company Europe, Maidenhead, England. ISBN: 0 07 707868 3.

Deming, W.E. (1986) *Out of Crisis.* Sterling Publishing Company Inc., New York, USA.

Dwyer, L., & Mellor, R. (1991) Organisational environment, new product process activities and project outcomes. *Journal of Product Innovation Management*, **6**. pp. 39–48.

Eales-White, R. (1995) *Building your Team.* Kogan Page, Town and Country ISBN: 0 7494 1342 5.

Ferguson, I. (1990) Process design. *Journal of Total Quality Management*, April. pp. 103–108.

Frankenberger, E., & Birkhofer, H. (1995) Teamwork in engineering design practice. *Proceedings of the International Conference on Engineering Design* (ICED 95), August 22–24, Prague. pp. 828–833.

French, M.J. (1971) *Engineering Design: The Conceptual Stage.* Heinemann Educational Books, London, England. ISBN: 0 435 71650 6.

French, M.J. (1985) *Conceptual Design for Engineers.* The Design Council, London, England.

Gallup, R.B. (1991) Unblocking, brainstorms. *Journal of Allied Psychology*, **76**(1). pp. 137–142.

Geschka, H., Kirchoff, G. & Flurius, G. (1993) An idea management software system, *Proceedings of the Fourth European Conference on Creativity and Innovation.* August 25–28, Danstadt, pp. 141–149.

Hauser, J.R., & Clausing, D. (1988) The house of quality. *Harvard Business Review*, May–June. pp 63–73.

Holt, K. (1995) Brainstorming – From classics to electronics. *Proceedings of the International Conference on Engineering Design* (ICED 95), August 22–24, Prague, pp. 279–283.

Jebb, A., Edney, R.C., Sivaloganathan, S., & Evbuomwan, N.F.O. (1992) Design function deployment – a platform for cross disciplinary product development. *Proceedings of the Institution of Mechanical Engineering Conference on Mechatronics*, September.

Korge, D.G., & Souder, W.E. (1989) Simultaneous new product development: reducing the new product failure rate. *Journal of Industrial Marketing Management*, **8**. pp. 301–306.

Kotler, P., & Armstrong, G. (1996) *Principles of Marketing.* (Seventh edition.) Prentice Hall International Inc., Eagle Cliffs, USA. ISBN: 0 13 228685 8.

Kuwahara, Y., & Takeda, Y. (1990) A managerial approach to research and development cost-effectiveness evaluation. *IEEE Transactions on Engineering Management*, **37**(2). pp. 134–138.

Malmqvist, J. (1995) Improved function – means trees by inclusion of design history information. *Proceedings of the International Conference on Engineering Design* (ICED 95), August 22–24, Prague. pp. 1415–1423.

Martin, M.J.C. (1994) *Managing Innovation and Entrepreneurship in Technology-based Firms.* Publ: John Wiley and Sons Inc., New York, USA. ISBN: 0 471 57219 5.

Oakland, J.S. (1997) *Total Quality Management.* Butterworth Heinemann, Oxford, England. ISBN: 0 7506 2124 9.

Pahl, G., & Beitz, W. (1996) In: *Engineering Design: A systematic approach.* Ed. K. Wallace. Publ: Springer-Verlag, London, England. ISBN: 3 540 19917 9.

Pinto, M.B., & Pinto, J.K. (1990) Project team communication and cross functional co-operation in new program development. *Journal of Product Innovation Management*, **7**. pp. 200–212.

Pugh, S. (1991) *Total Design*. Addison-Wesley Publishing Company, Wokingham, England. ISBN: 0 201 41639 5.

Rao, S.S. (1992) *Reliability Based Design*. McGraw-Hill Book Company Europe, Maidenhead, England.

Raven, A.D. (1971) *Profit Improvement by Value Analysis, Value Engineering and Purchase Price Analysis*. Cassell and Company Ltd., London, England. ISBN: 0 304 93770 1.

Rossetto, S., & Franceschini, F. (1995) Quality and innovation: A conceptual model of their interaction. *Journal of Total Quality Management*, **6**(3). pp. 221–229.

Taylor, A.J., & Ben, N. (1993) Enhancement of design evaluation during concept development. *Proceedings of the International Conference on Engineering Design* (ICED 93), August. The Hague, pp. 481–484.

Trost, R.L.A. (1993) The structure of CAC software: creativity in action. Newsletter of the Creative Education Foundation of the University of Buffalo, September, October and November, **4**.

Ulrich, K.T., & Eppinger, S.D. (1995) *Product Design and Development*. McGraw-Hill Book Company, Singapore. ISBN: 0 07 113742 4.

VDI (1987). *VDI Design Handbook 2221: Systematic approach to the design of technical systems and products*. Verein Deutscher Ingenieure Verlag, Düsseldorf, Germany.

Weaver, C.N. (1995) *Managing the Four Stages of TQM*. ASQC Quality Press, Milwaukee, USA.

Wright, I.C. (1995) *A survey of market segmentation for hairdryers*. Internal research report. Department of Mechanical Engineering, Loughborough University.

Wright, I.C., & Swain, I.C. (1995) New product engineering: The quality paradox. *Journal of Engineering Design*, **6**(1). pp. 49–55.

Wright, I.C., & McGuire, J. (1995) The utilisation of a methodological approach to ensure market compliance in the design of surgical stapling equipment. *10th International Conference on Engineering Design 1995* (ICED '95), Czech Technical University, Prague, 22–24 August. pp. 209–210.

Wright, I.C., Araujo, C.S., Benedetto-Neto, H., Campello, A.C. & Segre, F.M. (1996) The utilisation of product development methods: A survey of UK industry. *Journal of Engineering Design*, **7**(3). pp. 265–277.

INDEX